The Internet
& World Wide Web

THE ROUGH GUIDE

There are more than ninety Rough Guide travel,
phrasebook, and music titles, covering
destinations from Amsterdam to Zimbabwe,
languages from Czech to Thai, and musics
from World to Opera and Jazz.

To find out more about Rough Guides, and to
check out our USA titles on HotWired's
Worldbeat site, get connected to the Internet
with this guide and find us on the Web at:

http://roughguides.com/

Rough Guide to the Internet Credits

Text editor: Mark Ellingham

Design and lay-out: Henry Iles

Production: Susanne Hillen

Proofread by Kate Berens

This book is dedicated to A Certain Summer Feeling.

This second edition published Nov 1996 by Rough Guides Ltd
1 Mercer St, London WC2H 9QJ
375 Hudson Street, New York 10014
Internet: mail@roughtravl.co.uk

Distributed by The Penguin Group

Penguin Books Ltd, 27 Wrights Lane, London W8 5TZ

Penguin Books USA Inc., 375 Hudson Street, New York 10014

Penguin Books Canada Ltd, 10 Alcorn Avenue, Toronto, Ontario MV4 1E4

Penguin Books Australia Ltd, PO Box 257, Ringwood, Victoria 3134

Penguin Books (NZ) Ltd, 182–190 Wairau Road, Auckland 10

Printed in the United Kingdom by Cox & Wyman Ltd (Reading)

416 pages; includes index

A catalogue record for this book is available from the British Library

ISBN 1-85828-216-0

The Internet
& World Wide Web
VERSION 2.0

THE ROUGH GUIDE

by

Angus J. Kennedy
of **Internet**

Contents

Read Me

There's nothing worse than feeling left behind. When everyone is talking about something, but it just doesn't gel. The Internet's had this effect over the last couple of years. Everything you pick up. Internet this, cyber that. But, unless you've been connected, you're still in the dark. Getting to grips with the Net can be daunting, but it's a short (if steep) learning curve, and the basics don't take long to master. This small guide is crammed with nuggets of practical advice, troubleshooting tips, step-by-step tuition, and addresses of the places you'll need to go. We'll make you a Net guru in the shortest possible time. Guaranteed!

Internet books mostly fall into two categories: the brick-sized volumes that tell you far more than you want to know in unimportant areas and not enough on shortcuts; and the patronizing simplistic ones, that make it look easy in the bookstore with cute icons and catchy titles, but aren't much use once you start having problems. And, if they're written before mid-1996, they should be filed under ancient history. The truth is you don't need a fat book to get started on the Internet. It's too much work. And boring.

This Rough Guide gives it to you straight. In plain English. We think the Net is a pushover. If you can figure out how to use a word processor, you'll master the Net. Sure, you'll have teething troubles, but we show you how to solve them and where to go for help. Rather than compile everything there is to know about the Net, we give you the basics and show you how to use the Net itself to find out more. Since the Net and its associated technology changes almost daily, it's wiser to get your information from where it's always fresh.

What's more, we'll show you how to: get the best deal on Internet access, send messages across the world instantly for the price of a local call, find all the software you'll ever need free, become an expert in the most important Internet programs, and locate anything, anywhere, on the Net without having to learn any difficult commands. Or, if you're really impatient, you can wing it and go straight to our listings chapters to explore the weird, wild, and wonderful World Wide Web, or get those nagging questions off your mind in one of the special interest newsgroups. Who knows, you might even make a few friends along the way.

Well, what are you waiting for?

PART ONE

---

basics

Frequently Asked Questions

Before getting into the nitty gritty of what you can do on the Internet – and what it can do for you – here are some answers to a few Frequently Asked Questions (or FAQs, as acronym-loving Net users call them).

What is the Internet?

The **Internet** (or the Net) is not, as many people think, about computers. It's about people, communication and information sharing. It's a way of overcoming physical boundaries, like distance, to allow minds to meet.

Of course, without computers and computer networks none of this can happen. The formal definition of the Internet is an international computer network – but that could be expanded to include the content, too. The core of this network consists of computers permanently linked through high-speed connections. To join the Internet, all you have to do is connect your computer to any of these computers. Once you're online (connected), your computer can talk to every other computer on the Internet, whether they are in your home town or on the other side of the world.

What's it going to do for me?

Having the Internet at your disposal is like having 30 million consultants on your payroll. Except you don't have to pay them. You can find the answers to every question you've ever had, send messages across the world instantly, transfer documents, shop in another continent, sample new music, visit art galleries, read books, play games, chat, read the latest news in a range of languages, meet people with similar interests, obtain software, or just surf at leisure through mountains of visual bubblegum.

You can also use the Net as a **business tool**, both for communication by email, and for marketing and selling products. Indeed, we predict the Internet will become as integral to business as the telephone and fax machine.

Who's in charge?

Everybody, but nobody in particular. Various bodies are concerned with the Internet's conventions and operation. Foremost among them are the *Internet Network Information Center* (*InterNIC*), which registers domain names, the *Internet Society*, which acts as a clearing house for technical standards, and the *World Wide Web Consortium*, which discusses the future of the Web's programming language. No-one, however, actually "runs" the Internet. As the Internet is, in effect, a network of networks, most responsibilities are contained within the local network. For instance, if you have connection problems, you would call your connection supplier. If you object to material located on a server in Japan or Ireland, say, you'd have to complain to the administrator of that local server.

While it certainly promotes freedom of speech, the Internet is not as anarchic as some sections of the media would have you believe. If you break the laws of your country, and you're caught, you are liable to prosecution. For example, suppose you publish a document in the US outlining the shortcomings of a military dictator in Slobovia. It might not worry the US authorities, but it could be curtains for any Slobovian caught downloading the document. The same applies to other contentious material such as pornography, terrorist handbooks, drug literature, and religious satire. The Internet is not an entirely new planet.

But isn't it run by the Pentagon and the CIA?

The Internet was conceived in 1969 in the US, as the American Defense Department network (ARPAnet). Its purpose was to act as a nuclear attack resistant method of exchanging scientific information and intelligence. But that's old history in Internet terms.

In the 1970s and 80s several other networks, such as the National Science Foundation Network (NSFNET), joined, linking it to research agencies and universities. It was probably no coincidence that as the Cold War petered out, the Internet became more publicly accessible and the nature of the beast changed totally and irreversibly. These days, intelligence agencies have the same access to the Internet as everyone else, but whether they use it to monitor insurgence and crime is simply a matter for speculation.

Is this the Information Superhighway?

The Internet is often referred to as the Information Superhighway in the popular media. And no wonder. The Internet is the closest thing we have to a prototype for the Information Superhighway envisioned by US Vice President Al Gore, and talked up by Microsoft's Bill

Gates and associates. It has huge capabilities for cheap, global, and immediate communication; it may grow to dominate areas of education; it is already providing an alternative shopping mall; and it will almost certainly make inroads into banking and customer services.

Nonetheless, to get services like video on demand, we'll need a much faster network than today's Internet. It's already straining under the pressure of new users, and it will probably get worse before it gets better. Although with new digital alternatives such as ADSL, and cable and satellite links looming daily, the future is starting to brighten, the real digital "revolution" is still very much on hold.

What is electronic mail?

 Electronic mail or **email** is a method of sending text files from one computer to another. You can send messages across the world in seconds using Internet email.

Who pays for the international calls?

One of the greatest things about the Internet is the way it reduces the significance of political boundaries and distance. For example, suppose you're in Boston, and you want to buzz someone in Bangkok. Provided you both have Net access, it's as quick, easy, and cheap as sending a message across the street. You compose your message, connect to your local Internet provider, upload your mail and then disconnect.

Your mail server will examine the message's address to determine where it has to go and then pass it on to its appropriate neighbor, which will do the same. This usually entails routing it towards the backbone – the chain of high-speed links that carry the bulk of the Net's long-haul traffic. Each subsequent link will ensure that the message heads towards Bangkok rather than Bogotá or Brisbane. The whole process should take no more than a few seconds.

Apart from your own Internet subscription costs, **you pay only for the local call** to your provider. Your message will pass through many different networks, each with its own methods of recouping the communication costs – but don't worry, adding to your phone bill isn't one of them.

What's the difference between the Web and the Internet?

The Internet is the network that carries data between computers. The **World Wide Web** (or Web) is simply a user-friendly point-and-click way of navigating data stored on computers connected to the Net.

And what about Intranets?

The mechanism that's used to pass information between computers on the Internet can be used in exactly the same way in a local network such as in an office. When it's not publicly accessible, it's called an **Intranet**. Many companies are experimenting with Intranets as a way to distribute internal documents – in effect publishing Web pages for their own private use.

What is full Internet access?

You can access the Internet through several channels, but not all methods will let you do everything.

The World Wide Web, IRC, FTP, and Telnet – the main areas of the Internet, which we'll deal with later in this book – require **"full Internet access"**. You can get this using one of the **Online Services** (like CompuServe or America Online) or with what's called an **IP (Internet Protocol) account** from one of hundreds of local (or in some cases national and international) **Internet Service Providers** (ISPs).

You'll encounter a choice of IP accounts, which may include **SLIP** (Serial Line Internet Protocol) and **PPP** (Point to Point Protocol) for standard modem dial-ups, **ISDN**, and various types of direct connections. Regardless of what grade IP access you choose, you'll be able to do the same things, though at different speeds.

What's bandwidth?

A higher **bandwidth connection** means the capacity to carry more data at once – just as a thicker pipe means you can pump more water. But unlike water, where pressure can increase, data is limited by electron speed. When a connection is at full capacity, it can't be pushed faster, so data goes into a queue – thus forming a bottleneck that slows things down. So even if you have a high bandwidth connection to the Internet, you could be impeded by insufficient bandwidth between you and your data source.

What are IP addresses?

Every computer which is permanently connected to the Net has a 32-bit unique **IP (Internet Protocol) address**, so other Internet computers can find it. A typical address looks like this: 149.174.211.5 (that is, four numbers separated by periods).

Your computer will be allocated an IP address when you get full Internet access. If it's a SLIP (Serial Line Internet Protocol) connection you'll get a fixed address; if you access with a PPP (Point to Point Protocol) connection your host will allocate a new one each time you log in. The good news is that, other than when you first get connected, you'll probably never have to use these numbers. Why? Because there's a different system for humans called the Domain Name System (DNS).

Okay, then, what's the Domain Name System?

People don't like using numbers. Isn't it easier to remember a name than a telephone number? With this in mind, the Internet uses the **Domain Name System (DNS)** parallel to the IP number system. That way you have the choice of using letters or words, rather than numbers, to identify hosts.

Domain names look somewhat confusing at first meeting, but they soon become familiar. Indeed, you can often tell a lot about who or what you're connecting to from its address. For example, let's consider the email address: marvin@easynet.co.uk

As all Internet email addresses are in the format user@host, we can deduce that the user's name or nickname is Marvin while the host is easynet.co.uk. The host portion breaks down further into subdomain, domain type, and country code. Here, the subdomain is easynet (an Internet Service Provider), its domain type "co" means it's a company or commercial site, and the country code "uk" indicates it's in the United Kingdom.

Every country has its own distinct code, although it's not always used. These include:

au	Australia	nl	Netherlands
ca	Canada	no	Norway
de	Germany	se	Sweden
fr	France	uk	United Kingdom
jp	Japan		

If an address doesn't specify a country code, it's more than likely, but not necessarily, in the USA.

Domain types are usually one of the following:

ac	Academic (UK)
com	Company or commercial organization
co	Company or commercial organization (UK)
edu	Educational institution
gov	Government body
mil	Military site
net	Internet gateway or administrative host
org	Non-profit organization

What is a BBS?

Once upon a time **BBSs (Bulletin Board Services)** were like computer clubs, allowing members to dial in and post messages and trade files. However, these days the definition is far fuzzier. All Online Services, such as CompuServe and America Online, are technically BBSs. That is, they have a private network or file area which is set aside out of the public domain of the Internet. The big Online Services are not what most people refer to as BBSs, though. The term is usually taken to mean a small network which primarily acts as a place to download and trade files.

There are well over 100,000 private BBSs in the USA alone, most often devoted to particular or local interests, and in some cases access is free. They customarily have areas to play games, chat, use email, post messages, and sometimes get limited access to the Internet through their own private network connections.

What about Web servers and Web clients?

In Net-speak, any computer that is open to external online access is known as a **server** or **host**. The software you use to perform online operations such as transfer files, read mail, surf the Web or post articles to Usenet, is called a **client**.

A **Web client** is just another name for a browser program such as Netscape or Internet Explorer. A **Web server** is a machine where Web pages are stored and made available for outside access.

Can I shop online?

It won't be long before you can buy anything you want via the Internet. There are already hundreds of online stores but Net shopping has yet to take off in a big way. It suffers from the usual reticence people feel toward mail order, as well as much publicized (and frankly, inflated) concerns about credit card security. Netscape and Microsoft browsers already provide good security, so it can only be a matter of time before Net shopping gains mainstream acceptance.

Can I make money out of the Internet?

Yes, no, maybe – but maybe it's just as relevant to ask yourself the question "Can I continue to make money without the Internet?" The last few years have seen a gold rush in the computing hardware, software, training and publishing industries. People are making money getting others online and positioned on the World Wide Web – the **"commercial zone"** of the Net – and companies with good content are beginning to make real money from advertising "sponsors" who rent banner adverts at the head of their Web pages.

As yet, not too many companies are succeeding with **direct sales**, though that's likely to change – particularly for more specialist products (from oddball CDs to solar panels) for which the Net is an ideal medium. Right now, there's a lot more **marketing** going on, as well as use of the Net as a means of providing **customer support**.

Although online trading is acceptable these days on the Net – indeed a fair proportion of Web sites have something to sell – you should **forget traditional direct response methods**. If you try sending out junk email or posting commercial material in non-commercial areas, you might be cyber-assassinated (or "flamed" as it's called on the Net). If you want to see what that means, just post an urging advertisement in Usenet, or to a mailing list – and wait for the response!

So is the Net still basically a geek hangout?

There's no doubt about the Internet's geek-pulling power. There's stuff for Star Trek geeks, investment geeks, political geeks, alternative music geeks, movie geeks, health geeks, gardening geeks, sporting geeks, and every other sort of geek imaginable. Face it, geek's where it's at.

Okay, but what about deviants?

More than 30 million deviants worldwide have Internet addresses – including celebrities like the US President, Michael Jackson, the Sultan of Brunei, Stephen Fry, Bill Gates, and the British royal family, plus thousands of journalists, students, stockbrokers, scientists, doctors, and lawyers. That's if you'd call an inquiring mind a deviancy from the norm. Of course, there may also be perverts, gangsters, and con artists, but probably no more than you mix with every day in "real life".

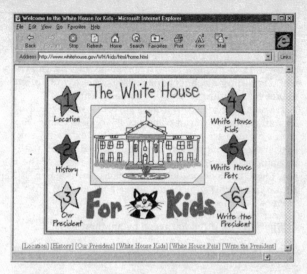

But is it yet another male-dominated bastion?

Well, there are more than twice as many men as women online, but for no particularly good reason. Some argue that women, more than men, are daunted by the technological hurdle and expense involved in getting online, others that women have less of men's "hobbyist" and "listing" obsessions. Whatever.

In theory, the Net is really as level as playing fields get – and its usage is likely to become little different from the phone, fax, and home video. After all, it's meant for communication and entertainment, and no-one can stop you, your views, your work, or your peers from getting online.

Will I make friends on the Internet?

It's certainly easy to meet people with common interests, just by joining in **Usenet (newsgroup) discussions**. And being able to discuss sensitive issues with strangers while retaining a comfortable degree of anonymity often makes for startlingly intimate communication.

Translating email pen pals into the real world of human contact, or even romance, is another thing. You won't be able to tell your new e-pal Alex's age, sex, appearance, or motives at first glance. And there's nothing stopping anyone from assuming the name of their pet, town, fantasy, or idol as an email user name or IRC nickname. So if you find yourself in council with a "Prince", don't swoon too soon.

What do I do if I'm harassed by another user?

The only way someone can harass you is by sending you unwelcome email, posting hostile replies to your comments in a Newsgroup, or pestering you in a Chat/Internet Phone channel. The simplest thing to do is to ignore them. If you've provoked them, then you'll just have to deal with it and take it as a lesson. If it goes beyond that, forward the messages or pass their details to your Internet Access Provider. Even if they've masked their identity, they're still traceable. Your provider should contact their provider, who'll most likely warn them or kick them offline.

It's very difficult to seriously harass someone via the Net and get away with it. After all, it generates evidence in writing.

Is there a lot of really weird stuff on the Net?

Yes, lots. Just like in real life, except it's easier to find.

What if children discover pornography or drugs?

Children will generally find what interests them and the deeper it's hidden, the harder they'll look. And even the bitterest old prude surely couldn't blame them for being curious. Face it, they're the Duke Nukem generation. Many educational bodies have taken steps to limit access to contentious matter, and entrepreneurs have been working on programs that deny access to material containing sexually explicit or drug-related key words. The major development at present is **PICS** (Platform for Internet Content Selection), a self-regulatory system of rating Web pages according to content, which will allow Internet software to be configured with a bar on "X-rated" pages. This or a similar system is likely to become a standard feature of Web browsers.

However, it's impossible to filter the Net completely, and perhaps just as well, because it's not the Internet's place to preach morals. If you are worried about kids becoming perverts on the Internet, comfort yourself with the fact that less than one percent of Internet "Newsgroups" are devoted to sex, and an even smaller percentage of the World Wide Web pages. How does that match up to the shelves of your local news-store?

You might also reflect on the idea that children exposed to the Internet might mature faster and learn to think more freely and independently. What they see of things like drugs, sex, and religious cults will be through first-hand interactive debates and discussions. If someone posts an article in a newsgroup advocating crack as an easy way to make money and friends, it might attract twenty negative postings in response. By following the trail of responses, children can understand reasoned argument, and form their own opinions based upon evidence rather than fashion and dogma.

Will I need to learn any computer languages?

No. If you can work a word processor or spreadsheet, you'll have no difficulty tackling the Internet. You just have to get familiar with your Internet software, which in most cases isn't too hard. The biggest problem most people have is in setting up for the first time, but with the "Internet made easy" packages available these days, that's no longer too much of an issue.

Once online, most people access the Internet by means of a graphical "icon-based" program, not too different from the way you use a Macintosh or Windows. And on the World Wide Web – the most popular part of the Net – you hardly even need to type: almost everything is accessible by a click on your mouse.

The only time you may need to use UNIX commands – the traditional computer "language" of the Internet – is if using Telnet to remotely log on to a UNIX computer. And that's something most of us avoid.

Can I use the Internet if I can't use a computer?

As mentioned above, even if you can't type, you can still use the World Wide Web – all you have to do is point your mouse and click. That's about as far as you'll get though. If you've never had any contact with computers, consider the Internet your opportunity. Don't think of computers as a daunting modern technology. They're just a means to an end. The best way to learn how to use a computer is to get one and switch it on.

How do I get connected?

Good question and worth a whole chapter. Read on.

Getting Connected

There are all kinds of ways to access the Internet – and if you live in North America, Europe, or Australia, you'll probably come in contact with a Net-connected terminal in the coming months – at your work, college, school, local library, or even your local coffee shop. But why wait? If you have a reasonably modern computer, all you need to get up and running is a modem (around $200/150) and an account with an access provider (around $15/£10 a month).

You don't need to be a computer expert

The most common barrier to getting connected is technophobia, or more specifically fear of computers. That's understandable, because the Internet requires a relationship with your computer. However, it's not that demanding. In fact, most people find it fun, once they've started. Internet programs are nowhere near as complex as the latest series of word processors. Even if you've never used a computer, you'll be able to figure out how to surf the Web within minutes. Finding your way around is another matter, but you're at an advantage – you have this guide.

Although using the Net is relatively simple, things tend not to work seamlessly, so be prepared for a period of modest confusion. Everyone goes through it, but you'll soon learn the ropes. And the online community is always willing to help, as long as you direct your queries to the right area. Before long, you'll be sharing your new-found expertise with others.

What you'll need

Before you can get connected, you'll need three things: a **computer** with enough grunt to handle the software; an account with an **Internet Access Provider**; and a hardware device – usually the fastest **modem** you can afford – to connect your computer to the Internet. How you connect to the Internet can make the difference between pleasure and frustration. You don't necessarily need state of the art computer gadgetry, but no matter what you have, you'll find a way to push it to the limit.

Computer firepower

It's possible to access the Net in some way with almost any machine you could call a computer, but if you can't run your Web browsing and mail software together without a lot of chugging noises coming from your hard drive, you're going to get frustrated.

To drive browsing software comfortably, you'll need at least a **486 SX25 IBM-compatible PC**, or a **Macintosh 68030** series, equipped with 8Mb RAM. While you can also connect to the Net with Ataris, Amigas, PC TVs, Psion Organizers, and even the Nokia 9000 cellular phone, you'll be severely restrained by the lack of software. If you want to do more than send email, you'll be far happier with something faster and more versatile.

To listen to music samples and sound effects, or use the Internet Phone, you'll also need an internal **sound card**, **microphone**, and **speakers** or headphones. Macs come with reasonable sound capability, but with PCs it's usually an extra. Unless your primary purpose is to create professional quality music, buy a Sound Blaster compatible card as it will work with almost everything.

Without **video hardware**, you'll be disappointed with the Web's short movies as they might only appear matchbox-size on your screen. If you'd like to improve the drawing time, quality, and size of your downloaded images and movies, you should consider graphic upgrade options such as accelerator cards, RAM additions, MPEG movie cards, and 3D accelerator cards.

If you can afford it and want the most out of the Net, **the ideal computer package** would be a fast Pentium, or 586/686, PC, 16+Mb RAM, 1+Gig hard drive, 32 bit sound card with wavetable synthesis, quad speed CD-ROM, at least a 15-inch monitor with a decent video card, and as your operating system **Windows 95** or **NT 4.0**. **IBM's OS/2 Warp** is in most ways a comparable, if not superior, operating system but less popular, and hardly mentioned in software releases. There's nothing wrong with **Power Macs** either, as any of their loyal (and productive) users will attest, except that most of the interesting software comes out for PCs first, and sometimes never makes it to Mac. But if you'd exchange user-friendliness for the cutting edge and you're more into art and publishing than twiddling, you might be happier with a Mac.

There's a lot to be said, too, for buying the same set-up as a friend, so you have someone to turn to for help.

Note: If you're on a network at work or college, don't attempt to connect to the Net without your systems manager's supervision. Networked PCs and Macs can use the same software listed later in this book, but may connect to the Net differently.

Connecting your computer to the Net

A powerful computer won't make up for a slow link to the Internet. Get the fastest connection you can afford. Unless you're hooked up through a network, you'll need a device to connect your computer to the telephone line or cable. There'll be a similar device at the Access Provider's end. This device will depend on the type of Internet account. The two main types are **Leased Line** and **Dial-up**. Leased Lines are expensive and aimed at businesses that need to be permanently connected. Dial-up suits the casual user. Investigate the Net through a Dial-up account before contemplating a Leased Line.

Modems – the plain vanilla option

The cheapest, most popular, but slowest, way to connect is by installing a **modem** and dialing up using the standard telephone network. Modems come in three flavors: internal, external, and PCMCIA. Each has its advantages and disadvantages.

The cheapest option is usually an **internal modem** – unless you have a portable, for which internal modems are often comparatively pricey. It must be installed inside your computer by plugging it into a slot called a bus. It's not a difficult job, but does require that you take the back off your computer and follow the instructions carefully (or get your computer store to do it). Because they're hidden inside your computer, internal modems don't take up desk space, clutter the back of your computer with extra cables, or require an external power source. They do, however, generate unwanted heat inside your computer, place an extra drain on your power supply, and lack the little lights to tell you if or how the call is going.

An **external modem** is easier to install. Depending on the make, it will simply plug straight in to your computer's serial, parallel, or SCSI port, making it easily interchangeable between machines (and simple to upgrade). External modems require a separate power source, maybe even a battery. And they usually give a visual indication of the call's progress through a bank of flashing lights (LEDs).

The credit card-sized **PCMCIA modems** are a mixture of both. They fit internally into the PCMCIA slots common in most modern notebooks but can be easily removed to use the slot for something else such as an external CD-ROM drive. They don't require an external power source. They are expensive, though, and don't like being dropped.

Whatever type you choose, the major issue is **speed**. Data transfer speed is expressed in bits per second or **bps**. It can take up to ten bits to transfer a character. So a modem operating at 2400 bps would transfer at around 240 characters per second. That's about a page of text every eight seconds. At 28,800 bps, you could send the same page of text in two-thirds of a second.

A 14,400 bps (V.32) modem is considered entry level for the World Wide Web. But if you can afford it, get a **28,800 bps (V.34)**, and preferably one that's upgradeable to 33,600 bps. They're a little more expensive but will reduce your online charges, and give you twice as much for your money.

Finally, make sure whatever you buy will work with your particular computer. PCs need a high-speed serial card with a 16550 or 16650 UART chip to be able to process any more than about 9600 bps reliably. Most modern PCs have them as standard, but check anyway. They're not an expensive upgrade.

Faster ways to connect

One good thing about modems is that they are the right-here right-now accepted standard everywhere in the world and work over the standard telephone system without any excess charges. But they are also slow and unstable, compared to what's around the corner.

The next immediately available option is **ISDN**. This provides three channels (1x16 kbps and 2x64 kbps) which can be used and charged for in various ways. ISDN Internet accounts don't usually cost more but, depending on where you live, the line connection, rental, and calls can cost anywhere from slightly to outrageously more than standard telephone charges. That's up to your telco. With ISDN, rather than using a modem, you'll need a slightly more expensive device called a Terminal Adapter, plus appropriate software, and possibly an upgrade to your serial card. For details on how to install ISDN under Windows 95 see: http://www.microsoft.com/windows/getisdn/

ISDN is a vast improvement on modem technology, not just for speed, but for superior line handling and almost instantaneous connections. However, just as it's gaining acceptance, several other copper-wire technologies promise to bring far higher bandwidths into homes at a fraction of the cost. One is the possibility of getting access, perhaps even a cheap permanent connection, bundled with a **cable TV** connection. Another is **ADSL**, which promises to deliver up to 6 Mbps in to, and 640 kbps out of, the home over the standard telephone cables via yet another type of adapter. Whether they will be superseded by optic fibre, ATM, or satellites before they reach mainstream acceptance is yet to be seen. Be sure to watch the press and ask around, because access to these sorts of speeds will make the Internet a whole new playground.

So, how do I get a connection?

To connect to the Internet, you'll need someone to allow you to connect into their computer, which in turn is connected to another computer, which in turn . . . that's how the Internet works. Unless you have a working relationship with whomever controls access to that computer, you'll have to pay for the privilege.

A firm in the business of providing Internet access is known as an **Internet Access Provider** (IAP) or **Internet Service Provider** (ISP). Once, Internet access was available only to the echelons of research and defense. Now, it has become a highly competitive business, with companies offering free trial periods and software to attract your custom, plus there's a host of "Internet Start Up Kits" on sale, which will connect you automatically to a local provider to fill in your credit card details. If a provider goes broke you could be left without access, and would need to open a new account – probably with a new email address. So choose your ISP carefully.

One alternative to the dedicated IAPs and ISPs is to subscribe to one of the major **Online Services** – such as CompuServe, America Online, or Microsoft Network – which offer full Internet access at increasingly commercial rates. Most of these commercial giants offer two separate services: access to the Internet proper and access to their own private network. On the Internet front, they can be appraised in the same way as any other ISP, and are reviewed in the following chapter.

How much is it going to cost?

Since the gates to the Net are in the hands of small as well as large business, a highly confusing array of Access Providers (and pricing structures) has emerged.

The biggest issue is whether you have time charges.

Where local calls are fixed or free, as in North America, Asia and Australasia, providers usually either restrict the number of access hours included in the monthly charge or charge by the minute. Otherwise you could stay on the line all day and keep others from using it. In countries such as the UK, where local calls are timed, lengthy connections mean hefty phone bills.

This means that in the UK charging is quite simple. It's common just to pay a single monthly fee of as little as £8 or an annual fee of £90. In North America and Australia there are usually time charges of some sort. For example, in the US, you might commonly pay $20 per month for the first 40 hours access and then $2 per hour thereafter.

One other factor to consider are **Points Of Presence** (POP) are crucial: they're the local dial-up numbers. You want to get an ISP with a local POP – and, if you travel, a range of access numbers – otherwise you can run up some serious phone bills. Often, in the US, if you need to call your provider from outside the state, it may offer a free 1-800 number with a flat fee of about 15¢ per minute including the call.

Wherever you're based, it pays to shop around and look for the optimum combination of price, service, availability, and extra features. To help with your quest, we've printed a list of providers at the end of this book. Inevitably, given the huge number of operators, it's far from complete (and no guarantee of quality), but it will get you started – and you can always change later on, exploring the Net itself to see what's on offer in your area. You could also check the computer classifieds in one of the proliferating Internet magazines. Many offer guides comparing local providers' prices, services, and points of presence.

In general, the best idea is to get started with someone who will give you all the start-up software and cheap access for the first month. Ring several Freecall numbers and ask for their latest information packs and access software. Alternatively, look in at your local computer store and pick from one of the packages offering easy-to-install software pre-programmed with a call-up to a local provider.

What to ask

Choosing an Access Provider is the single most critical part of getting connected. When shopping around, ask as many as possible of the following questions:

How long have you been in business, who owns the company, and how many subscribers do you have?

You need to know who you're dealing with. Big operators may offer certain advantages like national and even global dial-up points, security, guaranteed access, stability, and close proximity to the high-speed backbone. However, they can be slow to upgrade because of high overheads and may have dim support staff. Small younger providers can be more flexible, have newer equipment, more in-tune staff, cheaper rates, and faster access, but conversely may lack the capital to make future critical upgrades. There aren't any rules, it's a new industry and all a bit of a long-term gamble.

Can I access for the price of a local call?

If you have to pay long-distance rates, it's going to cost you more. Many providers give you the option of dialing a toll-free national number and charging you back. Get a local provider if possible. Ask if it has multiple points of presence (POPs).

What are your support hours?

It's not essential to have 24-hour support, but it's a bonus to know someone will be there when you can't get a line on the weekend or at 11pm.

Can you send me a copy of your network map?

A quality provider should be proud to provide you with a topology map of its peer connections. What you are really asking is who it buys its connection from, with whom it exchanges data, and the size of its internal network. It's easier to get it as a map so that you can try to make sense out of it and compare it with others at your leisure. You have to try to figure out whether its network is fast and reliable. Good signs are its own transcontinental and international links, close proximity to the backbone, multiple routing options, and high-speed connections. Of course, none of this matters if its overloaded with traffic.

What is your start-up cost ?

Avoid paying a start-up fee if possible – though if it includes a licensed copy of Netscape or a decent software kit, it could be worth the savings in download time and bother.

What software do you supply – is it 32 bit, and does it work with Netscape or Microsoft Internet Explorer?

Likewise avoid paying for start-up software. Some providers recommend commercial packages such as *CyberJack* and *Internet in a Box*; others provide their own. Whatever you're getting, if it doesn't work with Netscape or Internet Explorer, forget it – and if you're running Windows 95, you don't want 16 bit software. If you are reasonably confident with your computer try a free software alternative first. Spending more money is no assurance of long-term higher standards or simplicity.

What are your ongoing monthly charges?

Most providers charge a monthly fee, and with some that's your only cost. This is common in the UK where local calls are charged by time. Elsewhere it usually forms a base rate with certain time constraints.

What are your usage time charges?

In most countries where local calls are free or untimed, you'll be charged for the amount of time you're online (connected). In many cases your monthly charge will include a number of free hours per month or day. Find out if unused hours can be used as future credits.

Are there any premium charges?

Premium charges are one of the main drawbacks with the Online Service giants such as CompuServe, which provide quality commercial databases as well as Internet access. But having to pay extra to use certain services is not necessarily a bad thing, as you don't want to have to subsidize something you don't use.

Is it cheaper to access at certain times?

In an effort to restrict traffic during peak periods, providers may offer periods with reduced or no online charges. Think about when you're most likely to use your connection. Try during the cheap period. If you can't connect, it's slow, or you'd rarely use it at that hour, then it's no bargain.

Can you support my modem type and speed?

Modems like talking to their own kind. When modems aren't happy with each other, they connect at a slower rate. It's not much use if your 33.6 kbps modem can only connect at 14.4 kbps. Ask what connection speeds your provider supports. If it's lower than your modem's top speed, look elsewhere.

Do you offer full access, that is a SLIP or PPP connection?

To explore the World Wide Web, you'll need a full connection to the Internet. You may be offered SLIP or PPP access. Choose PPP, if available, as it supports error correction and compression. It's also easier to set up. If you only want email and Usenet, you could ask for a "shell" account, which can be substantially cheaper. Each provider will have several alternatives, at different prices — just ask.

Do you offer high-speed access such as ISDN or ADSL?

If the answer's yes, find out the cost all up, including the hardware, wiring, rental, and call charges. If it's affordable, ask for installation contacts. In some parts of the US, for example, installation is only about $20, and thereafter costs the same as a telephone.

Do you carry all the newsgroups in Usenet? If not, how many do you carry and which ones do you cut?

Usenet has more than 25,000 groups and it's still growing. That's 95% more than you'll ever want to look at in your lifetime. Most providers carry only a portion, but it's still usually over 60%. The first ones to be axed are often the foreign language, country specific, provider specific, and the adult (alt.sex and alt.binaries) series. If you particularly want certain groups, your provider can usually add them, but if it has a policy against certain material it may refuse. Unless you're concerned that particular groups could have a negative influence on whomever is using your connection, get as many groups as you can. You never know what you'll uncover.

Do you use POP3 for email?

POP3 is superior. It enables you to pick up your mail from a cybercafé, at work, or wherever you can get online. If a provider doesn't use it, ask if there's a way to pick up mail remotely. For example, you can pick up AOL (America Online) mail by logging in over the Net with its software. But that can be a pain.

What will my email address be, and how much do you charge to register a domain name?

You usually have the option to choose the first part of your email address. You might like to use your first name or nickname. This will then be attached to the provider's host name. Check if your name's available and what the host name would be. You don't want a name that could reflect badly on your business plans. For instance, if you register with the UK Service Provider Demon, your email address will end with **demon.co.uk** – perhaps not the ideal choice for a priest (although one vicar who used the first edition of this book reckons it's a conversation point). If you want your own domain name, a provider should be able to register your choice for you. For instance, if John Hooper trains ducks to use computers, he could register duckschool.com and give himself the email address **john@duckschool.com**. Then it would be easy to remember his address, just by thinking about who he is and what he does. Expect to pay an extra $200/£150 per year, or more, for this privilege. Note also that CompuServe – at present – assigns numbers rather than names to its users. This is a disadvantage, as it makes them hard to remember, but it's one they're aware of and may change.

How much does it cost for personal Web page storage?
Many providers will include a few megabytes of storage free so you can publish your own Web page. In general, if you go over that megabyte limit there'll be an excess charge.

Once you've done your calculations, drawn up your shortlist of providers, and received your start-up software, you should be ready to dial your provider of choice. If you've done your research well you should have come across at least one free introductory period. These can be worth having – but be wary. You'll often have to supply your credit card details and join before they'll let you in. Make sure the offer really is free and doesn't have any hidden costs.

Connection Software: TCP/IP

 It's standard practice for Access Providers to supply the basic **connection software** – usually for free. However, because the Internet is constantly evolving, no matter how good the starter kit, you'll soon want to replace or add components.

The basic kit

What you get from a provider, or from buying a start-up kit or disk in a computer store, varies from the bare minimum needed to dial in and establish an IP connection, to a full Internet toolkit.

At the heart of every package is the **TCP/IP** software, known as the **stack** or in Windows as the **winsock**. It enables the computer to talk the Net's language. It needs

31

to know your IP address and the address of the server your provider uses to convert domain names into IP addresses and thus connect you. All your Net software, such as your newsreader, Web browser, and mail client, relies on it to converse.

Once this TCP/IP software is correctly configured to your provider's details, you can pick and choose all the other components as you see fit. If you switch providers you just have to alter a few details in the TCP/IP configuration. Your provider will have no problem telling you what to change or will supply you with the TCP/IP already configured.

Windows 95, OS/2, or Mac?

If you're running **Windows 95**, IBM's **OS/2 Warp**, or Macintosh **System 7.5**, you already have all the TCP/IP software you need. And setting it up to dial its respective Online Service is just a matter of following menu commands. But, if you want to connect to another provider, you'll need help. Your provider will either supply you with the configuration settings on a file or give you written instructions on how to set up. Failing that, get someone to walk you through it over the phone. Once that's done the rest is easy.

Earlier systems

If you're using an earlier version of Windows, or a pre-System 7.0 Mac system, you'll need to either upgrade your operating system or obtain a **TCP/IP program**.

Of the several TCP/IP programs for the Windows 3.x, the most popular is **Trumpet Winsock**. It's available freely on the Internet and used as the core of many ISPs' Windows 3.x bundles. It's not actually free, though. If you want to use it after a trial period, you are requested to pay the author. Its dial-up scripting takes a while to figure out, but once you have it going it's rock solid and works with everything.

Other popular winsocks include Netmanage's **Chameleon** sampler, the free and best part of its commercial package and the one that comes with **Quarterdeck Mosaic**. They have less daunting interfaces which make them a little easier to configure and can dial multiple providers.

Macintosh users need look no further than **MacTCP**, which can be obtained separately from most Access Providers or from your Apple dealer as part of the Apple Internet Connection Kit.

Dialing different providers

Once your connection software is set up you should be able to forget about it, unless you have to **dial a different provider**. This is where problems can occur on PCs. When you install the TCP/IP software, it deposits its own version of a file named winsock.dll into your system path. If you install two TCP/IP packages you could have two such files in different directories, but both in your system path, or one could overwrite the other. Make sure this doesn't happen as it can cause conflicts.

If you change providers and you already have a TCP/IP program on your machine, or if you are running Windows 95, OS/2 Warp, or a Macintosh, ask your new provider's advice on configuration. Never install two TCP/IP stacks, it's asking for trouble.

Dialers

The other essential piece of connection software is the **dialer**. It is often integrated into the same software that enables the TCP/IP connection. The dialer is the place to enter your **user details**, **password**, and your **provider's telephone number**. After it's configured all you should ever have to do is click on "connect", or something similar, to instruct your modem to dial.

If it might be useful to you, get a dialer that enables you to enter several providers' details and alternative phone numbers. Windows 95 handles this supremely. To automate the log-in under Windows 95, get the Dialup Scripting Tool. It comes with the Plus Pack or you can download it free at:

http://www.microsoft.com/windows/download/dscrpt.exe

Did you get all that TCP/IP stuff?

If you didn't understand a bar of the last couple of pages on getting connected, don't worry! Internet connection and TCP/IP configuration is your Internet Access Provider's speciality. It's in their interest to get you up and running, so if things go haywire, or you're just plain confused, do things the easy way – give them a call. After all, if you can't get connected, they're not going to get paid.

Right – is that it, or do I still need more software?

The TCP/IP and dialer combination is enough to get you connected to the Net. But you'll need more software to use the Net's various areas – and you'll probably get most of it from your provider.

The one thing you absolutely definitely need is an **FTP client**, so that you can download all the best Internet software from the Net itself, for free. If you've been given Netscape, the Chameleon sampler, WinFTP, or Fetch, you're ready to start.

Your next step will be to get yourself programs to **handle mail**, read **Usenet**, use **IRC**, browse the **Web**, view graphics, encode and decode files, and whatever else you desire. Don't worry, they're not hard to find with the whole Internet at your disposal – and they needn't cost a penny. For more on how to do it, just read on.

CONNECTING FOR THE FIRST TIME

The best exercise for your very first connection is to get the latest Internet software.

First, install or configure your **TCP/IP**, dialing and **mail software** to your provider's specification. If your provider has done its job properly and supplied you with clear instructions, this shouldn't be too hard. You'll also need an **FTP program** (see the chapter on File Transfer, starting on p.67), which shouldn't require configuration, although it can be handy to set your email address as its default password.

Next, **connect your modem** (or terminal device) to the phone line, and **instruct your dialer** to call. It will make all kinds of mating noises while connecting, like a fax machine. Once the connection's negotiated, these sounds will cease. At some stage you'll have to **enter your user name and password**. This will be a one-off event if it's incorporated into your scripting, otherwise you'll have to do it every time. Keep this password private – anyone could use it to rack up your bill or, perhaps worse, read your mail (although you may be issued with a separate password to retrieve mail).

If you've been given a program called **Ping** as part of your software package, you can use it to verify that you have an IP connection by contacting another computer. Just open up Ping and key in any domain name such as www.microsoft.com or www.ibm.com If Ping fails to convert the domain name into an IP address on both attempts, you've either incorrectly configured your TCP/IP settings, your provider's Domain Name Server is not working, or you've failed to achieve an IP connection. Log off, recheck your settings and try again. If you can't get it to work, ring support and ask for help.

If you haven't been given Ping, skip that test and go straight to your **FTP program** – and if you can't connect to any FTP servers, ring support. Assuming you can, it's time to build your software collection. Just take your pick from the Software Roundup (see p.315). The latest version of Netscape would make a good choice, if you haven't been supplied it, but be warned – it's so big it could take over an hour for the full chat/Java/3D edition (at 14.4 kbps).

Once you've successfully downloaded something from the Net and verified it works, you're ready to launch into the World Wide Web, Usenet, or pretty much everything else on the Internet. Give yourself a pat on the back, the hardest part's over.

Okay, I'm connected – but it's very slow, or I keep getting a busy tone

This is an all too common lament. The Net is suffering badly from overload and **transfer rates slow down** due to bottlenecks between the computer where a file or Web page is stored and your computer. If transfers are slow from everywhere, however, the problem lies closer to home. It could be that your provider has too many users online, or accessing its Web area from outside, and the bottleneck is forming between it and the Net. In this case your provider needs to increase its bandwidth to the Net. Probably, it will, but as it's such a low-margin business, they often stretch things.

Another common problem is the **busy/engaged tone** when you dial in, especially at peak hours (the end of the working day is worst). Keep trying until you get in: even though you dial a single number, there are several modems at the other end. If this problem happens often, complain, or get a new provider.

Another common problem is that you can connect, but you **can't actually get on to the Net**. This could be due to several things, such as a malfunctioning DNS server, an

---

Dial-Up Networking   ⊠

⚠ The computer you are dialing in to is not answering.
    Try again later.

                        [OK   ]

---

incorrectly configured TCP/IP, failure to get an IP address, or a temporary outage. If you specify a few DNS servers in your configuration, the first won't occur. If you've already succeeded in getting on the Net and you haven't meddled since, your configuration should be all right. But check it anyway. If you can pick up your mail, and access local Web sites, but not others, there'll be an outage somewhere. Report it, and try later. If it's intermittent, chances are you're not getting an IP connection every time. Apart from dialing again, all you can do is complain or change providers.

Always call your provider when you have complaints with its service. You'll get to know what's going on and where it's headed. If you're not treated with respect, no matter how trivial your enquiry, take your money elsewhere. There's a prevailing arrogance within the computer industry. Don't tolerate it. You're the customer, they're not doing you a favor.

THE SINGLE BEST PIECE OF ADVICE

If you know someone who's a bit of an Internet guru, coax them over to help you hook up for the first time. Throw in enough pizza, beer, and compliments about their technical prowess, and you'll have an auxiliary support unit for life.

Online Services and Major ISPs

AOL, CompuServe, Microsoft Network, and Prodigy aren't exactly Internet Service Providers. They're what's classed as Online Services. That's because they supply more than just Internet access. They also provide private content, which is carried on a separate network and only available to members. These networks are similar to the Internet, though obviously on a much more limited scale. On the plus side, they are better organized, more secure, regulated, easier to navigate, and simpler to install, which makes them particularly attractive to newcomers. They also run some excellent bulletin boards or discussion groups, and, due to their international reach, offer a very broad range of Points Of Presence to dial in. If you want to pick up mail on your travels, this can be a big plus.

Following are brief summaries of what's on offer from the major Online Services. Even more than usual with the Internet, these comments carry a "sell by" warning: they are all in a state of flux as they migrate from their closed private networks to the Web proper. Also covered in this chapter are the major **international Internet Service Providers,** who offer full Internet access but don't provide a private network of their own, instead maintaining a presence on the World Wide Web where they offer customer support and information.

Bulletin Boards (BBSs)

Another presence on the Internet periphery are the **Bulletin Boards** (BBSs). These are usually small dial-up operations that only offer limited email and Usenet access to the Internet, if any at all. There are thousands of them worldwide, each with its own personality and range of facilities. Even if you already have full Internet access they may have something unique to offer, at a low cost, such as large games and software archives. However, they're increasingly becoming lairs for the less savoury types of files. To find specialist BBSs, try the classified adverts in PC magazines. Once you find one, you can use a program like Terminal, Hyperterminal, or Telix to log on and search for a file listing BBS activity in your area.

CHOOSING AN ONLINE SERVICE

Online Services make a great introduction to the online world. But many users end up spending most of their time on the Internet, and find they are paying extra for proprietary content, chat rooms, and forums they never use. However, if an Online Service has just one or two features that really do it for you, then it doesn't matter about all the rest.

So, try them out – all of them, if you have time. It won't cost you anything, because they're all mad on free trials. Between ten hours and a month is typical. Use them to do your Net research on where to go next and appraise them as we outlined in the Getting Connected chapter (p.19). If you enjoy one, then sign up. But don't do it until you've tried at least one dedicated ISP, so that you can compare them for speed and service.

AOL (America Online)

With well over six million account holders, **America Online (AOL)** is currently the largest Online Service. But the number of users could potentially be up to five times that, because each member is allowed five "screen names". In effect, this means five people – your friends and family, say – can each have a sub-account at no extra cost. They can then log in and do everything you can with a full account. With one exception. As account holder, you control how much they can access. So if you don't want your kids near binary newsgroups (the main area for pornography), you can bar them, or ban decoding and downloading.

These screen names are actually email addresses. So if you choose the screen name Shelley, your email address would be Shelley@aol.com. Unfortunately, with potentially thirty million screen names, it's hard to get the one you want. Especially as once you've taken one, and changed it, it can't be re-used.

AOL has been aggressively pushing its software to the point where any computer magazine buyer in the US or UK will have several copies of its software program. Still, signing up couldn't be easier. You just pop in the disk, type in a few personal details, click "yes" a few times, and within seconds you're asked to choose a screen name. And then you get a month's free access to not only all AOL's content but the full Internet as well.

AOL's own content is impressive and carries no premium charges. It differs from CompuServe's in being somewhat more aligned at leisure and kids than study and computing, and includes some lively forums or discussion groups. It has a bright cheerful interface, which can also be used for accessing AOL content and mail via the Internet.

For a free trial and local pricing call: ☎0800 279 1234 (UK); ☎800 827 6364 (US). AOL also offers Internet-only access in the US through **GNN**; for details on this, call: ☎800 819 6112.

CompuServe

CompuServe started Online Services in the late 1970s and now has over 5000 Points Of Presence in 187 countries, five million members, and a content range second

to none. It has support forums for just about everything supportable, online shopping, news, magazines, professional forums, chat, software registrations, program archives, financial data, flight reservations, and

more services than you could look at in a lifetime. It was also the world's first truly international full Internet access provider. So no matter where you join, you can dial in to any of its international numbers to browse the Internet or pick up your email. It's simple to register and provides all the necessary software, which now includes Microsoft's Internet Explorer, for free.

CompuServe has had well publicized problems over

the last year as its network strained under the weight of new users from its subscription drives. But it has been rewiring, rerouting its hubs (so that traffic doesn't all have to go through the US), and expanding its bandwidth, and as deals with Microsoft and AT&T come into effect, things should improve significantly. It has also promised to sort out its major bugbear of issuing numbers instead of names for its members, which makes its email addresses hard to remember.

Such glitches aside, CompuServe has already built the framework for global Internet provision, high quality content, and mass userbase handling. If it fulfills all its promises, it should move into the lead as the world's largest access provider.

CompuServe's charges can be quite complex, with premiums for some of its services, and different payment structures for different countries. Internet-only access is offered at a discount. It also has three age-bracketed US-only services under the WOW! banner.

For a free trial and local pricing call: ☎0800 289 378 (UK); ☎1800 025 240 (Australia); ☎0800 446 113 (NZ); ☎800 848 8199 (North America).

Microsoft Network

After a false start into a proprietary based network, **Microsoft Network** has established itself as a player, with over a million members signed. Like CompuServe, it's on its way to becoming a fully Web-based service – essentially, a pay-to-enter Web site.

Being the youngest on the block, and having the advantage of being hard-linked into every version of Windows 95, has clearly given it an edge. As Bill Gates admits, Microsoft doesn't need to make money out of its Internet presence. However, conversely, the Internet will be integral to everything Microsoft does from now on. So the Microsoft Network at its worst could become another Pathfinder (Time/Warner's colossal Web site). A place to get the latest product patches, plus a smattering of news and entertainment to keep you coming back. All it has to do is keep you exposed to its product range. So don't be surprised if it becomes free or drops its prices dramatically. At the moment it's way overpriced.

The dial-up side is a different issue. Unlike its Online Service rivals, Microsoft isn't in the access game. It has deals with other providers to supply access. This gives it the flexibility to pull out if need be, and switch providers, perhaps to cable or ADSL.

Right now, Microsoft Network's own content is sparse and mostly US-oriented, but what's there is generally first-rate, such as 3D chat rooms, secure email with drag-and-drop attachments, and NBC news. If you have Windows 95, you can just click on the icon and follow the instructions, but to save your phone bill call and get the latest software updates on disk.

For details call: ☎0345 002 000 (UK); ☎1800 386 5550 North America; ☎1800 257 253 (Australia), and ask how much they'd like to charge you today.

Prodigy
....

Prodigy was the first Online Service to add full Internet access. That used to be its drawcard. At the time of writing its Internet gateway was the least attractive of this field, bound by a shoddy browser and poor newsreader,

but it will soon be distributing Netscape Navigator and upgrading its TCP/IP compatibility.

It's not quite as content rich as the other Online Services, especially in product support and file downloads. However, it offers strong kids, travel, and business content, although sometimes at a premium, and has a strong focus on uncensored chat areas. It's also, at present, only available in North America.

Internet-only access is available through Access Direct. For a free trial call: ☎800 776 3449.

INTERNATIONAL ISPS

The big International Internet Service Providers are – like the Online Services detailed above – useful if you travel a lot, as you can make use of their local dial-in Points Of Presence. But they're also strong at home, and are likely to be among the major long-term players.

IBM Global Network

Big Blue is an odd company. It doesn't exactly welcome home users with open arms. In fact, it would prefer you to come back with an order for your whole building. Even then it would rather you sorted out the individual billings. When it comes to attitude, IBM has it in bottles. But it invariably has the product to back it up and Internet connectivity is no exception. In a recent online survey, IBM was ranked the #1 US provider across the board. However, although it's available in more than 100

other countries, outside the US, it appears to be in two minds whether or not it's in the consumer market.

So if you're after a clean, fast, internationally transferable connection, call your local IBM branch for details. Depending on where you are, be prepared for a bit of a run around, and in some cases (not in the US) substantially higher rates than usual.

Call: ☎0800 973 000 (UK); ☎132 426 (Australia); ☎800 775 5808 (North America); or your local IBM dealer. Or if you have Web access, see: http:/www.ibm.com/globalnetwork

Netcom

With around half a million subscribers, **Netcom** is possibly the world's largest regular ISP – a claim it looks set to dispute for some time with UUNet Pipex/AlterNet and the giant US newcomer AT&T. It still has less than a tenth of AOL's membership but it is a serious ISP, with close to 100% coverage in North America and the UK, and plans to expand into Europe, the Asia Pacific region, and Latin America.

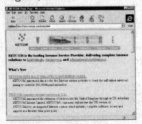

You're unlikely to have complaints about its service. Netcom's network and nonsense-free installation are as sound as you'll find, plus it has support staff on duty around the clock seven days a week. And most importantly, they know their stuff.

The only downside is that i the US you have to call a (408) number for phone support, so outside this area you'll be up for long distance rates. However, it does have an (800) fax-back number and swift online support. It's priced about average, and perhaps a little higher in the UK.

For more call: ☎0800 973001 (UK) or ☎800 501 8649 (North America); or see: http://www.netcom.com

UUNet Pipex/AlterNet

After the big Internet Service Provider shakeout which everyone's predicting, **UUNet Pipex** is well poised to remain among the major players. Not just because it's a solid provider now, but because it's already putting its footholds into next generation technology. Its recent merger with MFS, a cable owner and telecommunications carrier, should guarantee it can expand to meet bandwidth demand at competitive prices. Conversely, it does mean it's already taking risks, especially if traffic moves to the skies.

 Like IBM, UUNet Pipex's primary focus has been the corporate market, but its consumer products are far better defined through **Pipex Dial** in the UK and **AlterNet** in North America. On the home user front, it offers 33.6 kbps dial-up access throughout its network and a global roaming option that means you can dial in to any of its hundreds of presences worldwide. It's also one of the few providers to offer extra mail accounts as standard.

For details, call: ☎0500 474 739 (UK) or ☎800 4UUNET4 (North America); or see: http:/www.uunet.net

APC (Association for Progressive Communications)

APC is neither an Internet Service Provider nor Online Service, but an association of networked groups. It's specifically dedicated to serving non-governmental organizations and citizens working for social change. In the UK, it's represented by **GreenNet**; in the US by **IGC**; and in Australia by **Pegasus**. Plus it has members in places major ISPs wouldn't dream of going, such as Ethiopia and Uzbekistan.

That doesn't mean all APC members have full Internet access – there are still many places the Net hasn't reached in full. But it does mean if you have a GreenNet account, you have reciprocal access to any of its local networks, and a way of picking up your mail on the move. Plus the networks have special interest forums you won't find on the Net, on such issues as peace, human rights, the environment, social justice, indigenous rights, public health, and poverty. However, unless you are involved with NGOs, are politically active, or spend time in less connected areas like Africa and Latin America, it is unlikely to offer you anything extra.

For details call: GreenNet ☎0171 713 1941 (UK); IGC ☎415 442 0220 (US); or Pegasus ☎07 3255 0255 (Australia). Or see: http://www.apc.org/dial.html

Email

If you need one good reason to justify hooking up to the Internet, email should suffice. Once you get used to conversing by email, and you build up a base of contacts with email addresses, don't be surprised if it becomes your preferred means of communication. You will write more letters and respond a lot quicker – and that means you'll probably become more productive.

Why email will change your life

Email is such an improvement on the postal system that it will revolutionize the way and the amount you communicate. You can send a message to anyone with an email address anywhere in the world, instantaneously. In fact it's so quick that it's possible they could receive your message sooner than you could print it. All you do is key an address, or choose it from your email address book, write a brief note, and click "send". No letterheads, layout, printing, envelopes, stamps, or visiting the post office. And once you're online your mailreader can automatically check for mail at whatever interval you like. You don't have to wait for the postie to arrive.

Email is also better than faxing. It's always a local call to anywhere, at any time. You never get a busy signal and you don't wake people up in far-flung destinations with different time zones. Plus you receive the actual text and not a photocopy, or an actual image file and not a scan. So that means you can send color.

It's also an improvement on the phone. You can send a message to a part of the world that's asleep and have a reply when you get up the next morning. There's no need to synchronize phone calls, be put on hold, speak to an answerphone, or tell some busybody who's calling. With email, you take the red carpet route straight through to the top. And you don't have to make small talk, unless that's the purpose of the message.

Replacing the post and fax is not email's only strength. You can also **attach any file** to a message. This allows you to forward things like advertising layout, scanned images, spreadsheets, assignments, sound clips, or even programs. And your accompanying message need only be as brief as a Post-it note or compliments slip.

Challenging the establishment

One of email's great victories is in the war against stiff business writing. Ironically, some of its inherent limitations have proved to be assets. Because email messages are simply text files, there's no need to worry about fonts, letterheads, logos, typesetting, justification, signatures, print resolution, or fancy paper. It distills correspondence down to its essence – words.

But it has gone farther than that, it has encouraged brevity. This could be the result of online costs, busy users, or just the practical mindset of the people who first embraced the technology. Whatever the reason, it's good discipline and it means that you're able to deal with several times more people than you could ever manage before.

On the other hand, email is also putting personal correspondence back into letters rather than phone calls. Almost all new users remark on this – and its possibilities for a surprising intimacy.

Managing email

If you're charged by the minute to stay connected, whether by the phone company or your provider, it's wise to **compose and read your mail offline** (ie, when you are not connected by phone). That way, while connected you're actually busy transferring information, and getting your money's worth. Most mail clients give you the option to send your messages immediately or to place them in a **queue**, as well as to collect mail at regular intervals or on request.

Unless you're connected for long periods, you should use queuing and manual checking, otherwise the program will try to send and collect when you're offline. You can then go online, collect your mail, upload your queued mail, reply to anything urgent, log off, deal with the rest and send your new bag of letters next time you go online.

Filing

In the same way that you keep your work desk tidy, and deal with paper as it arrives, you should also keep your email neat. Most mail clients let you organize your correspondence into **mailboxes** or trays of some sort. It's good discipline to use several for filing. You should always have an **in-tray** and an **out-tray**. And choose the option to **keep copies** of outgoing messages, so you can keep track of what you've sent.

Filtering

Some mail clients offer **automatic and manual filtering** abilities to allow you to transfer incoming mail into designated mailboxes, either as it arrives or on selection. It looks for a common string in the incoming header, such as the address or subject, and transfers it directly into a mailbox other than the default in-tray.

This can be useful if you subscribe to a lot of mailing lists (see the following chapter) or get a lot of junk office email. But these apart, it's better to use the manual option. This way, you leave messages in the in-tray until they've been read and dealt with, and then you can transfer them into archives for later reference.

Etiquette and tracking replies

It's common courtesy – and netiquette – to **reply to email promptly**, even if just to verify receipt. After all, it only needs to be a couple of lines. Leave email in your in-tray until it's dealt with so you can instantly see what's current. Do the same with your out-tray. Just leave the mail that's awaiting reply.

As email is quick, and people tend to deal with it immediately, if you don't get a reply within a few days you'll know what to follow up. Once you've received your reply, you can either archive or delete your original outgoing message.

Sending email

Despite first appearances, Internet email addresses aren't so hard to recall. Compu-Serve numbers apart, their name-based components are a lot easier to remember than telephone numbers and street addresses. However, there's no real need to memorize them, nor do you have to type in the whole address every time you want to write to someone.

There are two common shortcuts: one involves using a previous message, the other setting up a shortcut or nickname (an "address book" entry).

To **use an address from a previous message**, simply select the message and, if it's one you've sent, choose "send again", or if it's one you've received, "reply". You'll then have the option of including the contents of the previous message. You can delete that and also change the subject heading if you want. If you select the option "reply to all", it will go to everyone who received the initial message as well as the sender. Beware!

The **nickname** or **address book** option is equally straightforward. All mail clients let you store addresses so that you can select them quickly without having to retype the address.

Forwarding and redirecting

You can also **forward** or **redirect** a message to somebody else. Forwarded messages are tagged like replies whereas redirected messages are transferred unaltered. You can also add your own comments or edit the messages.

Carbon copies (cc) and blind carbon copies (bcc)

If you want to send two or more people the same message, you have two options.

When you don't mind if recipients know who else is receiving it, one address will have to go in the "To:" field, and the other addresses can also go in this field or in the "CC:" **carbon copy** field.

When you don't want recipients to know who else is getting their message, put their name into the "BCC:" or **blind carbon copy** field. They will then be masked from the other recipients.

Subject

Once you've worked out who is to receive your message, let them know what it's about. Put something meaningful in the **"Subject:" heading**. It's not so important when they first receive it – they'll probably open it even if it's blank. However, if you send someone your resume and you title it "Hi," two months down the track when they're looking for talent, they're going to have a hard time weeding you out of the pile.

Filling in the subject is optional when replying. If you don't enter anything, most email clients will retain the original subject and insert **"Re:"** before the original subject title to indicate it's a reply. Pretty clever, huh?

Signatures

Almost all mailreaders allow you to add your personal touch at the end of your composition in the form of a **signature file**. This will appear automatically on your email, like headed notepaper. It's common

```
  ///\\     ///\\     ///\\     ///\\
 /`0-0'    ` @ @\    //o o//     a a
    ]         >       ) | (       _)
    ~         ~         ~          ~
  John      Paul     George     Ringo
```

practice to put your address, phone number, title, and perhaps round off with a witticism. Net geeks even construct monumental pictures and frames in ASCII art, but you'll have more taste than that.

Replying to mail

Another great email feature is the ability to quote from received correspondence. When you want to reply to incoming mail, simply click on "reply" – in most email clients – to automatically **copy the original message** and address it back to the sender. This message will appear with **defining tags** (>) prior to each line, and you have the option of including parts or all of the original message – or deleting it. So when someone asks you a question or raises a point, you can include that section and answer it directly underneath. This saves you having to type it in, or them having to refer back to the message they sent.

If your email client doesn't offer this automatic duplicating and tagging, you can do pretty much the same, by copying the text from the letter you want to reply to, selecting "reply," and pasting it in. You can then edit accordingly, indicating which sections have come from the previous letter by typing defining tags (>).

Whichever system you run, don't fall into the habit of including the **entire contents** of the original letter in your reply. It wastes time for the receiver and its logical outcome (letters comprising the whole history of your correspondence) hardly bears thinking about.

Attaching non-text files to your email

Suppose you want to send something other than just a text message – such as a **word processor document** or a **spreadsheet** or an **image** – via email. It's quite feasible, and no longer requires technical expertise.

It works like this. Internet mail messages are transmitted in plain ASCII text and must be no larger than 64 kb. That means to send anything larger than 64 kb and anything other than text it has to be processed first. This includes all **binary files** such as images, spreadsheets, word-processor documents, and programs. Thankfully, these days, your email program can handle this for you without too much thinking on your behalf. It simply converts the binary coding into 7-bit ASCII and chops the message into units less than 64 kb. When the message arrives, it's automatically decoded, and then lobbed into the designated download directory.

Well, it's almost that simple. First, both parties' mailreaders need to support a common encoding standard – otherwise it will appear in gibberish. The most used methods are **Binhex**, **UUencode**, and **MIME**. It doesn't really matter which you use as long as it works every time, so try a practice run first. To send the file, look in your mail menu for something along the lines of "Send Attachments" or "Attach File." Refer to your Help file on how to specify an encoding method, as it varies between packages. MIME is gaining acceptance across all platforms (it's all that Netscape's mailer recognizes), so if you have the option, choose it as default. On Macs it might be called Apple Single or Apple Double. Always choose Apple Double.

If your mailreader doesn't automatically decode attachments, ditch it for one that does. **Eudora Pro** is worth the expense for its reliability in this area alone.

The next generation: Microsoft Exchange

Microsoft Exchange (part of Windows 95) and Microsoft Internet Mail and News (part of Internet Explorer) go one step further. You can apply formatting directly to a message, and drag and drop binary files into the body. However, both ends must have it to appreciate all the features, otherwise the recipient will get all the formatting as a useless and time-wasting MIME attachment.

Additionally, although the concept of fancying up your email by adding colour, logos, and signatures might seem appealing, it's unlikely to increase your productivity and actually detracts from one of email's strongest features – simplicity.

The address – and returned mail

Internet addresses should appear along the lines of: user@host The user refers to the sender's identity and host identifies the server where they collect their mail.

If you submit an illegally constructed address, or an address that doesn't exist, your message will be bounced back to you with an error message telling you what went wrong.

This usually happens within a matter of minutes. Sometimes, however, your mail will be bounced back after a few days. This usually indicates a physical problem in delivering the mail rather than an addressing error. When it occurs, just send it again. If it's your end that's caused the problem, you might have a whole batch of mail to re-send.

Sending mail to Online Services

To make life a little harder, not all mailing addresses you encounter are going to be in the standard user@host format.

To send to **CompuServe subscribers**, for example, you have to use the host name compuserve.com and replace the comma in the user name with a period. Thus to send mail to CompuServe member 12345,678 you would have to change it to 12345.678@compuserve.com

Other Online Services maintain a regular Internet form in their addresses. For example, to send to Brian McClair at America Online, you would probably address it to brianmc@aol.com while Ryan Giggs at Prodigy might be giggsy@prodigy.com These Online Service subscribers get to choose their "nickname" address, just like regular Internet users.

Collecting from the road

With a **POP3 email account** (ask your Provider if that's the type you have), you can pick up your email from anywhere on the Net without even changing your email program's settings. If you're packing your computer, it shouldn't be a problem – all you have to do is connect to the Net via any full IP access provider and pick up your mail in the usual way. This is where the international big guns like CompuServe, IBM Global Net, UUNet, and Microsoft Network are handy. If you set up one of these accounts at home before you leave, you can dial in to any of their international points of presence and have it billed to you at home. But, if you intend to use the Net a lot in one spot, it may be more cost effective to get a temporary local account. But, of course, you still have to pay your usual provider to maintain your mailbox while you're abroad. (Although since you won't be dialing in, you may be able to negotiate a reduced monthly fee.)

If you'll be separated from your computer, you'll need to know your email configuration settings. That is, your POP3 mail account (e.g. jane@mail.fish.com), SMTP address (e.g. mail.fish.com), email address (e.g. jane@fish.com), user name and password. You can find these details in your mail client's configuration settings or by asking your Service Provider or system manager. Then you can get on any machine that's hooked to the Net anywhere in the world – at a cybercafé, say, or on a friend's or business associate's machine – and put your details in its email settings and collect and send your mail in exactly the same way as you do from your home account. But be careful to restore the original mail settings when you've finished, and delete your mail, otherwise someone may either deliberately or inadvertently use your mailbox and read your mail.

You might also find it useful to take a pre-configured copy of **Eudora Light** on a floppy. That way, you can conduct the whole exercise from a disk drive without having to change any settings. You can also save your mail to the disk and take it with you. Eudora Light is available free at: ftp://ftp.qualcomm.com/quest/eudora Remember someone else can pick up your mail in exactly the same way, so keep your password secure. And for the ultimate in mobile mail ease, read on.

Hot Mail – a free mailbox on the Web

Several companies specialize in giving away free mail accounts. The catch is you have to put up with a bit of advertising as well.

Our pick is **Hot Mail** at: http://www.hotmail.com Just log into the Web page, give a few details and you'll have a mail account in seconds. It's not like normal mail in that it's all done via the Web. That makes it great for collecting your mail on the road, especially as you can use the same page to pick up your POP3 mail, but a bit inconvenient for everyday use. As you can give any details you like, and recipients can't pick the header apart to tell where it's from, it's a perfect anonymous mailer – though abusers can still be traced.

UUNet Pipex offers a similar service to subscribers.

Staying anonymous

Occasionally when sending mail or posting to a newsgroup, you might prefer to **conceal your identity** – for example, to save embarrassment in health discussions. There are three main ways to send mail anonymously. As mentioned above, Hot Mail is one.

The second is less ethical. You can change your configuration so that it looks like it's coming from somebody else, either real or fictitious. However, if anyone tries to reply, their mail will attempt to go to the alias, not you. You might get a few laughs out of discovering this, as many people are unaware you can do it. But, be warned, they can trace the header details back to your server, if they're really keen. Your local law enforcement agency is that keen.

The third way is to register with a server dedicated to **redirecting anonymous mail**. These generally act as gobetweens. When someone receives such mail, it's plainly masked, as it comes from an obviously coded email address. When they reply, the anonymous server handles the redirection. That's as good as it gets, but if you break the law in the process, they can still find you by demanding your details from the server's administrator. For more information see: http://c2.net/remail

Privacy

Although there's been a lot of fuss about hacking and Net security, in reality email is still a lot more secure than the telephone or postal system. However, although not likely, it's still possible that your email could be intercepted by curious parties. If you're sending information that could threaten someone's reputation, affect stock prices, or get you in trouble, you should consider encrypting your mail. That usually involves scrambling the message using an encoding program.

PGP (Pretty Good Privacy), the most popular method, generates a set of public and private "keys" from a passphrase. You can distribute the public key but you must keep the private key secure. When someone wants to send you a private message, they scramble it using your public key. You use the private key, or your secret passphrase, to decode it.

It might not seem such a big deal to ensure a two-way conversation – you may have even thought it was one of your rights. Well, think again. In fact, most governments believe they have a mandate to monitor all forms of communication. You'll find that to guarantee absolute privacy, that is, to send a message even the CIA couldn't crack, using a relatively simple program, may place you, or the programmer, in breach of an arms export act. Some mail clients have built-in encryption, however it's likely to be what's referred to as "weak encryption" – something that could be cracked by someone relatively skilled. To get water-tight security you need to use a much bigger key (stronger encryption), like PGP's. (See our Software Roundup chapter.)

At present, the Net is ablaze with indignation at government moves to enforce restrictions on strong encryption, particularly across national divides. The reasons cited range from issues of national security and tax collection to the classification of encryption as a weapon during war times. If you believe in freedom of speech above all else, get involved. For more see: The **PGP FAQ** at http://www.prairienet.org/~jalicqui/pgpfaq.txt, the **Electronic Frontier Foundation** at http://www.eff.org/ or the newsgroups: alt.security.pgp and comp.risks and sci.crypt and talk.politics.crypto

Where to get an email program

For addresses of where to **download email programs**, see our Software Roundup.

If you are using Microsoft Exchange you should upgrade the Internet messaging or better still ditch it and use Internet Mail and News, which comes with Internet Explorer. See Microsoft's home page at: http://www.microsoft.com.

Finding someone's email address

See our chapter on **Finding It**.

The Net by email

If your Internet access is restricted to email only, you can still get to quite a lot via automatically responding mailservers (see the section following). No-one would suggest it's on a par with full access, but you're not shut out altogether. For example, if you can't use FTP, you could try using an FTP mail server to supervise the transfer. It's even possible to retrieve Web page text. There's more about these alternatives in the following chapters.

Mailing Lists

If you want to receive a lot of email, the surest way is to join a mailing list. There are thousands available via the Net, all intended to disseminate information or encourage discussion on a specific topic. This is the Internet's easiest way to keep up with special interest news and discussion, as all you have to do is collect your mail.

Joining couldn't be easier. In most cases, you simply **"subscribe"** by sending a single email message. Once aboard, you'll receive all the messages sent to the list's address, just as everyone else on the list will receive what you send. **Unsubscribing** is equally simple. Luckily so, as you may get a fright at the amount of mail some lists generate.

Mailing list basics

Each mailing list has two addresses: the **mailing address** used to contact others on the list; and the **administrative address** used to send commands to the server or maintainer of the list. Don't get them mixed up or everyone else on the list will see you're a bozo.

Most lists are **unmoderated**, meaning that they rebroadcast messages immediately. Messages on **moderated** lists must first be approved by human intervention. Moderation can be used as a form of censorship, but more often it's a welcome bonus, improving the quality of discussion and keeping it on topic by pruning out irrelevant and repetitive messages. It all depends on the moderator, who is rarely paid for the service. Certain other lists are moderated because they carry messages from one source, such as the US Travel Warnings. Such lists often have a parallel list for discussion.

If you'd rather receive your mail in large batches than have it trickle through, request a **digest** if there's an option. These are normally sent daily or weekly, depending on the traffic.

Most lists are maintained by computer programs these days, but some are still manual. For those, the administrative address is the same as the list's address with -request appended. For example, the administrative address of the list dragster-bikes@sissybar.net would be dragster-bikes-request@sissybar.net To subscribe or unsubscribe to such a list, send a one-line message to the administrator.

Listserv

The most popular automated list system, LISTSERV, is now widely available on the Net. Its lists use listserv as the administrative address, so to join the list muck@rake.com you'd send a subscription message to: listserv@rake.com

Requests are interpreted by a program which usually reads only the message body. Messages may contain several requests as long as they're on separate lines, but you shouldn't include your signature as it will confuse the program. Since all LISTSERV systems are hooked together, you can send your request to any LISTSERV host and your request will be redirected. If you're not sure which host to use, send your request to listserv@bitnic.bit.net (in North America) or listserv.net (in Europe).

To join a LISTSERV list, send the following message:
    SUB listname your name
To take yourself off, send:
    SIGNOFF listname
To find out what options are available, send:
    HELP
To find out all the lists on a LISTSERV system, send:
    LIST
To find lists throughout all LISTSERV systems, send:
    LIST GLOBAL (It's over 500 Kb, so brace yourself!)
To be notified of new lists as soon as they appear, join:
    new-list at listserv@vml.nodak.edu

Note that many LISTSERV lists are mirrored in Usenet newsgroups under the bit.listserv hierarchy.

MajorDomo

MajorDomo is another list manager similar to LISTSERV. It uses the address majordomo@host

To join a MajorDomo list, send:
    subscribe listname address
To be removed, send:
    unsubscribe listname address

In both cases adding your email address is optional but useful if you want to subscribe someone else.

To find out which lists you've subscribed to at any MajorDomo host, send:
    which
As MajorDomo hosts are independent, you can't request an overall list – you have to request it from each host individually. To receive a list, send:
    list

Finding a list to join

See our chapter on **Finding It**.

Starting your own list

To find out how to start your own list, mail:
    listserv@bitnic.educom.edu and listserv@uottawa.bitnet
see: The List Owners Survival Guide at:
    http://www.lsoft.com/manuals/owner/owner.html
and ask your access provider.

Vacation alert!

If you're going on vacation or are not going to be able to
pick up your mail for a while, consider unsubscribing
temporarily. It's amazing how quickly mailing list email
can build up.

File Transfer (FTP)

Before you can crack open the Internet's treasure chest, you'll probably need to stock up on software. Even if you bought a kit like CyberJack, Turnpike, or Internet in a Box, or were given a package by your access provider, it won't be long before you'll want to try out alternative components or add the latest multimedia gadgetry.

overview.html		
Host: ee.utah.edu		
Status: Getting		
State: Finished		
Transfered: 2753	**Bytes/Sec:** 550	**Time Left:**
226 Transfer complete.		

The good news is you can download almost all the Internet software you'll ever need free, from the Net itself. And, surprisingly, many of these freely distributed programs are actually superior to those bundled into commercial packages. In fact, they're almost always better. So don't be afraid to turf out components that you've acquired in a starter kit. As Internet software must comply with TCP/IP specifications, units should be seamlessly replaceable.

If your kit's **TCP/IP socket** causes problems (see TCP/IP on p.31), consider replacing it with something reliable like **Trumpet Winsock**, or reinstalling the one that comes with **Windows 95**. Any bundle that won't let you mix and match components isn't worth keeping. The only drawback is that if you install new components you might have to launch them by clicking on their icons and not from the menu in your all-in-one package. But that's no real concern.

Before you can download anything, you'll need an **FTP (File Transfer Protocol) program**. You can use a stand-alone dedicated program or do it all from your World Wide Web browser. Browsers such as Netscape and Microsoft Internet Explorer are continually improving as FTP clients, but dedicated programs are less demanding on system resources so may work better if you're short on memory. Dedicated FTP clients may also offer more features, such as the ability to enter identification and passwords.

We've dedicated a whole chapter of this book to a **roundup of Net software** (see p.315), giving the FTP or Web addresses to contact. You may want to refer to it in conjunction with this section.

Free software programs from the Net

While the Internet might be a veritable clearing house of freely available software, it's not all genuinely free. There are three types of programs you're allowed to use, at least for a while, without paying. They are called **freeware**, **shareware**, and **beta programs**.

Freeware

Freeware is provided by its author(s) without any expectation of payment. It could be a complete program, a demonstration sample with crippled features, a patch to enhance another program, or an interim upgrade. In some cases, a donation, or even a postcard, is appreciated.

Shareware

Shareware usually has certain conditions attached, which you accept when you install or run the program. One common condition is that you must pay to use the program if you continue with it after an initial free trial period. Another condition may be that you pay if you intend to use it commercially. Sometimes the shareware version, while adequate, is a shortform of a more reliable or heavily featured registered version. When you pay your registration fees, the author or software distributor will mail you the upgrade or grant you access to a password-protected FTP area.

Beta programs

Betas are distributed as part of the testing process in commercial software development. You shouldn't pay for them as they're not finished products. But they are often good enough for the task, and sometimes – for example, the popular Netscape World Wide Web browser (of which more later) – are at the cutting edge of technology.

With all beta programs, you should expect to encounter bugs and quirks now and again. Don't be too upset by having to restart the program or reboot (start it up again) occasionally – it's all part of the development process. But do report recurring faults to the developers, after all that's why they're letting you have it free. If you notice a pattern, email the distributors and ask for a fix. If it's just too buggy, get an alternative.

How to use FTP

Of the several techniques for transferring files across the Internet, by far the most popular is FTP. Obtaining files by FTP is straightforward if you have an **FTP client** with a graphical interface. They're all much alike – anything will do to get started. And if you don't like one, use it to download another.

Unless you've been granted special permission to log into a server and transfer files, you'll have to use what's known as **"anonymous FTP."** Sites which allow you to do this follow a standard log-in procedure. Once you're in, you can look through the contents of a limited number of directories and transfer files to your computer.

Many Net servers have areas set aside for anonymous FTP. Some even carry massive specialist file archives. And most software houses provide updates, patches, and interim releases on their own anonymous FTP sites. No single server will have everything you need, but you'll soon find favorites for each type of file. Even your access provider will have an FTP area, where you can transfer files for updating Web pages, download access software, and exchange files with colleagues.

FTP domains are often prefixed by ftp: but that's not a rule. When you're supplied a file location it could be in the form ftp.fish.com/pub/dir/jane.zip That tells you that the file jane.zip is located in the directory pub/dir on the ftp.fish.com server.

Logging in and downloading a file

Before you can download anything, you have to **log on to the server**. FTP programs use different terminologies, so it won't hurt to read its help or "readme" file. It should tell you what to key in where. Basically, though, the procedure is fairly routine and goes like this:

To retrieve ftp.fish.com/pub/dir/jane.zip, enter the server's address ftp.fish.com as **host name**, anonymous as **user name** and your Internet email address (in the form user@host) as a **password**.

Next, enter the **directory** you want to start looking in, in this case, /pub/dir Make sure the path and file details are entered in the correct (upper/lower) case. If you enter Dir instead of dir on a UNIX host, it will return an error because UNIX is case sensitive. If you have the file's full location, try entering that as initial directory. However, don't be surprised if a file isn't where it's supposed to be – system managers are forever shuffling directories. And it's not necessary to get the location exactly right: once you're in, you can just browse around until you find it.

Having entered the details above, you're ready to **log in**. If the site gets a lot of traffic, you may not be admitted the first time. Don't let that discourage you. If you can't get in within ten attempts, try again later, perhaps outside the local peak hours. If you're accessing a US site from Europe or vice versa, try when that continent is asleep. You're also likely to get a better transfer rate.

Once you're accepted, you'll see a listing of the initial **directory's contents**. Look for the contents file called readme, index, or the like. Read it if you're unsure of the contents, and read, too, any accompanying **text files** before downloading a program. You can usually do that by either clicking on them or selecting "view" or "read" from the menu.

Most FTP programs work in a similar way to Windows' file manager or the Macintosh folder system. That means when you click, something happens. Look at the top of the directory contents. Clicking on ".." will send you up a directory level. Clicking on "." will take you back to the root directory. Directories should be distinguishable from files by having a different color, type-face, having a folder icon, or at least not having extensions. **Clicking on a directory** will open it, **clicking on a file** will start the download.

Make sure you **select "binary transfer"** before down-loading any files other than plain text. If you're unsure of the file type, just choose binary. It can be used to transfer text files as well. Although it may be slightly slower, text files aren't usually that large, so it's not really an issue. But if you download a graphic, sound, or program as "text" it will be useless. Everyone makes that mistake at least once.

Your FTP client should give you a **transfer progress report** to tell you how long it's going to take. You can either sit and watch the bits zip into your hard drive or relegate it to the background while you do something else, like explore the Web.

Unfortunately, **if the transfer fails** or is canceled, you can't pick up where you left off. You have to start again from scratch. This is one of the Net's most annoying and frustrating features.

Uploading files

FTP isn't just for scoring files, you can **upload** as well. It might be more practical to submit stories, documents, graphics, and applications this way, rather than burden the email system with bulky attachments. For example, suppose you want to submit artwork to a magazine. You could FTP the scans to an area set aside for downloads (often a directory called incoming), and then notify the editor by email. The editor could then instruct staff to upload them for approval. If they're okay they could then be processed and moved to an outgoing directory for print house access.

In some cases an area is set aside where files can be uploaded and downloaded to the same directory. This could prove useful if you want to transfer files to a colleague who's having problems with handling mailed attachments (it happens!). It can be quite annoying to have to wait for several megabytes of mail attachments to download and decode before you can read your mail. Especially if it has to be re-sent.

FTP through the World Wide Web

It's approaching the point where you can do almost everything on the Internet from the helm of your **Web browser** (see our chapter on the Web, starting on p.155). You can certainly use FTP with your browser, and it is very useful as Web pages often have links to FTP addresses. In fact, this is where you'll encounter most of your archive leads.

To **follow an FTP link on a Web page**, just click and wait to be logged in (it will take longer than loading a Web page). Depending on the link, you'll either get a page of the directory's contents, or the file you want will be on its way to your hard drive. As with any FTP transfer, if the file has moved, you'll either be defaulted back to a higher directory or get an error message. If the file isn't where it should be, or you want to enter an unlinked location, just enter it as a Web address.

Instead of http: use ftp: in the first part of the address. So, to look for a file at: ftp.hen.com in the path: /pub enter: ftp://ftp.hen.com/pub Once connected, just click on what you want in the usual fashion.

The **Netscape Web browser**, in particular, is a superb FTP client. You can kick off multiple transfers and surf the Web while you wait for the downloads or uploads to finish. Most other Web browsers are FTP ready too, but very few automatically send the session to background and let you do something else while you wait. If your browser isn't so flexible, get another.

FTP by email

Several services offer **FTP by email**. They can take up to a few days, but may save access charges over slow networks – it's usually quicker to download your mail from a local server than to transfer files from a distant busy server. If you're in more of a hurry to get offline than get the file, give it a shot. To find out how, send a "Help" message to: ftpmail@gatekeeper.dec.com

File Service Protocol (FSP)

FSP (File Service Protocol) is a more robust method of file transfer. It hasn't caught on in the mainstream yet, but it's commonly used by the digital underground.

Although it fulfills exactly the same purpose as FTP, it has several advantages, and uses entirely different protocols. Its main advantage from a user's perspective is that if the server goes down or you break connection, you can pick up where you left off. With FTP, you have to start all over again. There is a small trade-off in speed, however.

For more on the practicalities download the FAQ at: ftp.germany.eu.net/pub/networking/inet/fsp And for a lot more, follow the Newsgroup alt.comp.fsp or join the mailing list: fsp-discussion@germany.eu.net

File types and compression

There are two reasons why archived binary files are usually **compressed**. One is to decrease their storage demands and the other is to reduce transfer times. After you download a compressed file, you have to **decompress** it to get it to work. Before you can decompress it you'll have to know how it's been compressed and have the right program to do the job.

	Helpers		
Mime Type	**Application**	**Action**	**Extensions**
video/x-msvideo	AVI to QT Utility	Launch	avi
video/x-qtc	Conferencing Helper Application	Launch	qtc
application/mac-binhex40	Stuffit Expander™	Launch	hqx
application/x-stuffit	Stuffit Expander	Launch	sit

It's usually easy to tell which technique's been used just by looking at the file name or where it's located. Unless the site is specifically targeted at one platform, you're usually offered a **directory choice** between DOS, PC/Windows, Mac, and UNIX. Once you've taken that choice everything contained in that directory and its subdirectories will be for that platform only. If not, you can usually tell by the file extensions. The following table shows common file extensions and the programs needed to decompress or view them.

Extension	File type	Program to decompress or view
.arc	PC Compressed archive	PKARC, ARC, ArcMac
.arj	PC Compressed archive	UNARJ
.bin	MacBinary	MacBinary, usually automatic in Macs
.bmp	Bitmap	Graphics viewer, MS Paintbrush
.cpt	Mac Compact Pro archive	Compact Pro, Stuffit Expander
.doc	MS Word document	Word processor such as MS Word or Wordpad
.exe	PC executable	Self executing from DOS or Windows
.gif	Graphic Interchange Format	Graphics viewer
.gz	UNIX Compressed archive	GNU Zip
.hqx	Mac BinHex	BinHex, Stuffit Expander
.jpg	Compressed graphic	Graphics viewer
.lha, .lzh	Compressed archive	LHA
.mpg	Compressed video	Video viewer
.pict	Mac picture	Graphics viewer
.pit	Mac PackIt	PackIt
.ps	PostScript	PostScript printer or GhostScript
.sea	Mac Self-extracting archive	Click on icon to extract
.sit	Mac Stuffit compressed archive	Stuffit Expander
.tif	Tagged image format	Graphic viewer
.txt	Plain ASCII text	MS Notepad, text editor, word processor
.uu, .uue	UNIX UU-encoded	UUDECODE, Stuffit Expander
.z	UNIX Gnu GZip archive	GZip
.Z	UNIX compressed archive	UNCOMPRESS
.zip	PC PKZip compressed archive	PKZip, WinZip, Stuffit Expander
.zoo	Compressed archive	ZOO

PC archives mostly end in .exe, .zip, .lzh, or .arj. The .exe files are usually **self-extracting archives**, which means that they contain a program to decompress themselves. All you have to do is execute them. Just transfer them to a temporary directory and double-click on them in

File Manager or Explorer. Or run them from DOS by changing into the temporary directory and typing what comes before the .exe.

If you're on a PC, get the latest copy of **WinZip**, which lodges itself within File Manager, and the latest **Stuffit Expander** for Windows and place it on your desktop. The great thing about this combination is that it will handle just about everything. And it's easily configurable to automatically extract archived files just by double-clicking them in File Manager or Explorer, or by dropping them onto the Stuffit or WinZip icons.

Compressed **Macintosh files** usually end .cpt, .sit, .sea, or .hqx. The .sea files self-extract by clicking on them, the rest by dropping on, or opening with, Stuffit Expander.

See our **Software Roundup** for details of how to obtain the above programs.

How to set up your directory structure

Before you start installing every Internet program you can find, first sort out your **directory structure**. Otherwise, you'll turn your hard drive into a tangled jungle.

Hard drives are organized into tree-like structures. In DOS and Windows 3.x, each level is called a **Directory**. In Windows 95 and Macs it's called a **Folder**. Both mean the same thing, they're just represented different graphically. For simplicity's sake we'll call them directories. The top level of a drive is called the Root Directory. It's for system start-up files only, so don't lob anything in there. No matter what system you're running, you should create the following first-level directories:

Programs: Install all programs into their own separate subdirectories under a first-level directory called Programs, Apps, or similar. It's wise to have a second level separating the types of programs such as Net,

Graphics, Office, and such. Thus, you'd install Netscape and Eudora into their own subdirectories under Net; Word and Excel under Office; ACDSee and PaintShop under Graphics, and so forth.

Download: Configure your Net clients to download to a common Download directory and create a shortcut (alias) on your desktop to open it. Think of it as an intray and clear it accordingly.

Temporary: Once you've downloaded an application, extract it to an empty Temporary directory and then install it under the Programs hierarchy. Once done, delete the contents of the Temporary directory. If you have the space, keep the original installation file in case you need to reinstall it. Put it in your Archive directory.

Archive: Rather than have files build up in your Download folder, dedicate an Archive directory with enough subdirectories to make it easy to find things again. As you download new versions of programs, delete the old. You could also open it to your peers through a Windows 95 Dial-Up, or FTP, server. It's also the first place to delete files to make space.

Data: Put irreplaceable files, such as those you create, into a Data directory tree and regularly back it up onto another medium such as a floppy disk, tape, or even an FTP site. Use WinZip or Stuffit to compress it all into manageable chunks.

Where to find an FTP client

See the **Software Roundup** (p.315).

Finding files

See **Finding It** (p.110).

Usenet Newsgroups

The Internet may be the best place to catch up on the latest bulletins, health warnings, celebrity gossip, sports results, TV listings, movie reviews, and all that stuff commonly known in the popular media as news. It can even be delivered by email, like a virtual newspaper run. But don't be confused, that's not what's called "news" on the Internet.

In Net-speak, if you're "downloading news," you're retrieving messages posted to **Usenet discussion groups**. These messages, or **articles** as they're called, are similar to email messages but are transmitted in a separate system. Articles are grouped by topic into **Newsgroups**. Each Newsgroup has a single theme and there's hardly a subject imaginable that's left uncovered. Whether you're interested in baseball, be-bop, Buddhism, or brewing beer, there'll be a Newsgroup deliberating over the issues closest to your heart.

With a growing total of over 25,000 Newsgroups accessible to more than 40 million users, you'll have access to the world's experts in every field. Want to know the recipe for Lard Surprise, whether it's safe to go to Kashmir, why Quake keeps crashing, or where to sell that unexploded land mine in your garden? Fine, just find the right Newsgroup, post your query, and wait for the results. It's the Net as virtual community in action: fun, heartwarming, contentious, and unpredictable – and, after email, the Internet's most valuable resource.

We've listed a selection of popular and interesting Newsgroups in our **Guide to Newsgroups** (p.288). This chapter covers the basics of how to access them and join the discussions.

Accessing Usenet

You can access Usenet in several ways. The easiest is if you have **full Internet access**; this allows you to read and post articles online, switching between Newsgroups as you please. You can read any article, in any group, as long as it remains on your news provider's system.

If you just have a **BBS (Bulletin Board) or "shell" account**, you usually have to subscribe to groups and then wait for articles to arrive. A third, more obscure route is **via satellite**. A few companies provide read-only access through a decoder that sits between the dish and your computer. They transmit the entire Usenet database overnight. You can subscribe to what you want and scan through it over breakfast. But, as it's a one-way feed, you still have to post conventionally.

Even a full Internet connection does not guarantee **access to all groups**. Sometimes Newsgroups are cut, due to logistics or because of a policy to exclude certain types. That decision lies with whoever supplies your newsfeed. Although most Newsgroups are discussion groups for enthusiasts of above-board hobbies, there's a percentage of pornographic, incendiary, provocative, and just plain moronic material. So it's not surprising that many government, educative, corporate, and conservative bodies want to filter them.

How it works

Your Usenet provider (usually your ISP) keeps a **database of articles** which it updates in periodic exchanges with its neighbors. It receives articles anywhere from once a day to every few minutes, and dispatches locally created articles as well as the articles it receives from other neighbors. Due to this pass-the-ball procedure, articles may appear immediately on your screen as you post them, but propagate around the world at the mercy of whoever's in between. Exactly how much you get, and what you see, depends on your provider's neighbors and how often they update their articles.

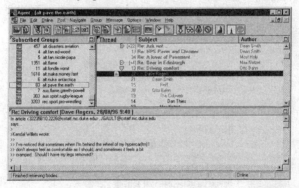

No provider can keep articles forever as it needs the space for new ones, so it **expires** them after a certain holding period. It's usual to delete articles after about four days and even sooner for large groups and binaries (articles containing encoded programs, images, or formatted text). Each provider has a different policy.

In addition, some Newsgroups are "moderated," which means that postings are screened before they appear.

Officially moderated groups are screened by whoever started the group or an appointee, but it's possible, though uncommon, that articles could be censored anywhere between you and the person who posted.

How to read addresses

Newsgroups are divided into specific topics using a simple **address system**. You can usually tell what a group's about just by looking at its address. The first part is the broad category, or **hierarchy**, it falls under. Here are some of the top-level and most popular hierarchies:

Hierarchy	Content
alt.	Alternative, anarchic, and freewheeling discussion*
aus.	Of interest to Australians
ba.	San Francisco Bay Area topics
bionet.	Biological topics
bit.	Topics from Bitnet LISTSERV mailing lists*
biz.	Accepted place for commercial postings
clari.	ClariNet subscription news service
comp.	Computing discussion*
ddn.	The Defense Data Network
ge.	German groups
k12.	Education from kindergarten through grade 12
misc.	Miscellaneous discussions that don't fit anywhere else*
news.	Discussions on Usenet itself*
rec.	Hobbies and recreational activities*
sci.	All strands of science*
soc.	Social, cultural, and religious groups*
talk.	Discussion of controversial issues*
uk.	British topics

* You'll find most of the activity within these groups.

Note that Newsgroup addresses contain periods (full stops), like domain names. But they're interpreted differently. Each part of the address distinguishes its focus, rather than its location. The top of the hierarchy is at the far left. As you move right, you go down the tree and it becomes more specific. For instance rec.sport.cricket.info is devoted to the compelling recreational sport that is cricket. Although several groups may discuss similar subjects, each will have its own angle. For example, while alt.games.sausages might have light and anarchic postings, biz.market.sausages would get down to business.

To find which Newsgroups discuss your area of interest, think laterally and use your Newsreader's filtering capabilities to **search its Newsgroup list** for key words. Or easier still, use a **search engine** (see "Finding It", p.110).

Getting access to more groups

Your newsfeed may not carry every hierarchy, nor every group within that hierarchy. Many local-interest categories, for example, will only be available within their particular locality. Your newsfeed provider selects which ones it wants to maintain and that's all you get to see. But that's not necessarily a fault, as it takes less bandwidth to keep the Usenet file up to date and thus reduces the general level of Net traffic.

But most providers are flexible. If, say, your provider has arbitrarily decided to exclude all foreign-language and minor regional groups, and you're interested in Finnish gardening and cooking, you should be able to get the groups added to the feed, simply by asking. However, sometimes omissions are due to censorship. Many providers remove groups on moral grounds, or to avoid controversy. The usual ones to get the chop are the alt.binaries.pictures.erotica (pornography), alt.sex and alt.warez (software hacking and piracy) hierarchies.

If you can't get the groups you want from your provider, either take your business to another provider, or, if that's not convenient, try a publicly accessible news server with a better selection. There's a list of them at: http://dana.ucc.nau.edu/~jwa/

Frequently Asked Questions (FAQs)

Every Newsgroup has at least one **FAQ (Frequently Asked Questions)** document. It describes the Newsgroup's charter, gives guidelines for posting, and compiles common answers to questions. Many Newsgroups carry several FAQs on various topics. They should always be your first source of information. FAQs are periodically posted, usually every couple of weeks.

A comprehensive list of FAQs can be found on the World Wide Web at: http://www.cis.ohio-state.edu/hypertext/faq/usenet/FAQ-List.html or by FTP from: rtfm.mit.edu in the path: /pub/usenet/news.answers

Choosing a Newsreader

There are several excellent **shareware Newsreaders** for every computing platform. Your access provider should supply one in your sign-up kit, and that should do to start with. Once you gain confidence on the Net, you might like to try a few alternatives.

Some mailreaders and **Web browsers** can also do the job of Newsreader. **Netscape**, for example, is useful in that you can seamlessly zip from the Web to Newsgroups and back. This saves memory by not having to open a second application and enables you to follow news links built into Web pages. However, at this stage in Netscape's development, it doesn't support automatic decoding, so it's not much use for binary groups, and it's a lot harder than most Newsreaders to figure out. Microsoft's Internet Mail and News, which comes with its **Internet Explorer** browser, is a satisfactory choice across all platforms, as is **AOL's** built-in Newsreader.

The specialist PC Newsreader that stands head and shoulders above the rest, however, is **Agent** from Forté. So far it's alone in allowing you to "queue" multiple articles for download. It has two versions: Free Agent, which is free; and Agent, the registered full-featured edition. A reasonable choice for **Macs** is **NewsWatcher**.

As ever, for download addresses of these programs, see our **Software Roundup** (p.315).

Getting started

Before you can get your news you'll need to tweak a few knobs on your Newsreader. It's hard to give definitive instructions because the features differ markedly between programs. However, here are the common things to look for.

Configuring the Newsreader

In the Newsreader configurations you'll need to specify your **newsserver**, your **identity**, and your **email address**. That shouldn't be hard – look under "Options" or "Preferences." Most Newsreaders also have a whole set of options on how long you want to keep articles after you've read them, how much to retrieve, and so forth. Leave those in the default settings and go back when you understand your demands. Right now, it's not so important.

Going online

When you first go online, you'll need to compile a **list of the Newsgroups** available on your server. Your Newsreader should do this automatically when you first connect – it could take up to several minutes. When the Newsgroups arrive, they usually appear in a window titled New Groups, though they may go straight into the main list.

The list of Newsgroups comprises just the names of the groups, not the actual articles. You have to retrieve these in a separate process. This generally involves selecting the group (usually by clicking on it), which will download the **headers**. The headers contain the article subject, posting date, and name of poster, and can be threaded by subject, or sorted by date or poster. When you see an interesting article, you can usually just click on it to bring it down. But again, that's not a rule, some readers use a combination of menu choices to go through the same motions. You'll have to either read the "Help File" or experiment.

You may be confused by the term **"subscribe."** Don't think of it like subscribing to a magazine, although it can work that way. It really means putting a Newsgroup into a special folder so that it's away from the main list. You might be able to give it special priorities, like automatically updating headers or retrieving all article bodies on connection, or it might just make it easier to locate.

Participating in Newsgroups

When a Newsgroup article raises a new topic, it's called **starting a thread**. Follow-ups to the initial article add to that thread. You can configure your Usenet reader to sort threads together to follow the progress of a discussion. But if you follow a group regularly you might find it more convenient to sort by date, to see what's new.

Posting

Posting is like sending email – and just as simple. You can start a new thread, follow up an existing one, and/or respond privately by email.

How you go about it depends slightly on your Newsreader software. It should automatically insert the Newsgroup you're reading in the "Newsgroups:" line. When starting a thread, pick a **subject** entry to summarize your query or statement. That way people scanning through the postings will know whether it's interesting. The subject line will also be used to identify the thread.

If you want to **crosspost** (post an article to more than one group), you just add those groups after the first group, separated by a comma, and then a space. Replies to crosspostings are displayed in all the crossposted groups. If you want replies to go to a different group, insert it after "Follow up – To:"

So, for example, if you want to stir up trouble in alt.shenanigans and rec.humor and have the responses go to alt.flame, the header would look like this:

Newsgroups: alt.shenanigans, rec.humor
Follow-up – To: alt.flame

Replying

Replying (or responding) is even easier than posting. Most Newsreaders give you the option of **following up** and/or **replying** when you read each message. This means you can send your contribution to the relevant Newsgroups (follow-up) and/or email the poster directly (reply/respond).

It's usually good practice to **reply as well as post**, because the original poster will get it instantly. It's also more personal and will save them having to scan through the group for replies. It's quite acceptable to continue communicating outside Usenet as long as it serves a purpose. Before long you'll have a circle of new virtual friends.

Like email, you also have the option of **including part or all of the original message**. This can be quite a tricky choice. If you cut too much, the context could be lost when the original post is deleted. If everyone includes everything, it creates a lot of text to scan. Just try to leave the main points intact.

Sending a test post

As soon as anyone gets Usenet access, they're always itching to see if it works. With that in mind, there are a few Newsgroups dedicated to **experimenting**. Post what ever you like to alt.test, gnu.gnusenet.test or misc.test You'll get several automatic (and maybe even humanly) generated replies appearing in your mailbox within a few days, just to let you know you're in good hands.

Kill files

If you don't like a certain person on Usenet, then kill their mail. Just add their email address to your Newsreader's **"kill" file**. Then you'll never have to download articles they've posted again. The same goes for any subject or topic: simply include the recurring string in your kill file. But don't make it too broad or you might filter out interesting stuff as well.

Image and sound files – and decoding

As with email, Usenet can carry more than just text. Consequently there are entire groups dedicated to the posting of **binary files** such as images, sounds, patches, and even full working programs. Such groups usually have .binaries in their address.

Again like email, binary files must be processed, most commonly in UUencoding, before they can be posted or read. You can use a separate program to handle the **encoding/decoding**, but it's far more convenient to leave it up to your Newsreader. As postings are restricted to 64 kb, the file may be chopped into several messages. Each part will have the same subject heading followed by its number. You just need to highlight all the parts and decode them in one go.

To **post a binary**, just attach it as in email and your Newsreader will look after the rest.

Beware of **downloading any program** that's posted to a Newsgroup. It's the surest way to contract a virus.

Starting your own group

With more than 25,000 Newsgroups in existence, you'll need fairly specialized tastes to get the urge to start your own group – and a fair bit of technical knowhow plus a lot of patience. It's one of the more convoluted and arcane procedures on the Net.

Before you can create a new Newsgroup, in anywhere but the alt. hierarchy, you need to drum up support. It's a good idea to start a **mailing list** first. To get numbers, discuss the proposal in the Newsgroups related to your topic and then announce your list.

Once you have a case, and support, you have to put it before the pedantic news.groups for a savaging. Then you go through a long process that culminates in an election where the number of "yes" votes must be at least 100 more than, and twice the number of "no" votes.

Starting alt. Newsgroups is much easier, as you just have to post a special control message. The hard part is getting people to frequent the group.

For more see:

Newsgroup creation companion
http://www.lib.ox.ac.uk/internet/news/faq/archive/usenet.creating-
Newsgroups.helper.html

How to start an alt. Newsgroup
http://www.math.psu.edu/barr/alt-creation-guide

How to write a good new group message
http://www.cs.ubc.ca/spider/edmonds/usenet/good-newgroup.html

Newsgroup netiquette

Apart from your provider's contract, the Net itself is
largely devoid of formal rules. Instead, there are certain
established, or developing, codes of conduct known as
netiquette (Net-etiquette). These apply principally to
Usenet Newsgroups.

If you breach netiquette, you may be ignored, lec-
tured by a self-appointed net-cop, or (if you're
committing some major offense) flamed. A **flame** is personal abuse. You don't have to breach netiquette to get
flamed – just expressing a contrary or naive opinion
will sometimes do the trick. When it degenerates into
name calling, it's called a flame war. There's not much
you can do to avoid compulsive flame merchants, but if
you follow these tips, you should be welcome to stand
your ground.

Read and locate

Most importantly, before posting to any Newsgroup,
read a range of its existing postings first. If it's a big
group you might get a good enough idea of what's
going on within one session, but more likely you'll need
at least a few. **Download all the relevant FAQs** first, to
make sure your article isn't old hat. Some Newsgroupies
are not too tolerant of repeats.

Next, make an effort to post in the most **relevant group**. If you were to ask for advice on fertilizing roses in rec.gardening, you might find yourself politely directed to rec.gardening.roses, but if you want to tell everyone in talk.serious.socialism about your favorite Chow Yun Fat film, don't expect such a warm response.

Type and language

Less obviously, **never post in upper case**, unless you're "shouting" (emphasizing a point in a big way). It is regarded as a sign of rudeness and ignorance. And keep your **signature file** short and subtle. Some people think that massive three-page dinosaurs and skyscrapers sculpted from ASCII characters tacked to every Usenet posting gives them credibility. That's unlikely.

In similar fashion, express yourself in plain English (or the language of the group). Don't use **acronyms or abbreviations** unless they reduce jargon rather than create it, or use affected misspellings. Avoid over-using smileys, and other emoticons (see "Net Language", p.350), too. Some might think they're cute, but to others they're the online equivalent of fuzzy dice hanging from a car's rear view mirror.

In addition, don't post **email you've received from someone else** without their consent.

Join in! Be positive!

These warnings aside – and they're pretty obvious – don't hold back. If you can forward a discussion in any way, contribute. That's what it's all about. **Post positively** and invite discussion rather than making abrasive remarks. For example, posting "All programmers are social retards" is sure to get you flamed. But: "Do programmers lead healthy social lives?" will get the same point across and invite debate, yet allow you to sidestep the line of fire.

Overall it's a matter of courtesy and knowing when to contribute. In Usenet, no-one knows anything about you until you post. They'll get to know you through your words, and how well you construct your arguments. So if you want to make a good impression, think before you post, and don't be a loudmouth.

Of course, if all this seems just a tad twee, you might appreciate 101 ways to be obnoxious on Usenet at: http://www.indirect.com/user/steiners/usenet.html

Posting commercial messages

Having such a massive captive audience pre-qualified by interests is beyond the dreams of many marketeers. Consequently you will occasionally come across flagrant **product advertisements** and endorsements within Usenet. There have been cases where many of, and even all, the groups were unselectively crossposted by a single advertiser.

This process, known as **spamming**, is a guaranteed way to incur the wrath of a high percentage of Usenetsters. It usually incites mass mailbombing (loads of unsolicited email) and heavy flaming, not to mention bad publicity. Use the hierarchy .biz for commercial announcements, or tread very subtly, if you must plug your new book, CD, or whatever, in a regular Newsgroup. It's entirely legitimate, for example, to **put a Web address in your signature**, so anyone can explore material you've posted on your own or your company's Web page. No-one objects to that.

Searching Usenet

See **Finding It** (p.110).

Surfing the World Wide Web

When you see something that looks like http://www.come/and/get/me.html taunting you in adverts or news articles, on TV shows or business cards, don't get shy. These cryptic addresses are simply invitations to the World Wide Web (or the Web), the world's most exciting and fastest growing communications medium. Unlike other more arcane areas of the Internet, it's remarkably simple to find your way around – and maybe even to find what you're after.

The Web's popularity is deserved, as it has made navigating the Internet as simple as pointing and clicking. But you'll need a little help to get started. That's why we've devoted a later chapter (see p.110) on how to find things and most of the second half of this book to Web site reviews. This chapter explains how to fit yourself out to explore the World Wide Web.

What to expect

The Web is the glossy, glamorous, user-friendly face of the Internet: a media-rich potpourri of virtual shopping malls, music samples, online magazines, art galleries, libraries, museums, games, job agencies, movie previews, self-promotions, and plenty more. Once you're online, for the most part, it's all free. Its coverage includes about half a million companies, everything from Disneyland to Wall Street, and everywhere from Iceland to Antarctica, all from the keyboard of your computer. If you can't find a reference to an event on the World Wide Web, chances are it's not happening.

Requirements

Make no mistakes. The Web is one hungry beast. It will lap up every bit of computer power and connection speed you throw at it, and still want more. While you can get away with yesterday's computers in the rest of the Net, the World Wide Web is far more demanding.

That means you'll need a **PC with at least a 486 DX33 processor and 8 Mb RAM**, a **Macintosh 68030 and 8 Mb RAM**, or the **equivalent Atari or Amiga machine**. It will need to be hooked to the Net at a modem speed of at least **14.4 kbps**, preferably 33.6 kbps, or better still via an ISDN, cable, or ADSL link. Sure, you can get away with less, but it will groan. You will too as you wait for graphic intensive pages and background sound to load.

In addition, you'll need a **browsing program** to provide the graphical interface. The most popular are Netscape and Microsoft Internet Explorer. We discuss these in depth, later in this chapter.

Home pages

On the World Wide Web, **home page** has two meanings. One refers to the document that appears when you start your browser and acts as your own "home base" for exploring the Web. Whenever you get lost or want to return to somewhere familiar, you can just click on the "Home" button. The other refers to any entity's representative Web document.

For instance, Rough Guides" own home page – to be found by keying http://www.roughguides.com/ – is the top page in its set of Web documents. Its Web site includes this home page, as well as numerous interconnected pages, published as a set. Each page is accessed simply by keying its unique Web address into your browser or by following a link from another page.

These Web addresses are formally known as **URLs** (Uniform Resource Locators).

The addresses

You've almost certainly been exposed to a few Web addresses. You might not have taken much notice at the time, but you'll need to in future because they will help you find what you want on the Web. To visit an address, you simply key it in to the "URL," "Go To," "Location," or "Open Location" box on your Web browser. If all works well, your browser will retrieve the page and display it on your screen.

Keying URLs

Remember, path names in UNIX are case sensitive. So you need to key URLs carefully, taking note of capitals.

Web (http) addresses

URLs look ridiculously complex at first glance, but they soon make sense. Consider an address as having three parts. Reading from left to right they are: the **protocol**, such as http://, ftp://, news:, or gopher://; the **host name** (everything before the first single forward slash); and the **file path** (everything after and including the first single forward slash). Consider the address:

  http://www.star.com.hk/~chow/Yun/fat.html

The http:// tells us it's a HyperText file located on the World Wide Web, the domain www.star.com.hk tells us it's in Hong Kong, and the file path indicates that the file fat.html is located in the directory /~chow/Yun/

Although the majority of URLs include the file's path, the trend is moving toward shorter addresses, especially for the home page. For example, if you key in: http://www.apple.com you'll reach Apple's home page, but key in: http://www.apple.com/documents/aboutapple.html and you'll find another document deeper within Apple's site.

With better browsers such as Netscape Navigator, you needn't key http:// as it's an automatic default. In fact, if you're after http://www.apple.com, just key: apple and it will fill in the rest. It's likely that most browsers will follow suit in later releases.

Other addresses

As discussed in earlier chapters, you can access FTP, Gopher, Telnet, and Usenet from the wheel of your Web browser.

To use FTP, just add ftp:// to the file's location. So, to retrieve duck.txt located in the directory /yellow/fluffy from the anonymous FTP site ftp.quack.com, you should enter: ftp://ftp.quack.com/yellow/fluffy/duck.txt (Netscape knows that any domain starting with ftp. is an FTP site, so Netscape users can omit the ftp:// part of the address.)

Gopher and Telnet work in exactly the same way, but Usenet omits the // Thus, to access the newsgroup alt.ducks, key: news: alt.ducks

Hypertext

Web pages are written in **HTML (HyperText Markup**

Language), which enables links to other documents to be imbedded within the text, thus creating a third dimension. If you've used Windows Help or Macintosh Hypercard, you'll be familiar with the concept.

Depending on how you've configured your browser, **text which contains links** to other documents (or to another part of the same document) is usually highlighted in another color and/or underlined. To pursue the link, simply **click on the highlighted text or object**. When the new document appears, it will be entirely independent of the one where you found the link. The previous document is now history. And as the new document needs no connection with it, there mightn't be a reciprocal link. However, there is an easier way to return, as you'll soon see.

Gopher

Before the Web's explosion, **Gopher** was the smartest way to archive data on the Internet. As the name suggests, Gopher is used to "go for" information. Although it stores data in an entirely different architecture, it looks and acts similar to the Web. In many ways, the Web is its natural successor and what used to be stored in Gophers is now on the Web – and for most purposes you need not read on. However, certain old battlers like government bodies and universities still use it to archive stuff, so it's useful to know how it works.

Gopherspace is a separate entity from the Web, although when you link out of the Web and into a Gopher site you may not recognize the difference. Its clickable directory listings work just

---

like hyperlinks, however these Gopher burrows are dead-ended. You can surf from page to page following links all day on the Web, but with Gopher, once you find your text file, you have to tunnel back out again.

To access a Gopher from the Web, key in gopher:// before the address in your Web browser. For example, to access the "Mother of all Gophers" at Minnesota University, key: gopher://gopher.tc.umn.edu:70/ It has all you need to know about Gophers, including how to search by subject or geographic region.

For more on searching Gophers, see **Finding It** (p.119).

Browser basics

Web browsers are a dynamic technology. By the time you read this, they will likely have moved forward several generations. **Netscape** – the industry leader – has been releasing updated browsers every couple of weeks since early 1995. There are now over thirty other browsers on offer, though with the notable exception of **Microsoft Internet Explorer**, few come close to Netscape's in terms of features or performance.

Despite the various quirks that distinguish different browsers, they achieve the same end through similar means. The following intrinsic functions are described for Netscape and Microsoft Internet Explorer but should be common to all latest generation brands. The actual menu wording changes between platforms, brands, and releases – Internet Explorer, for example, calls URLs "Internet Shortcuts" – but as long as you get the general drift, you'll figure it out.

At time of writing, these are the main features you'll find when you set a browser running:

A dialog box where you enter URLs

This box runs horizontally above the browser panel. In Netscape, when it's blank, it says **"Go to:"** beside it, and when it retrieves the URL the wording changes to **"Location:."** Irrespective of what it says, key the URL you want to visit in there, or choose **"Open Location"** or "Open" from the File menu, and enter it in there.

After you've typed in the URL, hit **"Enter,"** (or the **return key** on your keyboard) and wait. It rarely takes more than a minute or two to locate and load Web pages, and if you've got a fast connection it can be a matter of seconds.

Navigation buttons to take you back, forward, and home

The navigation buttons are located on the toolbar above the browser panel. Displaying them is usually optional,

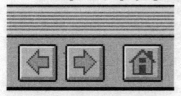

but they're hard ·to live without. To go back to a previous page, just click the **"Back"** button until you find it. To return to where you were, keep pressing **"Forward."** And to go back to your start-up page hit **"Home."**

You can go back and forward through pages pretty much instantly once you have visited them during a session, as your computer **caches** the document in its memory. How much material you can click through in this fashion, however, depends on the amount of cache allocated or the "number of documents stored" chosen in the configuration preferences of your browser.

Identifying links and the history file

An "active" link is like a signpost to a new page. You click on the link to go there. After you've been, nothing changes on the page, but your browser records your visit by storing the URL in a **history file**. It's then called a "followed" link.

You can customize links by displaying them as underlined and/or a special color. The default is usually underlined blue for active links and red for followed links. See how this works for yourself. Look at any page. Links you haven't followed should appear blue and underlined. Just click one and load the page. Now, click "Back" and return to the previous page. The link should now be red.

What's more, a link to the same URL will also be red on any other page. After all, a link contains the address of where you're going, not where you've come from. Just like the same signpost, but in different locations. So think of your history file as collection of signposts.

Customized links have an optional expiry period, after which they revert to the normal color. If you choose "Never," visited sites will stay red forever and remain in your history file. But it's wiser to keep the expiry short. A big history file can slow things down.

You can also use the history file to **return to a visited page**, rather than clicking the "Forward" and "Back" buttons. You'll find the file under the "Window" menu in

Netscape and the "File" menu in Internet Explorer. It will display where you've been in your current session and you can just click on a line and go there. One rather annoying glitch with current editions of Netscape is that once you do this it loses all the backtracked pages.

A button to stop transfers in progress

To cancel a transfer, because it's taking too long, or you've made a mistake, just hit the **"Stop"** button. In the middle of a transfer, you might have to hit "Stop" before "Back" will work.

The option of not loading images, or loading text first

The drawback of the Web's graphic richness is the time it takes to download images. To speed things up, you have the option of **not loading images**. To view the images after the page is loaded, either click on them individually, choose **"Load Images"** from the menu, or hit the "Images" button. You should also configure it to load text before images. That way, in theory, you don't have to wait until an entire page is loaded before you can read it. The only problem, in Netscape anyway, is that this hardly ever works.

The option of choosing your initial home page

Browsers usually come preconfigured with a **default home page** – their own, which often includes information about new products and a range of search options. This will come up every time you set the browser running, or if you hit "Home." If you'd prefer an **alternative home page**, just specify it in the preferences or options.

It's handy to have a page that links to your favorite **search tools** or perhaps one that gives regular sports or news updates. Be sure, however, to choose one that's quick to load or it will delay the start of each session.

Better still, select the option to load a blank page at start-up and then specify your favorite search tool as the home page. That way, you're ready to go immediately, and can just hit "Home" to conduct a search.

A hotlist, or bookmark file to store useful URLs

Whenever you find a page that's worth another visit, you can file its location. To do that, just "Add" it to your **"Hotlist," "Bookmarks," or "Favorites"** (browsers use different names for this feature). To share them with a friend, you can attach the "Hotlist" file to email. They can open it up as a local hypertext page or even specify it as their home page.

The ability to send mail

Browsers generally run "straight out of the pack," and need no configuration to run. However, there are several dialog boxes hidden away in the options or preferences that should be completed if you want to get the most from a session. For example, before you can send email and post to newsgroups directly from a browser, you'll have to complete your **email** and **news server** details. Your provider will supply this information. If you're not sure what to put, just ask.

Web pages offer various **email opportunities**. You'll often see a contact name inviting email. When you click on it, you'll either get a form, a dialog box, or a mail client will open, either your browser's or your main mailer, depending on your configuration. Just type your message and send it. Replies arrive through the normal email channels.

The ability to read newsgroups

You can use your Web browser to see a **list of all the available newsgroups**. Just type: news:* , or hit the

"Newsgroups" button, if available. The first time could take several minutes. If the browser builds a local index file, later attempts will be almost instantaneous. Once the newsgroups are listed, you can click on them to retrieve articles and post in the same way as with any newsreader. Again, the procedure differs between browsers and releases. So consult the "Help" file.

Browsers are convenient for accessing newsgroup references from Web pages and vice versa but lack many of the advanced features of dedicated newsreaders. Netscape started out with a basic, useful newsreader, integrated into its main window. Now it uses a counter-intuitive and confusing program tacked on the side. So, if you're planning a serious Usenet session, fire up a newsreader instead.

Plug-in support

Netscape Navigator has become so central to everything you do on the Net that it intends to move away from simply being a program, toward taking over the desktop. Thus, rather than design clients as separate entities, the latest trend is to make them **"plug in" to Netscape** and activate as needed. Over 100 programs can already be "plugged in" to do such things as read Excel spreadsheets, play Real Audio live music, view Fractal Image Files, deliver real-time stock

BrowserWatch Plug-In Plaza	Do you have a link to Plug-In Plaza on your web site? If so, you can now use this cool new GIF if you like!
The Full List	This is the whole list, but I gotta warn ya its getting big
Just Multimedia	Multi-Media Plug-Ins, AVI, QuickTime, ShockWave...
Just Graphics	Graphic Plug-Ins, PNG, CMX, DWG
Just Sound	Sound & MIDI Plug-Ins, MIDI, ReadAudio, TrueSpeech
Just Document	Document Viewer Plug-Ins, Acrobat, Envoy, MS Word...
Just Productivity	Productivity Plug-Ins, Map Viewers, Spell Checkers...
Just VRML	VRML & QD3D Plug-Ins
	By popular demand! We now have pages for each platform!
Macintosh	Macintosh Plug-Ins
Unix	Unix Plug-Ins
Windows	Windows Plug-Ins

quotes, display Virtual Reality worlds, and fix Netscape's shortcomings.

Over time, such programs that prove popular are likely to be built in or included with the shipped product. Microsoft, however, believes it's the operating system's job to handle such affairs, so it's moving toward "plugging" Internet Explorer and other applications into **Windows 95 Explorer**. Or building Windows into an Internet system. That way you're only running one operating system and can zip between all applications, Internet or otherwise, treating the Internet like just another disk drive. This seems a more logical plan, but only time will tell. In the meantime, Internet Explorer should accept the same plug-ins as Netscape.

See the **Software Roundup** (p.315) for a selection of the more useful plug-ins.

Playing live music, movies, and animations

Three essential plug-ins are: **Real Audio**, for live sound such as music, interviews, and news (if you have a sound card); **ShockWave**, for MacroMedia Director ani-

mations; and **QuickTime**, to play QuickTime movies. You'll find such files offered for downloading all over the Web – try the sites listed in the Entertainment, Music, and Radio sections of our Web Guide.

Unlike wav and au files, which must be downloaded in full to play, Real Audio plays live, enabling a whole spate of Internet radio stations and juke boxes. The sound has to be severely compressed, so the quality's not what you'd call hi-fi, but it should improve as bandwidth standards increase. And of course you can have it playing in the background while you surf other Web sites.

Mouse menus

Quality browsers enable or activate the most useful commands from your **mouse button** (the right button on PCs). Just hold it down and try them out. "Save this link as," for example, can come in handy to save time loading a large page. The saving process goes into the background while you continue in the foreground.

Copying and pasting

You can **copy text** from Web pages just like any other document. Just highlight the section, choose "copy" from the Edit menu (or use the shortcut keys), and paste it to a word processor, text editor, or mail program.

Saving pages as local files

When a page is saved as a bookmark, you must go online to access it. If it's not likely to change, and you want to read it offline, you may want to **save it to disk**.

Choose **"Save as"** from the File menu. It will give the option to save the page as **text** or **HTML**. If you select HTML, you can view it on your browser off or online by choosing **"Open local file"** from the File menu. Saving as a text file removes the hypertext tags, so you can view it in a word processor or Notepad.

A point to note is that Netscape doesn't convert HTML to text particularly well. It might even be worth keeping another browser or HTML editor handy just for this task. In this case, always save as HTML and do the conversion later. At this stage in browser evolution, images must be saved separately.

Retrieving images

Most Web pages display reduced images. In art galleries especially, such images are often linked to the full image. To **save an image**: either open it by clicking on it, and choose "**Save as**" from the File menu; choose "**Save this link as,**" and click on the link to the full image; or hold the mouse button down and choose "**Save this image as.**" Internet Explorer also gives the option of saving the image as wallpaper.

Viewing the document source

To see a page's raw **HTML coding**, you can choose "Source" from the View menu. This is a good way to learn how to design Web pages (see our section on this, beginning on p.126).

Transferring files

Some browsers, Netscape and Internet Explorer among them, are such good FTP clients, you may never need a dedicated FTP program. Just **click on an FTP link**, or **type it as a URL**, and the browser will treat it as any other link.

A good trick if you want to browse an FTP site rather than download a file straight from a link, is to copy the address using the mouse menu, paste it to the URL window, and delete the file name from the address. Then you can log into the server and browse it like a Web site.

Multitasking

Since things don't always happen instantly on the Net, it's often practical to do two or more things at once. You might as well download news, mail, and the latest software releases while you surf. If your browser supports multitasking, you can also have multiple Web sessions running. So if a page takes ages to load, just open a **"New Window"** or **"New Browser,"** and look at something else while you wait. And better browsers automatically send FTP transfers to background.

Bear in mind, however, that each activity is competing for computer resources and bandwidth, so the more you attempt, the higher the likelihood that each will take longer – or that your machine will crash.

Choosing a browser

A couple of years ago, there was only one decent browser – **NCSA Mosaic**. Then the NCSA team left and started **Netscape** and practically wiped Mosaic off the map. NCSA then licenced Mosaic to several developers who put out their own enhanced versions. Hence, these days, there are several different browsers called Mosaic and a few others, like **Microsoft Internet Explorer**, that mention it in credits.

Netscape v. Internet Explorer

While each browser has its own merits, all have one thing in common – they're playing catch-up to **Netscape**. That's because Netscape keeps introducing swags of enhancements to HTML. And whenever it announces support for something new, like animated images, frames, tables, backgrounds, or colored text, the Net reacts by putting it in a myriad of Web pages. Then they put up a warning: "this page looks best with Netscape." And such pages can look decidedly odd viewed with any other browser.

But it won't last forever. Microsoft is now pulling the same stunt with **Internet Explorer** by pioneering such gizmotry as inline video (video played on the page), background sound, font faces, and ActiveX. And that's resulting in similar warnings. It's also focusing more on the bigger picture – how the Internet is going to fit into everyday life, and its place in the operating system – by releasing Internet add-ons to its Office products and Windows 95.

Although at the time of writing, Netscape is still the superior browser, it could well be overtaken. It will be a battle to watch.

Other browsers

Although you'll be right at the cutting edge with either (or both) Netscape and Internet Explorer, some of the less advanced browsers do have their advantages. For instance, **Oracle's** free **Power Browser** comes with its own Web server, **Quarterdeck's Mosaic's** caching actually works, **CyberJack** updates itself automatically and has inbuilt Ping, and **WinWeb/MacWeb** requires less RAM. Others, like AOL's browser and Cello, are, at time of writing, almost devoid of things to praise. Whatever, there's no shortage to choose from – at least thirty, at last count, and they're nearly all free to test out.

That said, don't spend too much time worrying about which browser to get. Get the latest versions of Netscape Navigator and/or Microsoft Internet Explorer. And keep them both. They're free for personal use at present, though if you use the Net commercially you should read Netscape's licence agreement to see if you're obliged to pay. As much as it might alarm Netscape's shareholders, there's not much incentive to register. After all, most people use the latest betas – and betas, though time-limited, are always free. However, bear in mind that few developers are anywhere near as wealthy and diversified as Microsoft. They can't all afford to squeeze out competitors with free products. So when you settle on a program and you think it's value for money, keep it alive by paying. It's in everyone's best interests.

For more on these browsers, like where to get them, see the **Software Roundup** (p.315).

Java

Most browsers support or will soon support Sun's Web-oriented programming language, **Java**. This means that what once was a static environment is springing to life with all sorts of live or "animated" applications. Browsers that aren't Java-ready ignore the Java code, and display only the HTML text, or, often, crash.

Sometime in the near future, Java support will be built into the base operating systems like Windows, OS/2, and whatever Apple creates to save its skin. To find out more about Java and see the latest applications, see Gamelan at: http://www.gamelan.com

Finding It

Once you've selected an access provider, installed your software, and the whole thing's purring along, you'll be faced with yet another dilemma. How on earth do you find anything? Relax, it's easier than it looks, once you've learned a few tricks. How you find something depends on what it is, how new it is, where it's likely to be stored, and who's likely to know about it. In this chapter, we show you the first places to look, and as you gain experience the rest will fall into place. We also show you how to fix addresses that won't work. Assuming you have Web access, the only program you'll need is a Web browser.

What's out there

Anything you can link to through the Web, you can find using a **Web search tool**. Plus you can find anything that's been archived into an online database, such as email addresses, phone numbers, program locations, newsgroup articles, and news clippings. Of course, first it has to be put online, and granted public access. Just because you can access US government servers doesn't mean you'll find a file on DEA Operative Presley's whereabouts.

In the pages that follow, we examine the tools you'll use. You'll find their addresses detailed in our Web Guide, in the **Search Tools and Directories** section (p.158).

The main search tools

There are basically three types of Web search tools: robotically built indexes, intelligent agents, and hand-built directories. All have their specific uses.

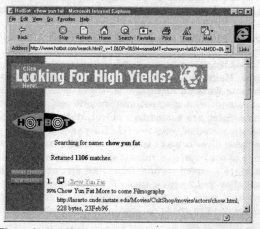

The robotically built indexes, or **search engines**, include very useful tools, such as **Altavista**, **HotBot**, and **InfoSeek Ultra**. Each of these runs a program called a trawler, crawler, spider, robot, wanderer, worm, or some such unsavory term, which scouts around the Web and then returns its findings. The pickings, such as each page's location, title, and an amount of text that varies between crawlers, are then stored in an online database. Using these tools, you can search for something specific by submitting **keywords**, or **search terms**, to this database through a simple Web page form. The results, which usually come back within seconds, are clickable like hot links on any other Web page.

Intelligent agents search the Net, or certain sites, live. There aren't too many on the Web yet, other than Bargain Finder Agent, which attempts to find the cheapest CDs for sale on the Net. But there are a few other dedicated clients, like **Netscape's Smart Marks**, which looks for changes in Web pages, **Quarterdeck's WebCompass**, which queries search engines, and a whole series at: http://www.agentware.com However, they're of specialized use so we won't discuss them here.

The third category are **hand-built directories** such as **Yahoo**, **Magellan**, **Point**, **What's New**, and **Stroud's Consummate Winsock Applications**. These usually sort sites into categories and sometimes include reviews or comments. Sites are sorted by subject, date, platform, or even their level of "coolness." In the pages following, we call these **directories** or **guides** when they cover a broad range of subjects (like Yahoo), **specialist sites** when they are more focused in one area (like Stroud's), or **lists** when they mainly rank sites (like Cool Site of the Day).

Finally, there are a few hybrids that might fit into a combination of these categories. If in doubt we'll call them **directories**.

As with just about everything on the Net, the easiest way to learn is to dive straight in. But before you do, pause to **read the instructions** first. Every search engine or directory has a page of tips on how to use them to their full potential. A few minutes reading these is guaranteed to make your searching more effective.

Search engines

Generally the quickest way to find specific reference to something on the Web is to use a **search engine**. These look like normal Web pages, with a form to enter the search terms of what you're looking for. It in turn feeds these terms into a database and returns a list of "hits" or correspondences.

Depending on the engine, the results should include enough information to judge whether the hits actually contain what you're after. However, each engine can only return its crawler's most recent findings, which may only be a small proportion of what's actually there and potentially months old.

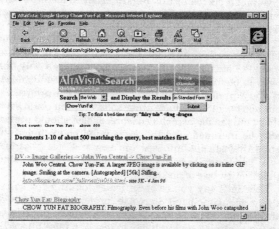

The various engines source, store, and retrieve their data differently. Always start with the best. Look for the biggest, freshest database and the ability to fine tune your search with extra commands and return the most relevant hits first. Currently, **Altavista**, **HotBot**, and **InfoSeek Ultra** (a new addition to the InfoSeek family) are the top candidates. **Excite**, **Lycos**, and **WebCrawler** can be useful when the others fail, but you often have to wade through a lot of poor-quality results as their search mechanisms are relatively crude.

Getting the most out of a search engine

Call up a search engine and study its instructions. The most important sections are how you state whether terms should be **included or excluded** (or more precisely, preferably included/must be included/must be excluded), and how to state that **multiple terms** are part of a set. At the time of writing only InfoSeek, HotBot, and Altavista give much choice in this regard. They're also the only ones to index the entire text, and not just extracts, of Web pages.

For example, if you're looking for something about Lotus software, and not Lotus cars, you'd want to include Lotus and exclude cars. Since there's only one term to be included, it automatically **must** be included. If you'd prefer information on spreadsheet programs, but don't want to exclude other software, you could state that Lotus **must be included**, spreadsheet should **preferably be included**, and that cars **must be excluded**. In both Altavista and InfoSeek you'd enter: +lotus spreadsheet -car The + sign says that it must be included, the - sign that it must be excluded.

Now let's say you're specifically looking for something about the band Stereolab, preferably a review of their album *Mars Audiac Quintet*. The album name is an unusual phrase, and unlikely to result in false hits, so it would be a good term to specifically include. However, specifically including it would exclude any pages about Stereolab that don't mention that particular album. Thus it would be wiser to state that it should, rather than must, appear. And you'll need to instruct the engine to treat the **three words as one phrase**, or you'll get hits on Mars, Audiac, and Quintet – and lots of links to NASA and chocolate bars. So to refine it further, you could state that "Stereolab" must appear, the phrase "Mars

Audiac Quintet" should appear, and "review" should appear. That way it's most likely that a page with all the terms will appear near the top of the results and the next most relevant under that. Altavista and InfoSeek have their own intricacies in grouping adjacent keywords into phrases, but joining them by dashes like this: mars-audiac-quintet works on both. The dashes state that a single space, not a letter, must appear between the words. You should read both help files for instructions on more complex searches – and observe how they interpret capitals.

Keep in mind that search engines are not the final word of what's on the Web. Just because they can't find it, doesn't mean it isn't there. It just means their trawlers haven't visited that site yet. Which means you'll have to turn to another, maybe fresher source. For instance:

Directories and lists

To browse the range of sites within a subject category, turn to one of the **directories**. There's no shortage of them, and they all seem to offer something unique. Indeed, they're so diverse that lumping them together is somewhat ambitious. What they all have in common is that humans, rather than automatons, collate the sites, and usually add a comment. The sites are then cataloged in some kind of logical fashion.

You usually have the choice of browsing directories by **subject group** and sometimes by other criteria like **entry date** or **rating**. Most directories also allow you to search their own sites through a **form**, rather like a search engine. Unlike search engines though, they don't keep the contents of Web pages, simply titles, categories, and sometimes comments or reviews. Naturally you'll have to adjust your searching strategy accordingly. Start with broad terms and work down until you hit the reviews.

Good all-purpose directories include: **Yahoo**, **Magellan**, **Point**, **The Internet Directory**, **World Wide Web Virtual Library**, the **InfoSeek Guide**, and the **Argus Clearinghouse**. You'll often find directories useful for finding specialist sites, which in turn can point you to the obscure cauldrons of your obsessions.

Specialist sites

Whatever your interest, you can bet your favorite finger it will have several dedicated Web pages. And there's probably a page somewhere that keeps track of them all. Such **mini-directories** are a boon for finding new and esoteric pages – ones that the major directories overlook. In addition, they sometimes run mailing lists to keep you posted with news.

If you have similar interests, you can email the Webmaster and introduce yourself. That's how the Web community works. You'll find hundreds of specialist sites all through our Web Guide, including the most popular in the Internet Search Tools category (see p.158).

Lists

If you're not looking for anything in particular, just something new, entertaining, or innovative, maybe you'll find it in a list. In fact, it can be worth checking into a few lists like **Cool Site of the Day**, **Geek Site of the Day**, **Stroud's What's New**, **Gamelan**, and the **Internet Chart Show** regularly to keep up to date. And to see what's popular, try **100 Hot Websites**. Again, addresses for all these are featured in our Web Guide (see p.165).

Finding stuff

If you start your search with the search engines and guides they'll invariably lead you to other sites, which in turn point you closer toward what you're after. As you get more familiar with the run of the Net, you'll gravitate toward specialist sites and directories that index more than just Web pages, contain their own unique content, and shine in specific areas. What's best depends largely on what you're looking for. When you find a useful site, store it in your **bookmarks**, hotlist, or favorites, so you can return. Here are a few examples of using a mixture of techniques to:

Find new and interesting sites

Search engines aren't good at finding the very latest sites. Nor do they give subjective advice, so you won't know what a site's like until you visit. Directories like Pointcom and Magellan are better because they review. But to find brand new sites, try: **What's New**, Internet magazine's **Essential Viewing**, and sites that showcase the latest technology, like **Gamelan**. Also scan newspaper technology sections and magazines like *Wired*, *Internet World*, *Internet*, *.Net*, and *The Web*. And as mentioned, lists like **Cool Site of the Day**, **Mirsky's Worst**, and **Geek Site of the Day** are all great value for finding the cream.

Find something from Usenet

The Usenet newsgroups are by far the best place to find opinions and personal experiences but they include a daunting amount of text to scan. Although it's sorted into like-subjected bundles, if you had to find every instance of discussion about something, it could take you days. And if it was tossed around more than a couple of weeks ago, the thread might have expired. But, with **archives** like DejaNews, InfoSeek, Altavista, and Excite, you can scan close to the entirety of Usenet, for up to a year in retrospect, depending on the archive.

DejaNews keeps articles the longest, bundles threads and profiles contributors. This makes it easier to follow a whole discussion, as well as check out whose advice you're taking and how well they're usually received. Plus the longer the history, the more chance you have of finding something obscure. **InfoSeek Ultra** archives the largest selection of groups, allows fine term tuning, and should thread results as well by the time you read this. Along with **Altavista**, it is best for crunching recent articles and weeding out the noise.

Like all search engines, these tools are pretty self-explanatory, but as ever it pays to read the help file.

Find someone's email address

Try **mail directories** like **Four11**, **Bigfoot**, and **WhoWhere**. These get most of their data from Usenet postings and visitors, so they're not in any way comprehensive, but they're pretty vast databases – and, of course, growing by the day. If that fails, try using the person's full name as a search term in a **search engine**

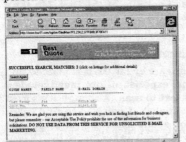

or Usenet archive. Alternatively, if you know where they work, search that company's Web pages – or better still (obvious but effective!) **ring up** and ask.

Find games, hints, and cheats

Try one of the big games sites like the **Games Domain**, **PCME**, or **Happy Puppy**, or search through Usenet as explained above. Stuck on a level? Look for a walk-through, or ask in Usenet.

Find something in Gopherspace

Gopherspace is just like the Web, but easier to navigate. Individual Gophers are internally searchable – just look for the menu entry. To search the menu titles in "all Gopherspace" use **Veronica**, the Gopher search engine. Veronica's database is compiled by trawling Gopher-space every couple of weeks, and retrieving the menu titles. All Veronicas contain the same data although some might be slightly fresher. Veronica searches produce a menu of Gopher items, which in turn point to Gopher data sources. It's on the "Other Gophers" menu on Minnesota's Gopher server, or at:
gopher://futique.scs.unr.edu/11/veronica

Some of the Web's search engines and guides, particularly Lycos and Yahoo, cover Gopher as well as the Web. You'll often find Gopher addresses interspersed among the Web addresses in Lycos. It may actually be more useful than Veronica, since it retrieves sample text, not just menu titles.

The Gopher of all Gophers has to be Gopher Jewels at:
http://galaxy.net/GJ/index.html or gopher://cwis.usc.edu/11/other_gophers_information_resources/gophers_by_subject/gopher_jewels
This provides a catalog of Gopher resources and contains over 2000 pointers by category.

Find the latest news, weather, finance, sport, etc.

Apart from hundreds of newspapers and magazines, the Net carries several large **news clipping archives** assembled from all sorts of sources. Naturally, there's an overwhelming amount of technology news, but there's also an increasing amount of services dedicated to what you would normally find in the news-stands, and it's often fresher on the Net. Occasionally there's a charge. For pointers, check our Web Guide under News, Fashion, Finance, Weather, and so forth.

Find out about a film or TV show

See the Film and TV section of our Web Guide or try the entertainment section of any major directory for leads to specialist sites. The **Internet Movie Database**, for example, is exceptionally comprehensive.

Find commercial support and services

Apart from being user-friendly, the major justification for joining an **Online Service** has traditionally been the quality of the content and the **user support forums**. AOL and CompuServe once had the market cornered in things like travel booking services, online banking, financial data, and product support. It's still a bit like that, but the Net is reaching out, and in some cases surpassing their standards. And soon the Online Services will move their content onto the Web on a pay-to-view basis. So even if you only have regular Net access, you can still get the best of both worlds.

Use the guides like Magellan, Point, Yahoo, and the Internet Directory to point you toward specialist databases, services, and companies in your area of interest. Or try one of the business directories from our Web Guide. The most professional outfits also buy banner advertising on popular sites like search engines. So you probably won't have to find them. They'll find you.

Some companies offer product support channels through their Web sites, but if you want advice from other users, go to Usenet.

Find the latest software

Most people start software searches using an Archie client to query one of the **Archie databases** that accumulate FTP listings in the same way as search engines trawl the Web. We don't. Nor do we use the Web version, which you'll find in the Internet Search Tools section of the Web Guide. It's too hard. For one, you have to know the program's exact file name, or at least part of it. Half the time you're not even sure of the program's name. Imagine you've heard about a beta program called Net Drill, Netdriller, Nedrilla, or something, that caches DNS queries locally. How are you going to find that with Archie when its program name's nedrrlb3.exe?

A much easier route is to try one of the **specialist file directories** like **Stroud's** or **TUCOWS**, and look under an appropriate category. Failing that, try coining search terms like "caches DNS" or "Netd*" and feeding them into the search engines, Usenet archives, and technical news clipping services like IWorld. As a bonus you'll likely find a description or review to tell you whether it's worth getting.

Once you've found a file, if it's proving slow to download, feed the file name into one of the **FTP engines** like **Snoopie**, **FTP Search**, or even **Archie** to find an alternative FTP site.

Find a mailing list

Tracking down a mailing list's a cinch. Subject search any of the directories in the **Mailing List** section of our Web Guide's Internet Search Tools. If that's not satisfactory, try the same search in a Usenet archive and check the FAQs from groups with hits.

Find help

If all else fails – and that's pretty unlikely – you can always turn to someone else for help. Just ask in an appropriate **Usenet group**. Summarize your query in the subject heading, keep it concise, and you'll have an answer within a few days.

How to fix broken web addresses

It won't take long to encounter a **Web link or address that won't work**. Don't get too perturbed, it's common and usually not too hard to get around. We already know that many of the URLs in our Web Guide will be wrong by the time you try them. Not because we're careless. They just change. For example, in the five months between the first edition's of this book's first and fifth printings, almost 100 sites needed addresses updating. That's the way of the Net. The most useful thing we can do is show you how to find the new addresses.

Error codes

When something goes wrong, your browser will pop up a little box with a message and **error code**. Either that or nothing will happen, no matter what you try. To identify the source of the problem, get familiar with the types of errors. Different browsers and releases will return different error messages, but they'll indicate the same things. As an exercise, identify the following errors:

Incorrect host name

When the address points to a nonexistent host, your browser should return an error saying "Host not found." Test this by keying: http://www.rufgide.com

Illegal domain name

If you specify an illegal host name or protocol, your browser will tell you. Try this out by keying http://wwwrufguide and then http:/www.ibm.com noting the single slash.

File not found

If the file has moved, changed name, or you've over-looked capitalization, you'll get a message within the page from the server telling you the file doesn't exist on the host. Test this by keying a familiar URL and slightly changing the path.

Busy host or Host refuses entry

Occasionally you won't gain access because the host is either overloaded with traffic, or it's temporarily or per-manently off-limits. This sometimes happens with busy FTP servers, like Netscape's. It's a bit hard to test, but you'll come across it sooner or later. You might also make a habit of accessing foreign sites when locals are sleeping – it's usually quicker.

When no URLs work

Now that you're on speaking terms with your browser, you're set to troubleshoot that problem URL. The first thing to verify is that you really have a connection. Try another site. If it works, you know the problem's with that URL.

If you **can't connect to any Web site**, try closing your

browser and reopening it. It could be a software bug. If that doesn't fix it, it might be your connection to the Net. First, check your mail. If that looks dodgy, log off and then back on again. Check it again. If it still doesn't work, ring your provider and see if there's a problem at their end.

If your mailreader connects and reports your mail status normally, you know that the connection between you and your provider is okay. But there still could be a problem between it and the Net. Try **Pinging** (see p.35) a known host, say www.ibm.com or logging in to an FTP site. If this fails, either your provider's connection to the Net is down, or there's a problem with your Domain Name Server. Get on the phone and sort it out.

If you've verified that all connections are open but your browser won't find any URLs, the problem lies with your **browser set-up**. Check its configurations and reinstall it if necessary. Ensure there are no winsock.dll conflicts. And finally, check you have the right browser for your operating system. For example, 32-bit browsers won't work properly with Win 3.1.

When one URL doesn't work

If it's only **individual URLs that don't work**, you know that either their address is wrong or the host at the other end has problems. Now that you're familiar with error messages you can deduce the source and fix that address. Web addresses disappear and change all the time, there's nothing you can do about it. It's often because the address has been simplified, for example from http://www.netflux.co.uk/~test/New_Book/ComPlex.html/ to http://www.roughguides.com

If you're lucky, someone will have had the sense to leave a pointer, but sometimes even that pointer gets out of date. Since the Web is in a constant state of construction, just about everything is a test site in transit to something bigger. Consequently, when a site gets serious, it might relocate to an entirely new host and forget the old address. Who said the life of a professional surfer was easy?

Finding that elusive URL

The most obvious clues in tracking elusive URLs are to use what you've deduced from the error messages. If the problem comes from the host name, try **adding or removing the www part**. For example, instead of typing http://roughguides.com try http://www.roughguides.com Other than that you can only guess. Host names are not case sensitive, so changing that won't help. If the host is busy, refusing entry, or not connecting, try again later.

When you succeed in connecting to the host, but the file isn't there, there are a few further tricks to try. Check capitalization. First try **changing the file name extension** from .htm to .html or vice versa, if applicable. Then try **removing the file name** and then each subsequent directory up the path until finally you're left with just the **host name**. In each case, if you succeed in connecting, try to locate your page from the links presented or by browsing through directories and hotlists.

If you haven't succeeded, there's still hope. Try using the main **key words** from the URL's address or title in one of the **search tools** such as InfoSeek Ultra or HotBot. Failing that, try searching on related subjects, or scanning through one of the subject guides like Yahoo, Point, or Magellan.

By now, even if you haven't found your URL, you've probably discovered half a dozen similar, if not more interesting pages. And in the process figured out how to find your way around the Net.

Creating Your Own Web Page

It doesn't take much time on the Web before you get the itch to have a go yourself, and publish your own Web page. You don't need to be anyone particularly important, or a company with something to sell. In fact, you just need three things: something to say, some way to convert it into HTML, and somewhere to put it. Finding a location isn't too hard, or expensive. The logical place would be on your access provider's server. Better providers usually include at least 1 Mb storage as part of the account. Or you could try one of the Web space and site development specialists.

Once you have the space, you can publish anything you like from the way you feel about your hamster to your Mad Cow conspiracy thesis. Or you can use it to publicize yourself, push causes, provide information, sell your products, or entertain. But before you leap out of the closet and air your obsessions or money-making schemes, do check you're not breaking any laws of decency or trade. Your Web space provider will know.

Putting your thoughts into HTML

Dozens of programs claim to simplify the procedure of **converting text into HTML**. A few even attempt to make it a WYSIWYG (What You See Is What You Get) affair. However well they succeed, you're well advised to spend a couple of hours coming to grips with how HTML works. The good news is that, unlike computer programming in general, it's not too hard. But it is rather tedious. It basically boils down to writing the page in plain text, adding formatting tags, inserting instructions on how to place images, and embedding links to other pages.

There's a small catch in that, like all Net protocols, HTML is under constant review – and particularly by Netscape and Microsoft. As such, although a drawn-up standard exists, certain new HTML enhancements only work on some browsers. Yes, as ever with the Net, the whole affair is quite a muddle.

Editing packages

The quickest way to get familiar with how HTML operates is to create a simple page from scratch. You won't need any fancy compiling software – a text editor, or word processor, will do. However, a specific **HTML edit program** can help by automating much of the mark-up process so you don't have to learn all the tag codes.

The competition between HTML editing programs is just as intense as with browsers, though they all have a long way to go to approach the ease of word processors. They can approach the task from various angles, such as converting word-processed documents, applying the tags from toolbar and menu choices, using step-by-step wizards, or by hiding the code altogether. With **HotDog Pro** (PC) or **BBEdit** (Mac), for example, you can see the code as you paste it, while with **PageMill** you can write a whole page without ever seeing any code. Despite the apparent advantages, even the least techy Web builders end up getting into raw code. So even if it looks pretty barbaric right now, just bear with it. It will pay off in the long run.

Plundering code

Once you're comfortable with mark-up logic, you can learn advanced techniques by hacking other pages. Just find a page you like and choose **"View Source"** from your browser menu to see the raw code. You can even cut and paste selections into your own page. If you save the file and view it with a text editor or word processor, you'll also see the code. However, it disappears when viewed with a browser.

The same applies to your own work. To see how it would look on the Web, you need to open it up as a **local file**. An easy way to do this on the PC version of Netscape is by typing a forward slash (/) as a URL. This will display your computer's file directory as a Web page. Then you can click your way through the directories until you find the file. You can even bookmark the directory or file for later recall. Alternatively, you can simply drag your html file into your browser window or onto your browser icon.

Tags

Next time you're online, view the source of any Web page. The first thing you should notice is that the text is surrounded with comments enclosed between less-than and greater-than symbols like this: <TITLE> My Home Page </TITLE>. These comments are known as **tags** or **styles**. Most, but not all, tags come in pairs and apply to their enclosed text. The first tag typically looks like: <TAG> and the closing tag like: </TAG>.

THE CODE

It's good practice, but not mandatory, to enclose HTML documents within the following structure:

<HTML>(identifies the document as HTML)
<HEAD><TITLE>(the title goes in here)</TITLE></HEAD>
<BODY>(everything else goes in here)</BODY>
</HTML>(end of document)

A Web document has two parts: a **head** and a **body**. The head contains the title, which is displayed on the top bar of your browser window. The body appears within the window.

Backgrounds and colors

It's possible to apply formatting to the entire body of a document by placing extensions within the <BODY> tag. For example, <BODY BGCOLOR="#00E4FF"> changes the **background color** to #00E4FF, the RGB code for aqua. Luckily, most HTML editors automate the color to RGB conversion, so you won't have to know these numbers. Some advanced browsers also recognize literal words such as blue, red, and purple (but don't rely on it).

To **change the color** of the document text, standard link, visited link, and active link, insert any or all of

TEXT="a", LINK="b", VLINK="c", or ALINK="d" respectively within the <BODY> tag, where a, b, c, and d are your chosen RGB color codes. And, to **display a background graphic**, insert BACKGROUND="(image file location here)". You can apply all sorts of fancy effects. However, until you're confident, don't go overboard, as fancy backgrounds often detract from readability.

Headings

In a word processor, when you want to emphasize something using larger or smaller text, you change its point size. In HTML you use a **heading** of the appropriate proportion. Headings are enclosed within <Hn></Hn> tags, where n is from 1 to 6 with <H1> being the largest and <H6> the smallest. The actual size it appears when read depends on the viewer's browser and the way it's been configured. Oddball browsers like AMSD's Ariadna differentiate headings by color and texture, not just size.

Playing with text

Standard HTML ignores multiple spaces, tabs, and carriage returns. To get around that, **enclose text** within the <PRE></PRE> (preformatted text) tag pair. Otherwise, any consecutive spaces, tabs, carriage returns, or combinations will produce a single space.

However, it's more conventional to end paragraphs with <P>, which creates a **single line break**. To create **multiple line breaks** use <BR>. One <BR> will start the text on a new line, two will create a line break, three will create two line breaks, and so on. Browsers automatically **wrap text** so there's no need to worry about page widths. To **center text** use: <CENTER>(text here)</CENTER>, and to indent from both margins use:

`<BLOCKQUOTE>`(text here)`</BLOCKQUOTE>`.

Three simple, but effective, ways to emphasize text are to use bold, italic (though beware this can be hard to read on the Web), or colored or enlarged type. To **bold text**, enclose within either: `<B></B>` or `<STRONG></STRONG>`. To **italicize**, use: `<I></I>` or `<EM></EM>`. To **change color or size**, use `<FONT COLOR="RGB" SIZE=n>`(insert text here)`</FONT>`, where RGB is the RGB color code and n (-7 to +7) is the increment above or below base font size.

Images

Placing **Web graphics** is an art form itself. The smaller they are in bytes and the fewer you use, the quicker your page will load. So reduce them first with an image editor. With practice, you can reduce size considerably without overly sacrificing quality.

The simplest way to **display an image** is to place it within the `<IMG>` tag, like this: `<IMG SRC="(image location here)">`. This will display it full size and bottom aligned with adjacent text. You can also insert extra specifications between IMG and SRC. For example,

`<IMG HEIGHT=300 WIDTH=400 ALIGN=TOP VSPACE=60 HSPACE=70 BORDER=100 SRC="image.gif">`

would set the dimensions of your image.gif to 300 high by 400 wide, align its top with the tallest item in the line, give it a border of 100 and separate it from the text by 60 vertically and 70 horizontally. All measurements are in pixels.

You can specify all manner of alignments including:
    ALIGN=right
Aligns image with left margin. Text wraps on right.
    ALIGN=left
Aligns image with right margin. Text wraps on left.

ALIGN=texttop

Aligns top of image with tallest text in line.

ALIGN=middle

Aligns the baseline of text with middle of image.

ALIGN=absmiddle

Aligns the middle of text with middle of image.

ALIGN=baseline

Aligns the bottom of image with the baseline of the current line.

ALIGN=bottom

Aligns the bottom of image with the bottom of the current line.

It is generally accepted as good practice to include an **alternative text version** for browsers with images switched off. To do this, insert ALT="description of image" anywhere between IMG and SRC. This is especially important if the image describes a self-contained link.

Lines

A horizontal rule can be created using <HR> or, in more detail, <HR WIDTH=X% ALIGN=Y SIZE=Z>, where X is the percentage proportion of page width, Y is its positioning (CENTER, LEFT or RIGHT) and Z is its thickness. The default is 100 percent, CENTER and 1. Or you could insert an image of a line or bar.

Lists

HTML offers three main types of **lists**: ordered, unnumbered, and definition.

Ordered lists

Ordered lists are enclosed with the <OL></OL> pair. Each item preceded by <LI> will be assigned a sequential number. For example:

```
<OL> On the command, "brace! brace!":
```
On the command, "brace! brace!":
```
<LI> Extinguish cigarette
```
   1. Extinguish cigarette
```
<LI> Assume crash position
```
   2. Assume crash position
```
<LI> Remain calm
```
   3. Remain calm
```
</OL>
```

Unnumbered lists

Unnumbered lists work similarly within the <UL></UL> pair, except that <LI> produces a bullet:

```
<UL>Suspected carcinogens
```
Suspected carcinogens
```
<LI>Television
```
  • Television
```
<LI>Red gummy bears
```
  • Red gummy bears
```
<LI>Toast
```
  • Toast
```
</UL>
```

Definition lists

Definition lists are enclosed within the <DL></DL> pair. The <DT><DD> pair splits the list into levels:

```
<DL>
<DT>Best screenplay
```
Best screenplay
```
<dd>Eraserhead II, Son of Henry
```
   Eraserhead II, Son of Henry
```
<DT>Best lead actor
```
Best lead actor
```
<dd>Chow Yun Fat, Duke Nukem
```
   Chow Yun Fat, Duke Nukem

```
<DT>Best lead actress
Best lead actress
<dd>Diana Spencer, Queen of Hearts
    Diana Spencer, Queen of Hearts
</DL>
```

Links

The whole idea of HTML is to add a third dimension to documents by linking them to other pages. This is achieved by embedding clickable **hot-spots** to redirect browsers to other addresses. A hot-spot can be attached to text, icons, buttons, lines, or even images. Items containing hot-spots usually give an indication of where the link goes, but the address itself is normally concealed. Most browsers reveal this address when you pass your mouse over the link. You can embed links to anywhere on the Net. Here's how to:

Create a link to another Web page

```
<A HREF="http://www.roughguides.com">Rough Guides</A>
```
Clicking on Rough Guides, would load the Web page at: http://www.roughguides.com

Create a link to a local page

```
<A HREF="trap.html">Step this way</A>
```
If the file trap.html is in the same directory or is mapped as a local file, clicking on Step this way will launch it.

Embed links in images

```
<A HREF="fish.html"><IMG SRC="fish.gif"></A>
<A HREF="bigfish.gif"><IMG SRC="fish.gif"></A>
```
In both cases, the locally stored image fish.gif contains the hot-spot. The first case launches the local Web page fish.html while the second would display bigfish.gif, which

could be a different image, perhaps a more detailed version of fish.gif.

Invite mail

`<A HREF="mailto:bigflint@ix.netcom.com">GPF Browne</A>`

On most browsers, clicking on GPF Browne would bring up the send mail dialog box, already addressed to bigflint@ix.netcom.com

Route to a newsgroup

`<A HREF="news:alt.elvis.sighting">Find Elvis</A>`

Clicking on Find Elvis would bring up articles in the alt.elvis.sighting newsgroup.

Commence a Telnet session

`<A HREF="telnet://pctravel.com">PCTravel</A>`

If the browser is configured to launch a Telnet client, clicking on PCTravel would initiate a Telnet session with pctravel.com

Burrow through to a Gopher

`<A HREF="gopher://gopher.scs.unr.edu>Veronica</A>`

Clicking on Veronica would transfer you to the Gopher at gopher.scs.unr.edu

Log in to an anonymous FTP server

`<AHREF="ftp://ftp.sausage.com/pub/hdp2inst.exe"> HotDog Pro</A>`

`<A HREF="ftp://ftp.microsoft.com/">Microsoft</A>`

Clicking on HotDog Pro would commence the download of hdp2inst.exe, clicking on Microsoft would bring up a listing of the root directory of ftp.microsoft.com

But wait, there's more

That's about all you'll need to know in about 99% of cases, but if you're more adventurous, there are no bounds to the things you can do with a Web page. At the first level there are dozens more fairly straightforward tags to create tables, frames, forms, blinking text, and assorted tricks. Then there are multimedia options like audio, video, animation, and virtual reality. And at the top level there's form processing and interactive pages.

 As you move up the levels of sophistication, you'll start to move out of the standard HTML domain, into complex scripting and programming languages like **ActiveX**, **Java Script**, **Java**, **PERL**, **CGI**, and **Visual Basic**. You may also need access to the special class of storage space reserved for Web programs, known as the CGI bin.

If you see something you like, look at the page source to see if you can work out how it's done, ask the Webmaster, or search the Web for a good DIY document. There are plenty of books on the subject, but beware: the technology's moving so quickly, they date instantly.

Java

The most invigorating thing to happen to the Web recently is the introduction of **Java**, a programming language which can be interpreted by any computer, and will soon be built into all operating systems. Netscape and Internet Explorer already include inbuilt Java interpreters, so you won't need any extra software.

Novice programmers will find Java pretty cryptic. It's a hard core language like C++. But you mightn't find it

so hard to copy
the Java Script
from pages cre-
ated by Java

eggheads. Just promise us not to vandalize the status
bar with scrolling messages. They make the page slower
to load, obscure link feedback, and sometimes cause
crashes. But then again, it's your page.

Your own Web or FTP server

Once your computer's connected to the Net, it can act as
a **Web or FTP server**, just by running the right software.
You can even run one on a dial-up account, however
your pages or files will only be accessible while you're
online. And if you're using PPP, you'll have a different
IP address each time you log in, so you won't be able to
pass it on until you're online.

Servers are remarkably simple to install – read the
help file and you'll be up within half an hour. But take
the time to set up your security options to allow only
appropriate access to the appropriate directories. That
means things like making your Web pages read-only
and your FTP incoming write-only. Otherwise you
might get hacked. You'll find server software detailed in
the Software Roundup (p.326).

How to publicize your site

Once you've published your page and transferred it to
your server, the real problems begin. You need to get
people to visit it.

Before you crank up the publicity campaign, consider
how you'd find such a site and whether, if you stumbled
across it, you'd bother stopping or returning. Most of
all, decide whether publicity now would be good, or if

you want to keep the site under construction awhile before you take out the full-page adverts in *The New York Times*.

On a basic level, most people will arrive at your site by taking a link from another or by typing in the URL. That means if other pages link to yours, or people can find your address written somewhere, you'll stand a chance of getting traffic.

The best publicity machines of all are the **search engines and directories**. Before you submit your URL to them (and you need to do so), find out how they work, whether they'll accept a brief review, scan your page for key words, or index it in full. You might find tricks like stringing repeated key words outside the HTML body, which can trick engines into prioritizing your page for that subject. Several sites such as Submit-it (http://www.submit-it.com) can send your details to a number of engines at once. You should also email other sites like yours and ask to exchange links. Scour the engines and directories to find similar sites. And don't overlook services that specialize in what's new, like http://www.emap.com/whatsnew/

Next, generate some **off-Web interest**. Announce your site in appropriate newsgroups and mailing lists. You can get away with posting the same message periodically in Usenet, but don't post to a mailing list unless you have something new to say. Include the URL on your stationery, business cards, and in all your regular advertising. And flash it in front of everyone you can. Finally, if it's really newsworthy, send a press release to whatever media might be interested. And just quietly, it mightn't hurt to throw a party, invite some journos, and wave some free merchandise about.

But before you tell anyone, install a **hit counter and statistics service** (see: http://www.digits.com/ and http://www.dbasic.com/counter/). Then sit back and watch them roll in.

Where to next?

For more about HTML, Web programming, and publicity try the Web Developer's Virtual Library at:

http://www.stars.com/

You'll find everything you need either on or linked to this site.

And for HTML editors see our **Software Roundup** (p.315).

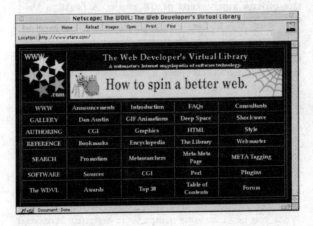

Internet Relay Chat

There's a facet of the Internet that is often described as the online equivalent of CB radio. A feature that enables you to hold live keyboard, and more recently voice and video, conversations with people all over the world. Part of that mechanism is called Internet Relay Chat (IRC) – and with other live Net chat techniques it's developing into a cheap alternative to long-distance telephone calls.

Since its inception in Finland in 1988, IRC has played a worthy part in transmitting timely eye-witness accounts of every major world event – including the Gulf war, LA riots, Kobe earthquake, Oklahoma bombing, and the Olympics. During the Gulf war, for example, IRC channels formed to dissect the latest news as it came in from the wire services. But, as you'll soon discover, politics, crises, and sport are not the only things discussed.

Unlike Usenet, on IRC your conversations are live. What you key into your computer is instantly broadcast to everybody else on your channel, even if they're logged into a server on the other side of the world. Some channels are obviously dedicated to particular topics, for example, #cricket, #quake, and #worldcup, but most are just informal chat lines. Who knows, your perfect match could be waiting for you in an online chat channel like

#hottub. You might think that's unlikely, but IRC has brought many couples together and some have even held their wedding ceremonies online. If you ever get to attend one, be sure to throw some rice, like this: """""""""". And if you want to find out where the real pointy-heads play, read on.

> **What's IRC?** A veritable online Love Boat,
> say Mr and Mrs D Elliot at:
> http://www.vantek.net/pages/delliott/

Requirements

When you enter something into an IRC channel, everyone else in that channel, wherever they are, will see it almost immediately. The only way that can happen is through **full Internet access**, or through a local chat server. However, you don't need a particularly fast connection nor a powerful computer. Ideally, you don't want to be paying **timed online charges** either, because it's another medium where, once you're hooked, you'll end up spending hours online.

Many users have free direct connections through university or work, so they can afford to leave their line open all day. That's one of the reasons why you'll often find idle occupied channels. When you enter the channel and "beep" an occupant, if they're in the vicinity of the terminal, they'll answer your call. It's also possible that they're chatting in other channels.

A caution

Of all the Internet's features, IRC is the one most likely to trip up newbies. Mainly because you can't hide your presence. For example, on Usenet, unless you contribute by posting a message, no-one will know you've visited. However, the second you arrive in an IRC channel you will be announced to all and your nickname will remain in the names list for as long as you stay.

Sleuthful chatsters can quickly find out who you are behind your nickname and probably tell whether you're a newbie from your settings. And the odd devious type may try to persuade you to enter commands which could hand over control of your computer. Never enter an unfamiliar command at the request of another user. If someone is bothering you privately, protest publicly. If no-one defends you, change channels. If they persist, get them kicked out by an operator.

Getting started

Net software bundles don't always include an **IRC client** or program. If that's your case, fire up FTP and get the latest **GUI client** (see our Software Roundup on p.315). Once it's installed, read its configuration instructions as well as all its tutorials and assorted text files.

It might sound a bit boring to have to read the instructions first but in this case it's necessary. GUI IRC clients have an array of cryptic buttons and windows that are less intuitive than most Internet applications. Before you start randomly clicking on things to see what they do, remember that people are watching.

Additionally, before you can get started, you'll need to **configure your client** to connect to a specific IRC server's address, and enter your nickname, real name, and email address. If you're worried about embarrassing yourself, try an alias. Some servers, however, refuse entry if their reverse lookups detect discrepancies.

The servers

To ease the strain on network traffic, try to use a nearby host. There are hundreds of open IRC hosts worldwide. The best place to get a list, or indeed any information about IRC, is from the alt.irc newsgroup. Failing that, you can get one from: http://http1.brunel.ac.uk/~cs93jtl/IRC.html

For starters, just choose one from your client's menu or try: undernet.org on port 6667.

IRC commands

IRC has over 100 commands. Unless you're very keen, you'll only need to know a few. However, the more you learn, the more you can strengthen your position. You can almost get away without learning any commands at all with GUI clients, but it won't hurt to know the script behind the buttons, and you may even prefer to use it. Your client won't automate everything, so each time you're online test a few more. Its "Help" file should contain a full list. If not, try: http://www.iac.net/~edge/irc.html or: www.undernet.org

There are far too many commands to list here, but those below will get you started. Anything after a forward slash (/) is interpreted as a command. If you leave off the slash, it will be transmitted to your active channel as a message and you'll look a right idiot.

Commands are NOT case sensitive

Command	Description
/AWAY <message>	Leaves a message saying you're not available
/BYE	Exits your IRC session
/HELP	Returns a list of available commands
/HELP <command>	Returns help on the specified command
/IGNORE <nickname><*><all>	Ignores output from specified nickname
/IGNORE <*><email address><all>	Ignores output from specified email address
/IGNORE <*><*><none>	Deletes ignorance list
/JOIN <#channel>	Join specified channel
/KICK <nickname>	Boot specified nickname off channel
/LEAVE <#channel>	Exit specified channel
/LIST <-MIN n>	Lists channels with a minimum of n users
/MOP	Promotes all to operator status
/MSG <nickname><message>	Sends a private message to specified nickname
/NICK <nickname>	Changes your nickname
/OP <nickname>	Promotes specified nickname to operator status
/QUERY <nickname>	Starts a private conversation with specified nickname
/TOPIC <new topic>	Changes the topic of the channel
/WHO*	Gives a list of users in the current channel
/WHOIS <nickname>	Displays identity of nickname
/WHOWAS <nickname>	Displays identity of nickname who has exited

Step by step through your first session

By now, you've configured your client, given yourself a nickname that you'll never use again, and are raring to go. The aim of your first session is to connect to a server, have a look around, get a list of channels, join one, see who's on, say something public, then something private, leave the channel, start a new channel, make yourself operator, change the topic, and then exit IRC. The whole process should take no more than about ten minutes. Let's go.

✦ Log on to a server and wait to be accepted. If you're not, keep trying others until you succeed. Once aboard, you'll be greeted with the MOTD (message of the day) in the server window. Read the message and see if it tells you anything interesting.

✦ You should have two windows available. One is for input and the other to display output from the server. Generally, the two windows form part of a larger window, with the input box below the output box. Even though your client's point and click interface will replace most of the basic commands, since you probably haven't read the manual yet, you won't know how to use it. So instead just use the commands.

✦ To find out what channels are available, type: **/LIST** You'll have to wait a few moments and then a window will pop up, or fill up, with hundreds of channels, their topics, and the number of users on them. To narrow the list down to those channels with six or more users, type: **/LIST -MIN 6** Now you'll see the busiest channels.

✦ Pick a channel at random and join it. Channel names are always preceded by #, so to join the mustard channel, type: **/JOIN #mustard** and then wait for the channel window to appear. Once the channel window opens, you should get a list of the channel's occupants, in yet another window. If not, type: **/WHO*** to get a full list including nicknames and email addresses.

✦ Now say something clever. Type: **Hi everyone, it's great to be back!** This should appear not only on the screen in your channel window, but on the screen in every other person's channel window. Wait for replies and answer any questions as you see fit.

✦ Now it's time to send something personal. Choose someone in the channel and find out what you can about them first, by typing: **/WHO** followed by their nickname. Your client might let you do this by just double clicking on their nickname in the names window. Let's say their nickname is Tamster. To send a private message, just type: **/MSG Hey Tamster, I'm a clueless newbie, let me know if you get this so I won't feel so stupid.** If Tamster doesn't reply, keep trying until someone does. Once you're satisfied you know how that works, leave the channel by typing: **/LEAVE** Don't worry, next time you go into a channel, you'll feel more comfortable.

+ Now to start your own channel. You can pick any name that doesn't already exist. As soon as you leave, it will disappear. To start a channel called shambles, just type: **/JOIN #shambles** Once the window pops up, you'll find you're the only person on it. Now promote yourself to operator by typing **/OP** followed by your nickname. Others can tell you have channel operator status because your nickname will appear with an @ in front of it. Now that you are an operator, you have the power to kick people off the channel, change the topic, and all sorts of other things that you can find out by reading the manual as recommended. To change the topic, type: **/TOPIC** followed by whatever you want to change topic to. Wait for it to change on the top of your window and then type: **/BYE** to exit IRC.

That's it really, a whirlwind tour but enough to learn most things you'll need. But before you can chat with other chatsters, you'll need to speak their lingo.

The language of IRC

Just like CB radio, IRC has its own dialect. Chat is a snappy medium, messages are short, and responses are fast. Unlike CB, people don't ask your "20" to find out where you're from, or type "breaker" when they enter a discussion, but they do use **short-forms**, **acronyms**, and **smileys** (:-). Acronyms are mixed in with normal speech and range from the innocuous (BTW = by the way) to a whole panoply of blue phrases. Don't be too shocked. It's not meant to be taken seriously. And don't be ashamed to use ordinary English language, either. You'll stand a better chance of being understood.

For a sample of some of the abbreviations and acronyms you might encounter, see our Glossary of Net language on p.350.

IRC netiquette

IRC attracts a diverse group for a variety of reasons. You're as likely to encounter a channel full of Indian expats following a ball-by-ball cricket commentary as a couple of lovers chatting intimately. Provided no-one rocks the boat too much, everyone can coexist. There's bound to be a little spontaneous mischief now and then, which usually just adds to the fun of the whole event.

However, some actions are generally frowned upon and may get you kicked from channels, or even banned from IRC. These include dumping large files or amounts of text to a channel, harassment, vulgarity, beeping channels constantly to get attention, and inviting people into inappropriate channels. Finally, if you make a big enough nuisance of yourself, some vindictive person might track you down and make you regret it.

IRC games

Many IRC channels are dedicated to games. You sometimes play against other people, but programs called **"bots"** are more common opponents. Such programs are written to respond to requests in a particular way, and even learn from the experience.

To find out more about IRC games,
send: info irc-games to listserv@netcom.com,
see: http://www.cris.com/%7Etrieger/irc-games.shtml and
http://www.yahoo.com/Recreation/Games/Internet_Games/
and the newsgroup: alt.irc.games

IRC picture gallery

Once you've used IRC a few times, you'll recognize many regulars, and they'll recognize you. If you'd like to put a face to their names, check out the IRC picture gallery on the World Wide Web at:

http://www.powertech.no/IRCGallery

You're welcome to add your own, and if your online pals haven't already done so, suggest it.

Internet telephony

The concept of using the Internet as an alternative to the telephone network is getting some quarters quite excited – mainly because it can cut the cost of calling long distance to that of a local call. But it's an area that's well and truly in its teething phase. Although it certainly works, don't expect the same fidelity as your local regular phone network.

To make calls on the Net, you need a **soundcard**, **speakers**, and **microphone** – standard multimedia fare. If your soundcard permits duplex transmission, you can hold a regular conversation, like an ordinary telephone, otherwise it's more like a walkie-talkie where you take turns to speak. As for your modem, generally 14.4kbps is ample to the task but the higher the bandwidth both ends are connected, the more likely you'll get decent sound quality.

There are several programs available for making calls now, including one built into **Netscape Navigator**. Some, like **Internet Phone**, work very similarly to IRC – you log into a server and join a channel. Others, such as **Webphone**, are a closer approximation to the conventional phone and start a point-to-point when you choose a name from a directory. It's worth trying a few to see what works best for your setup. One that's state-of-the-art is **Microsoft NetMeeting**, which has real-time voice conferencing, plus things like collaborative application sharing, document editing, background file transfer, and a whiteboard to draw and paste on.

You'll find a variety of these clients in our Software Roundup (see p.315).

Video conferencing

You might like the idea of being able to see who you're talking to, but even with ISDN connections and snazzy graphics, **Internet video conferencing** is more like a slide show than real-time video. But if it means seeing live footage of a loved one across the world, perhaps it's worth it, even at 14.4 kbps.

Again, see our Software Roundup (p.315) for a selection of video-conferencing programs.

Chat worlds

There's no doubt that Virtual Reality can look quite cute, but there's not much call for it. The best applications so far seem to be among the plethora of **chat worlds**, **virtual cities**, and **avatars**. These tend to work like IRC, but with an extra dimension or two. So rather than channels, you get rooms, playgrounds, swimming pools, and so forth. To switch channels, you might walk into another building or fly up into the clouds. You might be represented by an animated character rather than a text nickname and be able to do all sorts of multimedia things like build 3D objects and play music.

This all sounds pretty futuristic and it's certainly impressive at first, but whether you'll want to become a regular's another matter. Some interesting ones include **World's Chat**, **The Palace**, and **VizScape**. Once again, you'll find them in our Software Roundup (p.317).

Online games

Many say the Internet's next "killer applications" will be inspired by **networkable PC games** like **Duke Nukem**, **Command & Conquer**, **Doom**, and its successor **Quake**. Play them on a lone PC, and you'll become adept with a whole new range of virtual cutlery like chainsaws, flame tanks, and rocket-propelled grenades. But over a network, they take on a whole new dimension. It's no longer just a computer game, it's a battle of mate v mate. And things get serious.

To bring in another player, you need to establish a connection between two machines. The easiest way is over a phone line via modems, but that limits it to two players. To conscript more victims, you need a proper network. A **local area network (LAN)** is best. That's where you connect all the machines via network cards and cables. It doesn't cost much to set up at home, though everyone will have to bring their machines around. Easier still is to use a LAN at work. Just be sure to invite your boss to take the flak if things go wobbly.

The other way to bring in more players, or to play over long distances, is to use the Internet in conjunction with – if needed – an intermediary emulation program like **Kali** to sort out the protocols. However, at best it's erratic, and when the Net's slow, it's pretty much unplayable.

To find out more, including where to download the games, try the general games sites detailed in our Web Guide (see p.212).

Where to find the real propeller heads

Before Space Invaders (apart from the ubiquitous paddle game Pong) the only computer games to speak of were of the adventure variety. The ones where you'd stumble around **imaginary kingdoms** looking for hidden objects, uttering magic words, and fighting monsters. They were pretty tame compared to the likes of today's Quake and Duke Nukem 3D. But the funny thing is, these adventure games are still going strong in the UNIX world of the Internet.

Admittedly, they've come a long way, and blended with the whole Dungeons and Dragons caper, but they're still mostly text-based. That's "mostly," because a few are starting to appear with graphical interfaces. What sets them apart from conventional arcade games is the community that evolves from them. Within each game, participants develop complex alter egos enabling them to live out their fantasies and have them accepted within the group. But it can also become an obsession where the distinction between the alter ego and the self becomes blurred, and players retreat into the reassurance of the game. If they're dialing in from a home account, it can also become an expensive one. In other words, it's about as geeky as it gets.

On the Internet, such games are known as **MUDs (Multi User Dimensions or Dungeons)**. If they have a graphic component, they're called **GUI MUDs** (gooey muds). They can be classified further into combat, role play, and social MUDs. **Combat MUDs** are the original medieval adventure games, **role play MUDs** have more flexible modern themes, while **social MUDs** involve more interplayer activities. A social MUD can also be called a **MOO** (MUD Object Oriented), **MUSE** (Multi User Shared Dimension), or **MUSH** (Multi User Shared Hallucination). Got that? If so, drop everything and see a doctor.

Connecting to MUDs

You usually connect to MUDs via **Telnet** (see Software Roundup – p.331), although initially you might find the link on a **Web page**, where they are fast migrating. As every MUD is different, be prepared to learn some complex commands before you can play. However, don't let that intimidate you as newbies are always welcome, and other players will help point you in the right direction.

For more about MUDs, see: http:www.cis.upenn.edu/~lwl/mudinfo.html and the newsgroup hierarchies: alt.mud and rec.games.mud

PART TWO

The Guide

World Wide Web

Usenet Newsgroups

Software Roundup

A Guide to World Wide Web Sites

It's impossible to say exactly how many addresses are accessible from the World Wide Web, but it's likely to be hundreds of millions. That's because the Web is an ever-evolving beast with tentacles reaching into Usenet, Gopher, Telnet, and FTP. It's far and away the most popular part of the Internet, and with its graphic and sound capabilities, the most exciting. In fact, it's a little like having your own library, including magazines, business catalogs, academic journals, and fanzines from just about every obsessive, enthusiast, and wacko out there.

Technically, Web site addresses start with the prefix http: – anything else, although accessible from the Web, really belongs to another system. What sets the Web apart is its **hypertextual navigation**. Any Web page can link to any other Web page, whether it's on the same system or on the other side of the world.

Almost all Web sites contain **links** to similar sites as well as to some of general interest. It's entirely up to the whim of whoever owns the site. For example, at the Virtual Pub, you'll find original content as well as links to other beer-related sites. Take one of those links, and you'll most likely arrive at another site with links to even more related sites. So even though there are only about 700 sites reviewed in the following pages, use them as launchpads, click around, and you'll have access to millions more.

Finding what you want

The keys to finding your way around the Web are the **Internet search tools and directories**. See **Finding It** (p.110) for the lowdown on this and the directories following for addresses.

How to get there

To reach a site, carefully enter its **address** (taking note of capitalization) into your browser's **URL (or Location) window**. If you're using Netscape or Internet Explorer, you needn't type the http:// part of the address.

How to find a site again

When you see something you like, save its address to your **bookmarks, favorites, or hotlist**. That way you can access it from your browser's menu at a later date. Alternatively you can save the page to disk. But remember, you have to save the images separately.

When it's not there

Some of the Web sites we've listed will have disappeared, but don't let that deter you. Refer to p.122 for advice on how to track them down. The easiest way is to enter the title, and/or related subjects, as keywords into one of the search engines such as InfoSeek Ultra, Altavista, or Hot-Bot. Once you've mastered the Internet Search Tools & Directories, you'll be able to find anything.

So, wax up and get out there!

Web Sites Directory

Most human life has found its way onto the World Wide Web, so it doesn't exactly lend itself to **categorization**. Headings below are the ones we've adopted to make the listings in our guide easier to navigate. Obviously, they blur into each other at the slightest opportunity. So, if you're into music, you might want to explore "Music," "Entertainment," "Ezines," "Shopping," and "News, Newspapers, and Magazines." If you're up for fun, check under "Comedy," "Entertainment," "Weird," "Ezines," and "Games," and so on. To **search the net by subject or keyword**, try out some of the tools in our "Search Tools and Net Directories" section.

PART ONE

SEARCH TOOLS AND DIRECTORIES

This first section of our Web sites guide is devoted to guides to the Web on the Web, and in particular to all the tools you'll need to find sites and get oriented.

You'll find more as they're announced at Netscape's Search page at:

http://home.netscape.com/home/internet-search.html which can be accessed direct from Netscape's Menu and button bar.

WEB AND GOPHER SEARCH

Altavista
http://www.altavista.digital.com
A quick, huge database that usually delivers.

Gopher Searching

gopher://gopher.scs.unr.edu

Find text stored in Gophers using Gopher Jewels or Veronica.

HotBot

http://www.hotbot.com

First-class Web database, sponsored by *HotWired*, with several useful search options. Particularly adept at finding instances of people's names on sites.

InfoSeek/InfoSeek Ultra

http://www.infoseek.com

http://ultra.infoseek.com

InfoSeek has a range of engines with varying front ends, all with superb searching algorithms. Some involve charges to users after a trial period. One to watch for new products.

Internet Tools

http://www.itools.com/

All-in-one search and publicity forms.

Lycos

http://www.lycos.com/

Large database, but sometimes tediously indiscriminate.
Indexes page summaries, not whole pages.

WebCrawler

http://www.webcrawler.com

Fast, but merely searches page summaries or titles.

WEB DIRECTORIES

You'll find other specialist directories in their respective
sections.

Argus Clearinghouse

http://www.clearinghouse.net/

Directory of links to specialist directories, sorted by subject.

Electric Library

http://www.elibrary.com/

Simultaneously searches databases of newspapers,
magazines, newswires, classic books, maps, photographs,
and major artworks.

Global Online Directory

http://www.god.co.uk

European search aid.

GNN's Whole Internet Catalog

http://www.gnn.com/gnn/wic/index.html

Excellent and dependable selections of reviewed choices by
category – plus a business directory.

IBM InfoMarket

http://www.infomarket.ibm.com/

Simultaneously searches a wide selection of predominantly
technical journals, newsletters, newspapers, newswires, and
corporate databases.

Internet Directory

http://www.internet-directory.co.uk

This is the biggest, freshest, UK site directory and is
connected to *Internet* magazine's What's New.

Internet Magazine's Essential Viewing

http://www.emap.co.uk/review/

Monthly site reviews from *Internet* magazine. Even some
from this author.

Magellan

http://www.mckinley.com/

Invaluable source of reviewed and captioned sites.

Muscat

http://www.muscat.co.uk/

European site index.

New Rider's Official Yellow Pages

http://www.mcp.com/nrp/wwwyp/

Online edition of the fat yellow book.

NlightN

http://www.nlightn.com/

Searches databases, newswires, reference services, journals,
and book titles.

Point Communications

http://www.pointcom.com

The Web's most popular sites reviewed in depth, and sortable
by Presentation, Content, and Experience ratings. Compiles
the top 5%, whatever that means.

Starting Point

http://www.stpt.com/

Selection of the best tools to get going.

WebSource

http://www.websource.com.au

Everything Australian on the Internet.

What's New

http://www.emap.com/whatsnew/

New sites listed as they're announced. Archives are searchable by category or country.

What's On

http://www.whatson.com/

Internet magazine's directories, pick of the day, and charts.

WWW Virtual Library

http://www.ww3.org/hypertext/DataSources/bySubject/Overview.html

Consortium of subject-specific directories scattered all over the Web.

Yahoo

http://www.yahoo.com

Big and easy to navigate by subject, if light on reviews. But it includes loads of specialist stuff on the side, like Reuters news. Indispensable.

Yell

http://www.yell.co.uk

UK-specific guide, including company A–Z, film finder, and business phone directory.

YellowWeb Europe Directory

http://www.yweb.com

European Web guide.

Your Personal Net

http://www.ypn.com

Online version of Michael Wolff's *NetGuide* series of books.
That means particular strengths in Travel (a joint venture
with Fodor's), Music, Games, Medicine, Money, and (mainly
US) employment opportunities.

BUSINESS AND PHONE DIRECTORIES

See also: Business and Telecommunications.

Big Book

http://www.bigbook.com/

Lists over 11 million US businesses, plus street maps,
reviews, and free home pages.

Big Yellow

http://www.bigyellow.com

US business and shopping directory.

Commercial Sites on the Net

http://www.directory.net/

A huge directory useful for product searches.

Switchboard

http://www.switchboard.com

Trace people and businesses in the US.

Telstra Yellow Pages

http://www.yellowpages.com.au

Australian business phone directory. Sydney addresses
include UBD maps. Links to the White Pages for residential
numbers and addresses.

UK Multimedia Handbook

http://www.handbook.co.uk

Free contact directory for the UK multimedia industry.

Web100

http://fox.nstn.ca/~at_info/

The 100 biggest US, and non-US, businesses on the Web, ranked by revenue, with commentary and links.

World Wide Yellow Pages

http://www.yellow.com/

Global business contact directory. Search by name, industry, and location.

Yell

http://www.yell.co.uk

Includes UK business phone directory.

EMAIL SEARCH

These email searches source addresses from Usenet Newsgroup postings and visitors. Four11 is probably the pick, but they're all much of a muchness.

Bigfoot
http://www.bigfoot.com

Four11
http://www.four11.com

Internet Address Finder
http://www.iaf.net/

WhoWhere?
http://www.whowhere.com

LISTS AND PICKS

100 hot Websites
http://www.hot100.com
The hundred most visited Web sites each week, overall or by category. Not necessarily accurate, but close enough.

Cool Site of the Day
http://cool.infi.net
So popular that it's sent some winners enough traffic to crash their servers.

Internet Chartshow
http://www.emap.com/chartshow/
Top 10 new sites of the week, as chosen by EMAP Online.

Mirsky's Worst
http://mirsky.com/wow/Worst.html
Some genuine shockers, but most are entertaining in their ineptitude. Something of a lucky dip.

Netguide Now!

http://techweb.cmp.com/net

Weekly bulletins from *Netguide* magazine. Also available by email.

Netsurf Central

http://www.netsurfcentral.com

Hotwired's Web picks of the day.

Netsurfer Digest

http://www.netsurf.com/nsd/

Subscribe to receive weekly site updates and reviews.

The Revolving Door

http://asylum.cid.com/revdoor/revdoor.cgi

Dynamic, quasi-democratic hotlist maintained entirely by visitors.

Shareware top 20

http://www.clicked.com/shareware/

Top 20 shareware picks in several categories, along with reviews.

Stroud's What's New

http://www.stroud.com/new.html

The latest Internet shareware releases, daily.

MAILING LIST DIRECTORIES

InReference

http://www.reference.com

Search Usenet and thousands of mailing lists.

Liszt

http://www.liszt.com/

Searchable directory of mailing list topics.

Publicly Accessible Mailing Lists

http://www.neosoft.com/internet/paml/

Thousands of specialist email discussion groups organized by name or subject, with details on traffic, content, and how to join.

Search the Net

http://www.statsvet.uu.se/maillist.html

List of mailing list directories.

SOFTWARE GUIDES

Archie

http://pubweb.nexor.co.uk/public/archie/servers.html

Dated, slow, and cumbersome, but a popular method of searching public FTP sites.

Browser Watch

http://www.browserwatch.com

All the latest browsers and plug-ins.

FTP Search

http://ftpsearch.ntnu.no/

Powerful, but complex, Norwegian FTP search engine.

InfoMac HyperArchive

http://www.lcs.mit.edu/HyperArchive/HyperArchive.html

HTML version of the InfoMac Macintosh software site.

Jumbo Shareware

http://www.jumbo.com

Mammoth shareware archive for all platforms.

Shareware.com

http://www.shareware.com

Search several major file archives for all platforms.

Snoopie

http://www.snoopie.com

Lightning-fast searches of a crawler-built FTP database.

Stroud's Consummate Winsock Applications

http://www.stroud.com http://www.cwsapps.com

Windows Internet applications posted and reviewed as released.

TUCOWs

http://www.tucows.com

More Windows Internet applications.

The Well Connected Mac

http://www.macfaq.com/

Guide to Mac software and resources.

Windows 95

http://www.windows95.com

The latest Windows 95 applications.

Winsite

http://www.winsite.com/

BBS-like Windows archive.

World Catalog of Software Websites

http://ssrl.rtp.com:443/library/

Web sites sorted by category; it's easier to find developers here than products, however.

USENET SEARCH

Altavista

http://www.altavista.digital.com

Fast, big, and reliable Usenet database.

DejaNews

http://www.dejanews.com/

http://www.dejanews.co.uk

Gives the most power over results, and keeps articles longest, but may not cover all groups.

InfoSeek/InfoSeek Ultra

http://www.infoseek.com

http://ultra.infoseek.com

These archive possibly the most groups and allow the finest tuning to eliminate chaff.

Newsgroups in Oxford

http://www.lib.ox.ac.uk/internet/news/

Automatically compiled hypertext list of Usenet groups, FAQs, and reviews.

Open NNTP Sites

http://dana.ucc.nau.edu/~jwa

If you're behind a firewall at work or your ISP's Usenet coverage is lacking, try an open news server. This list is generated by a bot that looks for open ports. But if it's left open unintentionally, and they notice a marked increase in traffic, they may shut the door.

INTERNET STUDIES

Forrester Research

http://www.forrester.com

Few research firms are as switched on to new media as
Boston-based Forrester. Consequently its views on the
Internet don't always come free. Those that do are here.

GVU's WWW User Survey

http://www.cc.gatech.edu/gvu/user_surveys/

The biggest and oldest periodic Web user survey. Its latest
results shown a marked change in profiles, reflecting the
Net's convergence with the mainstream.

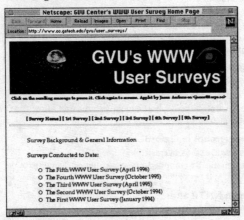

Hermes Study

http://www.umich.edu/~sgupta/hermes/

Analyzes the demographic profiles of Web users from a
commercial perspective. If you intend to market on the Net,
it's worth your while reading the latest results to size up
your quarry.

Neilsen Interactive

http://www.neilsenmedia.com

Results of the people meter people's Internet surveys.

Values and Lifestyles

http://future.sri.com/

The VALS program is digging deeper into the psychographic profiles of Net users with each new questionnaire. Complete the survey and discover whether you're regarded as an Actualizer, Fullfilled, an Achiever, an Experiencer, a Believer, a Striver, a Maker, or a Struggler. Marketeers, like astrologers and royals, need to class people to help justify their existence.

OTHER INTERNET STUFF

Blacklist of Internet Advertisers

http://math-www.uni-paderborn.de/~axel/BL/

Find out how to deal with electronic junk mail and pesky advertisers buzzing your favorite newsgroups. There's also a list of crafty Net abusers, which aims to discourage you from joining their ranks.

Gamelan

http://www.gamelan.com

Java headquarters. Great for finding innovative sites.

GeoCities

http://www.geocities.com/

Build your own free "homestead" in a virtual city that suits your style. It's all done through forms so you needn't know HTML.

HTML Converters

http://union.ncsa.uiuc.edu/HyperNews/get/www/html/converters.html

Convert almost any document to a Web page.

NetNames

http://www.netnames.com

If you'd like to register your own domain name, but it all seems too hard, try a third party specialist. But check here first to see if your choice has been taken. The lookup only takes seconds.

Realm Graphics

http://www.ender-design.com/rg/

You can pinch these background textures, bullets, icons, buttons, and arty bits and put them on your own Web page.

Silicon Toad's Hacking Resources

http://www.netwalk.com/~silicon/episteme.html

Crawl through the Net's very underbelly. Hackers, crackers, phreakers, and warez traders – it's business as usual here in Geek Alley.

Staking your claim in cyberspace

http://www.links.net/webpub/domains.html

How to register your own domain name, using official or subversive means.

World Wide Web Consortium

http://www.w3.org

Trying to convert something into HTML format to put it on the Web? Here's where to find help. You can also see the future of the Web being hatched by checking in for the latest HTML proposals.

PART TWO

WEB SITES SUBJECT GUIDE

First off, a disclaimer. This guide is not intended to be a roundup of the greatest Web sites in existence. Instead, we've tried to give as broad a range of sites as possible, so you can get started on a subject – and keep going by following the links from their pages.

ART, PHOTOGRAPHY, ANIMATION, COMICS, AND GRAPHICS

@art gallery
http://www.art.uiuc.edu/@art/

A digital sample of what's being cooked at the University of Illinois School of Art and Design.

24 hours in Cyberspace
http://www.cyber24.com/

Collective output of over 1000 photographers and 100 photojournalists documenting the impact of the digital revolution on 8 Feb 1996 everywhere from the Sahara to Times Square.

Art in Response to Censorship
http://www.sva.edu/WGTB/flypaper.html

Here's proof that the more that something is condemned or hallowed, the more it is embraced or challenged by the artistic community.

Art on the Net
http://www.art.net/

A friendly gallery to post your own art or look at that of others. There's even an area for hackers.

ArtAIDS Link

http://www.illumin.co.uk/artaids/

An Internet equivalent of the AIDS patchwork quilt.
Participation is encouraged: upload your own tribute to this
ever-growing mosaic of love, loss, and memory.

Big Fire Anime

http://www.bigfire.com/bigfire.htm

Monstrous archive of Japanese animation, cartoonery, and
software.

Comix'n'Stuff

http://www.phlab.missouri.edu/~c617145/comix.html

Unless you have a mega-bandwidth connection, you'll find
reading comics on the Net pretty tedious. But if you're into
comics as a communications medium, or art form, there's
ample fodder here.

Computer Graphics

http://mambo.ucsc.edu/psl/cg.html

Directory of computer-generated art resources, using distinct
thumbnails as captions.

Core-Industrial Design Resources

http://www.core77.com/

Are you a budding industrial designer, just waiting for a break? Maybe you'll find some help here. It has marketing tips, employment opportunities, and discussion forums, as well as listings of industry associations, business contacts, recommended reading lists, and design school addresses. If you're still stuck, maybe the student projects from Pratt's in New York will provide some inspiration.

Font Net

http://www.type.co.uk

As with almost everything Neville Brody – uber-designer of *The Face*, *Arena* and *Actuel* fame – touches, his Web debut oozes style at every turn. But there's substance as well in the form of various font samples and *Fuse* magazine posters, and persistent urging to subscribe to FontWorks' range of type products.

Kodak

http://www.kodak.com/

Details of Kodak's products, services, and latest developments, particularly its PhotoCD technology. Plus a gallery of JPEG and ImagePac stills, and the necessary viewing software for download.

OTIS (operative term is stimulate)

http://www.sito.org/

Photos, drawings, tattoos, ray-traces, video stills, record covers, sculpture, art links, and more.

Ping Datascape

http://www.artcom.de/ping/mapper

Add to a 3D flight through the Web. It was meant to become a television test pattern but seems to have come off the rails.

Pitchford Place

http://www.pitchford.com/QTVR.html

Gallery of QuickTime Virtual Reality images that can be viewed through 360 degrees with you in the center.

Sandra's Clip Art Server

http://www.n-vision.com/panda/c/

Somewhere down the artistic spectrum beneath Pierrot dolls, velvet prints, muzak, and butt photocopies lies clip art. For some reason, this soulless dross is often used to inject life into documents and overhead transparencies. To make your next presentation look thoroughly canned, dig in here.

Scooter Boy

http://www.iac.co.jp/scooterboy/

Cute interactive Japanese comic.

Stereogram pages

http://www.ccc.nottingham.ac.uk/~etzpc/sirds.html

Create your own Magic Eye pictures or download others' spotty 3D creations. In no time you'll be able to induce a migraine at will.

Strange Interactions

http://amanda.physics.wisc.edu/

Intriguing exhibition of prints, etchings, and lithographs by physicist John E Jacobsen.

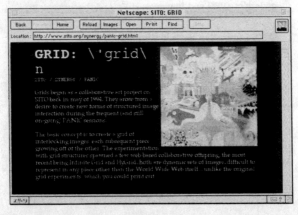

Synergy Grid

http://www.sito.org/synergy/panic-grid.html

Find out how to create collaborative image grids or use the infinite grid selector to tailor a multi-layered psychedelic collage to your favorite of 12,288,000,000 possible configurations.

Writing on the Wall

http://www.gatech.edu/desoto/graf/Index.Art_Crimes.html

Diverse collection of international graffiti art, showcasing the works of youths with little to say, speaking their minds.

BANKING

Bank of America

http://www.bankamerica.com

Reconcile your books, monitor check clearances, transfer and stop payments, and view your balance, all via your PC. That is, if you're with Bank of America.

Barclays

http://www.barclays.com

As staid as you would expect from the UK's largest banking/stockbroking/insurance conglomerate. In the future it promises serious online features such as credit card applications and a help desk but at this stage it's just the leaflets you avoid as you're waiting for service.

DigiCash

http://digicash.com

DigiCash is one of the frontrunners in the race to develop an acceptable "smart" currency for Net transactions. Right now, it's all experimental but it hopes its ecash will soon become a global standard. Pick up some electronic fun-tickets and purchase various intangibles at hundreds of participating shops around the Net. You won't get anything in return except the satisfaction of helping build the future of commerce.

European Union Bank

http://www.eub.com/

Antiguan offshore banking services via the Net.

First Virtual

http://www.fv.com/

Third party clearing house for Net transactions on electronically transferable items such as software, text, and advice. Participating vendors deliver the goods first. If you're satisfied, you instruct First Virtual to pay. Purchases are accrued and charged against your credit card monthly. Since you phone in your credit card details upon joining, no sensitive information ever passes over the Net.

MasterCard International

http://www.mastercard.com/

Like Visa, Digicash, and First Virtual, MasterCard appears well poised to profit from developments in electronic payments, smart cards, and online transactions. You'll get a somewhat biased idea of where it's all heading by delving through these pages, plus whatever MasterCard information you could possibly want other than your balance.

Network Payments and Digital Cash

http://ganges.cs.tcd.ie/mepeiroe/project.html

Some say paper cash is going the same way as pieces-of-eight, sea shells, and salt. Judge for yourself how close we are to obtaining an alternative global currency or, more urgently, an acceptable method of completing online transactions.

Visa Expo

http://www.visa.com

Will Visa achieve "One World, One Currency – Visa"? Who knows, but they certainly have an edge in electronic banking. As this site drums home.

World Bank

http://www.worldbank.org

The World Bank's major role is to help developing countries

reduce poverty and sustain economic growth. These pages extensively document the bank's projects and aspirations. If you're perplexed by how it can give away so much money and still stay afloat, you might come away a little more enlightened, if not somewhat optimistic for the future.

BOOKS AND BOOKSTORES

Amazon Books
http://www.amazon.com

Order from over a million titles, write your review, and read others'. Fully searchable by author, title, and key words.

Atomic Books
http://www.atomicbooks.com

John Waters, director of such bizarro movie classics as Pink Flamingos and Hairspray, frequents this Baltimore shop in search of "insane books about every kind of extreme.". Now you can order the same oddities online.

Banned Books Online
http://www.cs.cmu.edu/Web/People/spok/banned-books.html

This exhibit of controversial books is presented by Carnegie Mellon University, where the administration recently removed more than 80 sex newsgroups, a matter still contested by the students. See which books have been banned or come under attack, and why, by reading the contentious extracts. Many titles are now considered classics.

Blackwells
http://www.blackwells.co.uk

This UK academic bookseller has one of the best-organized sites for browsing subject catalogs and ordering.

Cambridge University Press
http://www.cup.cam.ac.uk

Online catalog plus updates on future and featured titles such as the Cambridge Encyclopedia.

Coupland Files

http://www.interlog.com/~spiff/coupland

Douglas Coupland interviews and articles, as well as analyses of *Microserfs*, *Generation X*, *Shampoo Planet*, *Life after God*, and other writings. The perennial 20-something's own home page is at: http://www.coupland.com

Dillons

http://www.dillons.co.uk

An excellent UK bookstore site, strong on both general and academic books – and serious about its online presence.

Educational Texts

http://www.etext.org/

Hundreds of thousands of words, ranging from the complete works of Shakespeare to the script of a lost episode of Star Trek. Plus links to similar archives of religious, political, legal, and fanzine text.

Eland Books

http://www.travelbooks.co.uk

This small specialist publisher has a model site, showcasing in elegant, unfussy layout its travel narratives, with well-chosen excerpts from each, and a full ordering facility.

Elsevier Science

http://www.elsevier.nl

Elsevier claims to be the world's leading supplier of scientific information. On board is an exhaustive list of its journals, publications, and multimedia products, plus news of forthcoming releases, reviews, and ordering facilities.

Future Fantasy Bookstore

http://futfan.com/home.html

Palo Alto's Future Fantasy Bookstore specializes in fantasy, horror, science fiction, and mystery books. You can search through its online library and, if anything takes your fancy, order it by email.

Future Fantasy Bookstore

Copyright 1994, Future Fantasy

A Bookstore of Science Fiction, Fantasy, and Mysteries

The Internet Public Library

http://ipl.sils.umich.edu

Links to thousands of online books, magazines, and newspapers.

Kaiser Books

http://kbc.com/

If you're after books and magazines, on or off the Net, you'll find a way to get them from here. If not in the book and magazine marketplace, then maybe amongst the hundreds of links, or from a shop in the worldwide secondhand bookstore directory.

Laissez-Faire Books

http://www.lfb.org/

Laissez-Faire has been a source of libertarian books and tapes for over twenty years. It offers titles by the likes of Ayn Rand, Thomas Jefferson, Ludwig von Mises, P.J. O'Rourke, Milton Friedman, Thomas Szasz and, of course, Adam Smith, on topics like education, drug policy, gun control, free marketeering, economics, and humor. You can email order from anywhere in the world.

Literary Kicks

http://www.charm.net/~brooklyn/LitKicks.html

This shrine to the beats has a mass of fine material, audio clips and links on the likes of Kerouac, Corso, Ginsberg and Cassady, and all who came into their orbit.

Loompanics

gopher://gopher.well.sf.ca.us/00/Business/catalog.asc

It's best to save this long, single-page catalogue as a text file, and read it offline. It's crammed with reviews and ordering details of subversive, strange, and sometimes downright nasty gems of anarchic and alternative writing.

Macmillan USA

http://www.mcp.com/

The Macmillan USA Information SuperLibrary goes further than most publishers, putting searchable contents pages and full chapter samples for many of its thousands of books online. What's more, you can download copies of any software included with computer titles, here or from its FTP site. It's a massive site.

Online Books

http://www.cs.cmu.edu/Web/books.html

There are complete texts tucked away in obscure archives all over the Net. Here's an index of about a thousand titles as well as links to almost 100 specialist repositories.

Online Bookshop

http://www.bookshop.co.uk/

Close to a million titles available from myriad publishers – plus links to numerous other bookstores. All books are cross-referenced by subject, with brief synopses and links to related material. Some are available through its central ordering mechanism, others direct from publishers.

Outpost:Culture

http://www.lb.com:80/~outpost/

Another book/bookstore/publisher finder, this time from US small press distributor, Inland Book Company.

Penguin Books

http://www.penguin.com

http://www.penguin.co.uk

Penguin maintains Web sites for both its US and UK companies, and they're introducing some neat features, including preview chapters of novels, and even a specially created hypertext novel. Worth watching.

Poetry Society

http://www.bbcnc.org.uk/online/poetry/

UK halfway house for budding poets and their victims.

Project Gutenberg

http://jg.cso.uiuc.edu/PG/welcome.html

Fifty years after authors die, their copyrights pass into the public domain. With this in mind, Project Gutenberg is dedicated to making as many works as possible available online in plain vanilla ascii text. Not all the books are old, however – some, such as the computer texts, have been donated. As great as that sounds, in practice you might prefer the convenience of the hard copy.

Pure Fiction

http://www.purefiction.com

For pulp worms and writers alike. Packed with book
previews, author interviews, and hundreds of links to the
sort of stuff you need to get off the ground and punch out
your first best seller. See also: alt.books.purefiction

Thomas Pynchon Home Page

http://www.pomona.edu/pynchon/

The reclusive author is ideal fare for the Net and this is a
wittily constructed site – courtesy San Narciso Community
College, of course – with complete text of Pynchon esoterica,
such as letters, articles, publishing blurbs, and the more
obscure short stories. Links, too, to the extensive Pynchonia
to be found elsewhere.

Romance Novel Database

http://www.sils.umich.edu/~sooty/romance/romance.html

Romantic fiction catalogued and rated, plus links to authors'
pages and similar sites.

Shakespeare

http://the-tech.mit.edu/Shakespeare

The Bard's complete works online.

Sun Tzu's The Art of War

http://www.cnu.edu/~patrick/taoism/suntzu/suntzu.html

Discover Sun Tzu's "The Art of War," with or without a guide.
At 2400 years old, it's believed to be the world's oldest
military treatise. Like other Chinese wisdoms such as the
teachings of Confucius, much of it still rings true and its
adages can be applied to any conflict. So much so, that it
became the Yuppies' surrogate bible. Oh well, battles do have
their casualties.

Tech Classics Archive

http://the-tech.mit.edu/Classics

Searchable archive of hundreds of translated Greek and
Roman classics.

Ventana

http://www.vmedia.com/

Order online from Ventana's range of popular computer texts, or download programs from its companion disks. The Internet section carries full text of Net selections, including Walking the WWW, Official Netscape Navigator 2.0, Internet Business 500, and Internet Roadside Attractions, complete with thousands of Web site reviews.

Wyvern Business Bookshop

http://www.cityscape.co.uk/users/ab96/

Buy direct from Wyvern's online business book catalog.

BUSINESS

@dmarket

http://www.admarket.com

Web advertising and marketing resources courtesy of *HotWired* and *Advertising Age*.

Barcode Server

http://www.milk.com/barcode/

Not only can you find out how bar codes work, you can even generate your own.

Business Index

http://www.dis.strath.ac.uk/business/index.html

Although it's very low-key, if you start here, you'll be no more than a link or two away from almost any business-related site.

Cyberpreneur's Internet Guide

http://asa.ugl.lib.umich.edu/chdocs/cyberpreneur/Cyber.html

Links to tips for new players in Net commerce.

Direct Marketing World

http://www.dmworld.com/

Direct marketing resources, such as lists, list-builders, copywriters, consultants, and agencies. There's a growing

employment section, literature for sale, and guides to direct
marketing on the Internet.

FedEx

http://www.fedex.com/

Federal Express has revolutionized the way carriers haul
freight, take orders, and service customers. This foray into
online parcel tracking and Net-distributed shipping software
marks yet another transport industry first.

Friends and Partners

http://solar.rtd.utk.edu/friends/home.html

US-Russian joint venture to help create a better understanding between the two nations. There's plenty of info on
such topics as economics, education, geography, music,
weather, and health, plus a literature section which contains
the full text of *The Brothers Karamazov* and *Anna Karenina*.
Its prime focus, however, is encouraging trade.

Internet Business Resource Directory

http://www.netsurf.com/nsf/v01/02/resource/index.html

Links to ISPs, business directories and publications,
advertising agencies, lawyers, bankers, venture capitalists,
and other commercial resources to help get your outfit flying
on the Net.

Internet Magazine's Marketing Hotlist

http://www.emap.com/internet/hot.htm

UK godfather of new media, Roger Green's one-stop guide to
working the Web.

US Patents

http://town.hall.org/patent/

Links to several patent abstract and securities databases,
such as the US Patent and Trademark Office and EDGAR,
plus advice on how to register your ideas. If you have the
patience, you might stumble across tomorrow's technology
long before the media.

Virtual Africa

http://www.africa.com/

This Cape Town service encourages trade with and within the newly acceptable South Africa. The facilities are in place, but at this stage not many have taken up the offer. But if you want to do business in the region, or are curious about opportunities and protocol, it's an inexpensive way to put your feelers out.

Who's Marketing Online

http://www.wmo.com

What's new in Web marketing trends, including new site reviews from an ad campaigner's perspective.

COMEDY

Bonk Industries

http://www.telegate.se/bonk/

In a subtle satire of corporate propaganda, Bonk highlights how we're conditioned to accept unethical business practices when they're cloaked in the right language.

Complaint Letter Generator

http://www-csag.cs.uiuc.edu/individual/pakin/complaint/

Someone getting on your goat, but stuck for the right words? Just mince their details through here for an instant dressing down.

LaughWeb

http://www.misty.com/laughweb

Bundles of jokes sorted into categories, and rated by readers. Expect at least a few smirks.

Milk Kommunications

http://www.milk.com/

This selection of incredible or shameful but true stories, anecdotes, and jokes is well worth a scan down every menu. Don't miss the original name-change press release from the artist formerly named after a dog.

Practical Jokes

http://www.umd.umich.edu/~nhughes/htmldocs/pracjokes.html

Larks and laughs at the expense of others compiled from the Usenet archives of alt.shenanigans

Pythonline

http://www.pythonline.com

Terry Gilliam-illustrated Monty Python mayhem, juvenilia, and humor, plus info on where they all are now.

Quote Generator

http://www.ugcs.caltech.edu/~werdna/fun.html

Get random quotes, excuses, and insults from various sources and then dig in to the extensive Usenet humor archives.

Spatula City

http://www.wam.umd.edu/~twoflowr/index.html

Tons of pointedly and pointlessly odd pages brightened by eye-catching 3D renderings. Don't push the big button. It really doesn't do anything.

The Whitehouse

http://www.whitehouse.net

A different parody of the official White House site every time you hit reload.

COMPUTING

Adobe

http://www.adobe.com

Information, support, and download areas for Adobe's desktop publishing software, including Adobe Acrobat, the browser plug-in or standalone that reads PDF (portable document format) files.

Apple

http://www.apple.com

Essential drop in for all Mac users and developers to get the latest product info and system updates.

Compaq

http://www.compaq.com

Product literature, software, and support for Compaq computers.

Computer Currents

http://www.currents.com

Various computing resources including an encyclopedia, hardware directory, and bookshop.

Dell

http://www.us.dell.com

Online access to Dell spare parts, technical support, BBS files, catalogs, press releases, and its international phone list. The site has all the charm of a chartered accounting firm's year-end report, but if you use Dell and need files or support, it's probably very efficient.

Hewlett-Packard

http://www.hp.com

Product support, literature, tutorials, drivers, and patches for HP products.

IBM

http://www.ibm.com

http://www.ibm.net

Key the first address for info on IBM's corporate world, products, and international operations. The "net" address has IBM Global Network contact details, plus a helpful set of tutorials and links to get you started on the Net.

Microsnot

http://www.microsnot.com

Spoof of the next site and a dig at Bill Geek's presidential claims. Plus more at: http://www.upx.net/~subcultr/wb95/swipe.html

Microsoft

http://www.microsoft.com

http://www.msn.com

Once it gets started, Microsoft rarely does things in half measures. Consequently this site is crammed with support documents, files, updates, development tools, and product news. If you're running any Microsoft apps such as Windows, Excel, or Word, you'll find all the latest upgrades, fixes, and tips herein. It's also the place to retrieve the latest version of Internet Explorer. The msn.com address is the default Microsoft Network and Internet Explorer home page, and it's not a bad one to keep. It has ample tutorials and helpful areas, but best of all can be tailored to display your choice of the latest news, weather, sport, finance, search tools, TV listings, fave sites, and much more.

Silicon Graphics

http://www.sgi.com/

Silicon Graphics' stylish site has all the corporate and product resources you'd expect from these state-of-the-art Net developers, plus demonstrations and samples of some of the things its high-end graphics workstations can do. That makes it quite a bit more entertaining than the usual hardware manufacturer pages. For example, check out VR Showcase for a taste of what's to come in virtual reality.

Software.net

http://software.net/

The time can't be far off when it's standard practice to distribute commercial software either via a secured Internet connection or by direct-dial access. This is almost there, with several titles for download through a secured link. Most, though, are conventionally boxed for Fedex delivery.

Sun Microsystems

http://www.sun.com/

Sun is the Net's biggest hardware player and a major sponsor in the development and use of new Net technology, such as the much hailed Java programming language. From here you can link to any of Sun's globally scattered Software Information and Technology Exchanges, which provide easy access to public domain software, government information, product support, and hundreds of innovative projects such as the Sunergy broadcasts and Internet radio.

Symantec

http://www.symantec.com

Free software, online updates and support on Symantec/ Norton's award-winning range of virus, disk management, communications, and Java utilities. Registered users will soon be able to automatically upgrade all Symantec software online. There's also talk of an upcoming online clinic to diagnose your computer's health.

Tidbits

http://www.tidbits.com/

Macintosh newsletter, from the author of the Internet Starter Kit.

Windows 95 Annoyances

http://www.creativelement.com/win95ann/

Fixes and replacements for many Windows 95 "features" and omissions.

Windows95.com

http://www.windows95.com/

The transition to Windows 95 was not so simple as Microsoft
makes out. Here's one of the best independent places to find
tutorials, tips, advice, Windows 95 shareware, and remedies
for the things that the Benevolent Empire neglected.

Yahoo! Computing

http://www.yahoocomputing.com

Computing site directory.

EMPLOYMENT

America's Job Bank

http://www.ajb.dni.us/

Links to over 1800 US State Employment Service offices and
over 100,000 vacancies. As a state project it's free for all.

CareerMosaic

http://www.careermosaic.com/

Search for vacancies among a rapidly growing field of
heavyweight clients, such as Chemical Bank, Intel, and
National Semiconductor, or through opportunities posted in
Usenet. As with most employment sites, there's plenty of
advice on resumes, career trends, and salaries. Each client
has its own set of pages outlining its employment conditions
and corporate activities.

E*Span

http://www.espan.com/

Thousands of jobs and seekers frustratingly concealed
behind a clumsy search interface.

EagleView

http://www.eagleview.com

Post your details to hundreds of Fortune 500 companies.

Jobs at Microsoft

http://www.microsoft.com/Jobs/

Join Big Brother's march across the globe.

Middle Eastern Job Market

http://www.xs4all.nl/~tgf/jobs/jobs/home.htm

Professional jobs offered and wanted in the Middle East.

Monster Board

http://www.monster.com/

Search for professional employment in the US and abroad. Like E*Span, the content's there but it's cumbersome.

Price Jamieson

http://www.pricejam.com

This international recruitment agency places all its professional job listings online, updating them at least weekly. It's well organized and high quality.

Reed

http://www.reed.co.uk

Top-notch service from the UK's largest employment agency, covering such diverse vocations as nursing, computing, catering, accounting, driving, charity, insurance, and project management.

Virtual Headroom

http://www.xmission.com/~wintrnx/virtual.html

Post your headshot and resume here to take a shortcut to the stars. It'll cost you to post but not to scout for talent. Then, of course, there's the couch to deal with.

ENTERTAINMENT

A Thousand Points of Sites

http://inls.ucsd.edu/y/0hBoy/randomjump1.html

Go blindly where ye have not been before.

Avenger's Handbook

http://www.cs.uit.no/~paalde/Revenge/index.html

There'll be no more Mr Nice Guy once you've paid a visit to
this armory of extreme nastiness. Much of it is compiled
from the archives of the Usenet group alt.revenge, the
definitive meeting place for suburban terrorists. It includes
vicious programs, things to do before you quit your job,
school pranks, and oodles of treacherous anecdotes about
getting even. John Steed would never stoop this low.

Build a Card

http://buildacard.com

Compete for the tackiest virtual Valentine or greeting card,
with this ingenious step-by-step online art studio.

Centre for the Easily Amused

http://www.amused.com

Hundreds of sites where thinking's banned.

Conspiracies

http://www.cjnetworks.com/~cubsfan/conspiracy.html

Create your own conspiracy theory.

Cyber Stars

http://www.realitycom.com/cybstars/stars.html

Look here for weekly updated astrological predictions,
astrology FAQs, and links to other soothsayers. There's still
no forecast for the thirteenth sign.

Disney.com

http://www.disney.com

Most of Walt's wonderful world of books, theme parks, music,
TV, film, video, and Mickey Mouse merchandising gets space
in this surprisingly dry promotional vehicle. Film gets
thorough coverage with loads of video clips, storybooks,
interviews, and Buzz Lightyear stuff, yet Donald Duck is
overlooked. Guess he knows how Woody felt.

Freeminder

http://www.cvp.com/freemind

Send yourself a timely email reminder.

Hidden Mickeys

http://www.oitc.com/Disney/Disneyland/Disneyland.html

Subliminal Mickeys hidden around Disneyland? Must be
something in the drinks.

HK Starcam

http://www.htkstar.com/starcam.html

Live bird's-eye view of downtown Hong Kong.

I Ching

http://www.facade.com/Occult/iching/

If the superior person is not happy with their fortune as told
by this ancient Chinese oracle, they can always reload and
get another one.

Internet Casino

http://www.casino.org

This online casino caused quite a legal stir when it
announced it would be operating a Bahamian gambling
haven open to anyone on the Internet. While it doesn't
encourage you to break the gambling laws of your state, it

does automatically deposit your funds into an offshore account and will even pay for your connection if you're a high enough roller. See also: http://www.casino-network.com

Kellner's Fireworks

http://www.kellfire.com/fireworks.html

Kellner has been in fireworks for almost fifty years and will ship to anywhere in the world. You can order its catalog online, but not as yet its products.

Lockpicking

http://www.lysator.liu.se/mit-guide/mit-guide.html

Thanks to the great minds at MIT, an indispensable illustrated lock-picking guide for potential felons. They laughed when I told them I was learning to housebreak, but when they came home . . .

MicroMovie MiniMultiplex

http://www.teleport.com/~cooler/MMMM/MMMM.html

Potpourri of animations and browser tricks.

Miss America

http://www.missamerica.com

It says here that to be a modern Miss America you need more than just long legs and a fancy name like Shawntel or Sharlene. You also have to be a bit of a genius. Thus a panel will toss you topical teasers like whether you approve of this Info SuperHighway thingy and how you'd stop kiddies from logging into sites like this to download pictures of swimsuited girlies. Of course, you should blitz it in the brains department. So now let's concentrate on your smile.

Penn and Teller

http://www.solinas.com/penn-n-teller/

While, regrettably, the Penn and Teller input here is fairly minimal, it has enough links to other magic and entertainment sites, including other P&T exhibits, to make it worth the visit. Although you can't email the duo directly, it does offer a forwarding service.

Rome Lab Snowball Camera

http://www.rl.af.mil:8001/Odds-n-Ends/sbcam/rlsbcam.html

Step right up and try your luck throwing virtual snowballs.

Say

http://wwwtios.cs.utwente.nl/say/

Enter your profanity, hit return, and it will speak the phrase back for the mirth of all within earshot. Try spelling words phonetically for greater success.

Sony

http://www.sony.com/

News, service and support, product information, and assorted material from Sony's huge stable of movies, music, broadcast, publishing, video, Playstation, and electronic interests. It's like ten major sites under one roof, with hundreds of corners to explore. For example, it has full biographies, discographies, and in some cases audio clips, from all its artists, such as the The High Lamas, St Etienne, and Leftfield. And that's just a taste.

Tarot Information

http://www.facade.com/Occult/tarot/

Choose from several different packs to find out what your future holds. For a second opinion, link up to the master site and try your luck at the I Ching, Biorhythm, Bibliomancy, Stichomancy, or Runes predictions. If you suspect it's all a great pile of randomly generated nugget, the Cindy Crawford Concentration exercise will surely set you straight.

The Postcard Store

http://postcards.www.media.mit.edu/Postcards/

Send a groovy e-postcard. Instead of mailing the actual card it sends a PIN number for access to a pick-up window.

Trading Card Dealers

http://www.wwcd.com/scdealer.html

Find that elusive baseball, football, or phone card through this directory of US trading card dealers.

UK National Lottery

http://www.connect.org.uk/lottery/

Everything you need to know about the UK lottery –
statistics, winning numbers, draw details, numerical
analysis, and instructions. Everything, that is, except the
only thing that matters.

Web Voyeur/Peeping Tom

http://www.eskimo.com/~irving/web-voyeur/

http://www.ts.umu.se/~spaceman/camera.html

Spend a night peeping through the Net's many cameras, then
go to bed safe in the knowledge that you've sat with pioneers
at the very cutting edge of technology. Now, tick that off the
list and get on with your life.

Zodiac Forecasts

http://www.bubble.com/webstars/index.html

The UK *Daily Mail*'s Jonathan Cainer presents free daily
forecasts in text or Real Audio.

EZINES

It's a fine distinction as to what's a net magazine (ezine) and a magazine posted on the net; below are the former. See also "News, Newspapers, and Magazines."

Addicted to: Stuff

http://www.morestuff.com

Quirky ezine where readers share obsessions.

Anorak

http://www.anorak.co.uk

A neat little British daily ezine, designed to be read inside ten minutes, in your lunch break. Features top stories from the day's tabloid newspapers, all the footie news, and nostalgic music quizzes. Boys' stuff, but well done.

Brillo

http://www.virago-net.com/brillo/

Ever get the sneaking suspicion the Net is a tad boys' club and patriarchal? Brillo ("Extra Abrasive") is out to challenge the whole sexuality of the new technology. And it's got style.

C'Lock

http://www.clock.co.uk

London culture, style, news, and views served up weekly.

Channel Cyberia

http://www.cyberiacafe.net

TV-style hourly updated news, sport, finance, entertainment, and Web reviews from the original cybercafé, Cyberia London. Unlike real TV, if you miss something you can catch up with it in the archives. A glimpse of the future?

E-Zine-List

http://www.meer.net/~johnl/e-zine-list/index.html

The Net's definitive guide to electronic magazines is easier to navigate now that its reviews can be filtered by keywords. But with over a thousand to scan, it still might be quicker to download the entire list and whip through it offline.

FiX Magazine

http://www.widemedia.com/fix/

British lifestyle ezine with stories on sex, travel, music, fashion, and health as well as free online counselling, a 48-hour dream analysis service and a settee where they sit around and spin Barry White. It's irreverent, stylish, and claims to be the "world's widest magazine."

FutureNet

http://www.futurenet.co.uk

Daily news, plus features from the UK magazine publisher's many titles such as .net, arcane, Mountain Biking UK, EDGE, Comedy Review, First XV, Total Guitar, Total Football, and, uhh, Needlecraft.

Geek Girl

http://geekgirl.com.au/geekgirl/

RosieX's plugged-in Australian cyberfemme magazine.

HotWired

http://www.hotwired.com

HotWired's hipness could only be rivaled by its hard copy brother Wired magazine (whose back issues it archives). It carries clear, well written features on the stylish edge of the techno-recreation world, covering new journalism, gossip, music, the arts, and commerce. Plus there's a "deep database" co-venture with our very own Rough Guides, making available the entire text of Rough Guide travel books, including, to date, the USA, Canada, Mexico, and Northern Europe.

J Pop

http://www.j-pop.com/index.html

Japanese pop culture features on the likes of manga, anime, games, and Pizzicato 5.

Phrack Magazine

http://freeside.com/phrack.html

Phrack has printed controversial articles for the hacking community for over ten years. You can download or browse back issues and subscribe free to the quarterly.

Psyche Journal

http://psyche.cs.monash.edu.au/

"An electronic interdisciplinary journal of consciousness research" with articles, commentaries, and book reviews on such subjects as vagueness, semantics, the language of thought, delineating conscious processes, and contrastive analysis. When you've figured that lot out, you can try the links to philosophical Gophers and other brain tapping stuff.

Salon

http://www.salon1999.com

This Apple-sponsored venture is intended as a kind of *New Yorker* for the Net: a stylish ezine full of provocative arts, literature, society, politics, and dinner-party natter.

Slate

http://www.slate.com

Microsoft's heavyweight political and literary weekly got off the mark by opening a forum on its business ethics, with EVP Steve Balmer in the Benevolent Empire's corner taking the blows. As could be expected, it came under heavy knee-jerk criticism from many commentators. For all the fuss, this is just another ezine, albeit better funded than most. What's most notable is it's geared more towards being downloaded and printed than read online.

Student Outlook

http://www.pro-net.co.uk/student/

UK student news, reviews, and opinion.

Suck

http://www.suck.com

Daily, smug, gossip-jammed, Netcentric news analysis that invariably hits its mark with dozens of

topical links scattered subtly throughout the copy. And
smart enough that many Net insiders keep it as a start-up
page.

The Spot

http://www.thespot.com

Glossy cult online soap about the twenty-something residents
of a seven-bedroom Malibu party house. Each day at least one
posts a diary entry and fills us in on the goss. Bed-hopping,
tears, and superbitches. Or your money back.

Urban Desires

http://desires.com/

Calls itself an interactive magazine of metropolitan pleasures
and delivers modern city stories on technology, food, sex,
music, art, performance, style, politics, and more.

Utne Online

http://www.utne.com

Selected articles from the progressive US alternative press
digest, *The Utne Reader*, bi-weekly Web-only content and a
gender-discriminatory café area for discussion.

Women's Wire

http://www.women.com

Instantly dispels rumours that the Net's a "man's man's
world". But slots in closer to *Elle* than *Hecate*.

Z Times

http://www.zpub.com/z/

Monthly time-capsules as viewed from the Web.

Zug

http://www.mediashower.com/zug/

Irreverence, Henry-Root-style email pranks, and quite a few
chuckles.

FASHION

Angel of Fashion Award
http://www.wp.com/SST/angel.html

Unless you have a super-fast connection, fancy fashion sites can be pretty frustrating. And unless they're kept up to date, they hardly qualify as fashion. Angel of Fashion singles out groundbreaking sites for praise and supplies links to many others.

Elle Magazine
http://www.ellemag.com http://www.elle.fr

This doesn't match the US or French glossies, but it still sports enough swish types in bright duds to make you feel undershopped in any language.

Fashion Internet
http://www.finy.com

Sort your togs out, tip to toe, with top tips ranging from the clueless guy's guide to buying a suit, to Bobbi Brown's makeup forum for thinking women.

Fashion Net
http://www.fashion.net

More fashion links than you could poke a chapstick at.

Fashion UK
http://www.widemedia.com/fashionuk/fuk.html

Minimal monthly e-mag with quality features, shoots, reader advice, shopping directories, and vanity links centered primarily around the London scene.

Is Fashion Silly?
http://www.softeam.it/pittimmagine/

Insider analysis of the Italian fashion industry.

The Lipstick Page
http://www.users.wineasy.se/bjornt/Lip.html

Cosmetic appliances for fun and profit.

Surgeon.com

http://www.surgeon.com

Cosmetic surgery service for men, with a gallery of stunning
before and after shots.

FILM AND TV

All Movie Guide

http://allmovie.com/index_text.html

A colossal sound and screen directory, easily navigable, and
complete with reviews and synopses.

Beavis And Butthead

http://calvin.hsc.colorado.edu/

Not only does this rabid fan of the dysfunctional duo have
nothing to do with MTV, he uses this page as a platform for
his wrath against its programmers. Apart from that, there's
an entertaining selection of B&B gossip, extracts, episode
guides, and an archive of his hate mail.

Capt James T Kirk Sing-a-Long

http://www.ama.caltech.edu/users/mrm/kirk.html

Audio excerpts from William Shatner's bold vinyl masterpiece
"The Transformed Man."

Channel 4 TV

http://www.channel4.com

Program support text, links, contacts, and follow-ups from
the UK's adventurous Channel Four.

Encyclopedia Brady

http://www.primenet.com/~dbrady/

The collected antics of "three very lovely girls," their
stepbrothers and folks.

FBI X-Files Division

http://www.ssc.com/~roland/x-files/x-files.html

This improbable, popular television drama is up there with
Star Trek in attracting obsessives, particularly on the

Internet, despite their being mocked by respective leading actors David Duchovny and William Shatner. Now this tongue-in-cheek X-Phile warehouse has started its own controversy by blocking AOL's 5 million users. The posted reactions are often more entertaining than the site itself.

Hollywood Reporter

http://www.hollywoodreporter.com/

Check out the gossip in the Hollywood dailies, and cruise round town with this site's Hollywood Hyperlinks.

Hong Kong Movies Home Page

http://www.mdstud.chalmers.se/hkmovie/

Get intimate with the action director's director John Woo's catalog, plans, and regular actors such as the genius **Chow Yun Fat**. If you've seen his early gems like *Hard Boiled*, *The Killer*, or *God of Gamblers*, you'll understand his cult status. But it's not all Woo and Fat, there's much more, including a searchable database, movie clips, pictures, FAQs, interviews, news Gophers, and even the Hong Kong Popstars Archive.

Internet Movie Database

http://www.imbd.com

You'll be hard pressed to find any work on or off the Net as comprehensive as this exceptional relational database of screen trivia from over 90,000 movies and one million actors. It's all tied together remarkably well – for example, within a couple of clicks of finding your favorite movie, you can get full filmographies of anyone from the cast or crew, and see what's in the cooker. Unmissable!

Le Simpsons

http://www.unantes.univ-nantes.fr/~elek/simpson.html

Listen to how the French have to hear Homer, El Barto, et al, and maybe you'll go a bit easier on them in future.

MCA/Universal Cyberwalk .

http://www.mca.com

See what the MCA/Universal movie and music stable has in store. All sorts of fun promo gimmicks, such as being able to interview the stars by email and download short clips.

Movies.com

http://www.movies.com/

Preview forthcoming Touchstone and Hollywood Pictures. All have short synopses, minute-long sample clips, interviews, stills, and assorted press releases.

MovieWeb

http://www.movieweb.co.uk

Customizable UK movie and video listings, reviews, previews, and interviews. See what's playing in your area.

Power Rangers

http://lc.www.media.mit.edu/Personal/manny/power/

Save this one for when a noisy junior Power Ranger interferes with your hangover. Point their head this way while you go back to bed. Downloading all the heavy graphics should give you ample time for some shut-eye. Bad news is it's yet another unofficial site with legal hassles.

Soap Links

http://www.cts.com/~jeffmj/soaps.html

Keep up with who's doing what to whom, who they told, and who shouldn't find out, in the surreal world of soap fiction.

Tardis TV Archive

http://www.tardis.ed.ac.uk/~dave/guides/

Episode guides, actor bios, and fan info on hundreds of TV shows from the US, UK, Canada, Japan, and Sweden.

The Picture Palace

http://www.ids.net/picpal/

Only weird, daring, and truly offbeat films get shelf space in
this online video store. There's some really choice gear in the
Exploitation, RIP, Japanimation, Hong Kong, Horror, and
Film Noir genres. All are reviewed and some include
samples. Have your credit card ready.

The Simpsons

http://www2.best.com/~jnc/simp/simpage.html

There's no shortage of Simpsons sites and you can get to
several from here. Then you'll be able to listen to Homer
drool "Two all-beef patties, special sauce… " and the like. The
flicks are as good as you would expect and the sound files
have a certain cuteness that many fans will enjoy tirelessly.

Tromaville

http://www.troma.com

Here's your lucky break. Troma, home of class films like
Toxic Avenger, *Chopper Chicks from Zombie Town*, *Space
Freaks from Planet Mutoid*, *Subhumanoid Meltdown*, and
Fatguy goes Nutzoid, needs acting outcasts and writers for
its Troma Army Bizarre productions. Form a line here.

TV Net

http://tvnet.com/

As close to everything televisual as is mentally healthy. That
includes places to vent your gripes, email addresses and
home pages of broadcasting networks, schedules, job
vacancies, and links to fan pages of just about every show
ever made. By the time you get through this lot, you'll be
lucky to have any time left for the neon bucket itself.

FINANCE

Current Oil and Gas Quotes

http://baervan.nmt.edu/prices/current.html

Get the latest spot and future prices on oil and gas.

Experimental Stock Data

http://www.stockmaster.com

Not all the S&P 500 stocks and mutual fund prices are available but still a generous amount for a free experimental service. Generate daily price/volume charts or download a year's back-data for import into your own analysis package.

PAWWS, Wall Street on the Internet

http://pawws.secapl.com/

Free North American quarter-hourly updated stock quotes, charts, fundamentals, and news. Pay and you'll get more meaty stuff like online brokerage, portfolio management, real-time quotes, research, and all the other services you would expect from a stockbroker.

QuoteCom

http://www.quote.com

More free trading data, news and charts, plus a multitude of subscription services.

Shareholder Action Handbook

http://www.bath.ac.uk/Centres/Ethical/Share/

When you buy shares in a public company, it gives you certain voting rights. By putting the entire text of the Shareholder Action Handbook online, this site hopes that you'll exercise those rights to the benefit of your community.

Silicon Investor

http://www.techstocks.com

Outstanding selection of free technology stock quotes, charts, forums, advice, and sentiment surveys. If you want to bet on the Net's success, this is the perfect place to start your research.

Stocks and Commodities

http://www.onr.com/stocks.html

More and more financial data, albeit mainly NYSE quotes, is becoming available on the Web every day. You'll find links here to investment research, charting services, economic sources, small business assistance, exchanges, online brokers, and Java investment applets, all of them reviewed.

TaxNet

http://www.purple.co.uk/purplet/tax.html

Get free help with filling out your UK tax claim.

Wall Street Directory

http://www.cts.com/~wallst/

Technical analysts contend that market prices reflect fear
and greed or supply and demand rather than inherent
fundamental value. Extreme wings such as Elliott Wavists
believe that the indices follow predestined cycles, or mass
psychological trends, which unwittingly requires certain
spiritual assumptions. It can seem far-fetched and complex,
but investing without understanding at least a few basic
tenets is akin to reckless gambling. This massive directory
should help point you in the right direction.

Wall Street Journal on the Internet

http://webserve.dowjones.com/

The Journal's not quite as generous as the majority of Net
newspapers – it intends to charge for this presently free
online edition of its market-leading finance paper. Choose
from a shortform version of the daily, an interactive live
edition, or a personalized dial-in service.

FOOD AND DRINK

"Nothing can bring you peace but yourself."
- Ralph Waldo Emerson

Celestial Seasonings

http://www.usa.net/celestial/

Unless you live in the
US, you won't be able to
order from Celestial
Seasonings' diverse
range of exotically
flavored teas, tea-related
gifts and apparel. But
you'll know what to look
out for at the
supermarket.

Chile-Heads

http://www.netimages.com/~chile/

Dip into chile recipes, chemistry, botanical facts, gardening tips, and general pepper talk. You can find out what's the hottest pepper, what makes it hot, how your body reacts, and identify that mystery one in your kebab.

Chocolate Lover's Playground

http://www.godiva.com/

This page almost hurts, with its mouth-watering chocolate recipes and meanderings into chocoholism. It delivers, too, but only within the US.

Epicurious

http://www.epicurious.com

Web-only marriage of Condé Nast's *Gourmet*, *Bon Appetit*, and *Traveler* magazines, crammed with recipes, culinary forums, advice on eating out around the world, dining tips, and articles on ways to stave off hunger with panache.

Mamma's Kitchen

http://www.ragu.com

How to fix up Italian nosh with bottled sauces.

Over the Coffee

http://www.cappuccino.com/

Enough coffee trivia, mail order firms, reviews, anecdotes, and links to similarly minded sites to keep any caffeine addict happy. An ideal companion for a brew up.

Pizza Net

http://www2.ecst.csuchico.edu/~pizza/

What a shame this experimental and example-setting online pizza delivery service only delivers graphic facsimiles and not the real McCoy. Wouldn't it be great to sit down to a piping hot feast of bugs, bolts, kittens, hammers, footballs, and road signs? Nevertheless, it does lay the foundation for a successful fast-food scheme.

Ribbets

http://www.odyssey.com.au/wtc/ribbets

How's this for lazy? Just say you're online, in the middle of a
Duke Net match, and you feel like ribs or pizza. If your only
phone line's tied up, you could switch to the Web, contact
Ribbets, and have one in front of you within half an hour.
But you have to answer the door – and live in Brisbane.

Spencer's Beer

http://realbeer.com/spencer/

Here's the place to find out how to perfect your brew. It
carries several hypertext home-brew recipe books, including
the entire Cat's Meow series. Bottle-spotters will be thrilled to
find a gallery of 228 labels in 128 shimmering colors.

Virtual Pub

http://lager.geo.brown.edu:8080/virtual-pub

None of the usual beer yarns like waking up in a strange
room stark naked with a throbbing head and a hazy
recollection of pranging your car. In this virtual pub, beer is
treated with the same dewy-eyed respect usually reserved for
wine and locomotives. You get all the beef down to the
specific gravity, bottle color, and alcohol content, but nothing
about those nasty side-effects like loss of motor skills,
blurred vision, and parking your lunch.

Wine Net

http://wine.net/index.html

Sniff *Uncorked*, an online wine journal, join in viniforums,
or link to vineyards, vendors, and wine fanciers' pages.

GAMES

The Chess Server

http://www.willamette.edu/~tjones/chessmain.html

Find, and play, a live opponent with any number of
spectators.

Connect 4

http://www.pobox.com/~pomakis/c4/

Challenge the computer to connect four, or any number for that matter. For tips on how to beat the system, read Victor Allis's masters thesis on expert play.

Crime Scene

http://www.quest.net/crime/

Help two detectives analyze forensic evidence and track down suspects in an ongoing murder investigation. Move along folks, nothing to see here.

DoomGate

http://doomgate.cs.buffalo.edu/~sven/

Billed as the best place to make new enemies, this site acts as a dating service to meet other Doomsters, so you can hunt them down and kill them via your modem. If you don't fancy killing fellow keyboardsters, join forces and fight together.

Fred

http://langevin.usc.edu/Fred/

Network Doom prototype using Java applets.

Frogger

http://speech.ee.yeungnam.ac.kr/htdocs/lsw/Java/applet/froggie/

Classic arcade game as a Java Applet.

Imperial Nomic

http://www.mit.edu/people/achmed/inomic/

You'll take ages to figure out this strange Web game. It's not that it has no rules. On the contrary, the object is to make them up. If they are accepted, your score changes in a way you won't be able to understand until you've spent some considerable time here. Confused? That's the general idea.

Interactive Web Games

http://www.yahoo.com/Recreation/Games/Internet_Games/Interactive_Web_Games/

Pit your wits against the computer or remote opponents on a whole variety of games.

Play Battleships

http://manor.york.ac.uk/htdocs/bships.html

Play battleships against the computer. Unfortunately, there's a simple way to cheat.

The Riddler

http://www.riddler.com

Use your Web scavenging, lateral thinking, literary, trivia and other skills to compete across the Net for prizes.

Sega

http://www.segaoa.com

News, special events, promotions, new releases, hints, product details, screen shots, audio/video clips, and support for Sega computer games.

The Talker

http://ss002.infi.net/broadcast/login

Choose an icon, alias, and attitude and bluff your way through this virtual party. Bear in mind that whoever else you meet must also have little else to do.

Virtual Vegas

http://www.virtualvegas.com

Showgirls, VRML slot machines, Shockwave blackjack, Java poker, shopping, and a chat-up lounge. VV bucks are virtual, but occasionally the prizes are real.

PC Games

For reviews, news, demos, hints, patches, cheats, downloads and other PC game necessities, try:

Game Center

http://www.cnet.com/Gamecenter/

Games Domain

http://www.gamesdomain.co.uk/

Gamers Realm

http://www.websolutions.mb.ca/realm/

Gamespot

http://www.gamespot.com

Happy Puppy

http://www.happypuppy.com/

King Link & Games

http://www.whiterock.com/kinglink/

Online Gaming Review

http://www.ogr.com

PCME

http://204.191.209.2/users/pcme

GOVERNMENT

CCTA Government Information

http://www.open.gov.uk/

Here's where to come for information on any UK government authority. Just open its colossal directory, scan down the list, make your choice, and before long you'll be nodding off, just as if you were actually there.

Central Intelligence Agency

hhttp://www.odci.gov/cia

Find out about the CIA's role in international affairs, the intelligence cycle, its history and real estate. But that's not what you're after is it? You watch TV and read the Weekly World News. You want to know about political assassinations, arms deals, Latin American drug trades, spy satellites, conspiracy theories, phone tapping, covert operations, government-sponsored alien sex cults, and the X-files. This must be another CIA.

Declassified Satellite Photos

http://edcwww.cr.usgs.gov/dclass/dclass.html

Here's what you've been expecting to stumble across on the Net: the first spy pictures taken from satellites and then dropped to earth by parachute. They're freshly declassified and plenty more will follow. Look closely and see Soviets knitting socks in preparation for a bleak winter.

FedWorld

http://www.fedworld.gov

Find US federal government servers, contacts, and documents.

Her Majesty's Treasury

http://www.hm-treasury.gov.uk

Another spine-tingling UK site. Read press releases, ministerial speeches, minutes, economic forecasts, and the budget, and decide whether your tax pounds are going to worthy causes.

US Census Bureau

http://www.census.gov/

There are more statistics here about the US and its citizens
than you'll ever want to know. You can search the main
census database, read press releases, view the poster gallery,
check the projected population clock, listen to clips from its
radio broadcasts, or link to other serious info-head sites.

US Federal Government Servers

http://www.fie.com/www/us_gov.htm

Extensive directory of US federal government servers.

Welcome to the White House

http://www.whitehouse.gov

Slick Willy might not really be at his PC when you choose to
"speak out" through the White House's official suggestion
form, but you never know, something just might filter
through. It's easy to be cynical about this PR exercise,
particularly the moribund guided tour, but it does show the
doors of democracy are at least ajar.

HEALTH

Alternative Medicine

http://www.pitt.edu/~cbw/altm.html

Part of the Net's ongoing research function is the ability to
contact people who've road-tested alternative remedies and
can report on their efficacy. Use this page as an index to
more specific sites and newsgroups.

Biorhythm Generator

http://www.facade.com/Occult/biorhythm/

The Skeptic's Dictionary says biorhythms are a con. Generate
your own and put it to the test.

The Drugs Archive

http://hyperreal.com/drugs/

Articles, primarily accumulated from the alt.drugs newsgroup,

that provide first-hand perspectives on the pleasures and
dangers of recreational drugs.

First Aid Online

http://www2.vivid.net/~cicely/safety/

Advice that could save a life.

Guide to Women's Health

http://asa.ugl.lib.umich.edu/chdocs/womenhealth/womens_health.html

Abundant pointers relating to women's emotional, physical,
and sexual health, on such topics as partner violence,
shyness, bulimia, dating, and contraception.

Interactive Patient

http://medicus.marshall.edu/medicus.htm

Determine whether you're really cut out for the quackhood
with this doctor/patient simulation. You get to fire a lot of
questions, make an examination, x-ray, diagnose, and finally
prescribe a remedy. It's just a shame you can't send a bill and
then take the afternoon off to get blotto at the golf course.

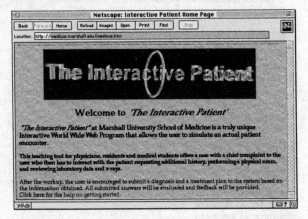

Medscape

http://www.medscape.com

While this medical forum is primarily aimed at health
professionals and medicine students, it's of equal interest to
anyone who's concerned with their general well-being.

Online Allergy Center

http://www.sig.net/~allergy/welcome.html

Online advice, news, and diagnosis for allergy sufferers.

Online Birth Center

http://www.efn.org/~djz/birth/birthindex.html

Support for midwives and parents, especially anxious
expectant mothers.

Pharm Web

http://www.mcc.ac.uk/pwmirror/pwb/pharmwebb.html

Pharmaceutical Yellow Pages.

Poisons Information Database

http://vhp.nus.sg/PID/

Directory of plant, snake, and animal toxin cures,
information centers, and practitioners.

Smart Drugs and Nootropics

http://www.damicon.fi/sd/

If nootropics really make you smarter, how can we afford not
to take them? Both sides of the argument are presented here,
as well as mail order catalogs, government regulations, case
studies, and information on smart drugs.

The Virtual Hospital

http://indy.radiology.uiowa.edu/VirtualHospital.html

Continuously updated medical database intended to provide
patient care support and distance learning to practicing
physicians, via online multimedia tools such as illustrated
surgical walkthroughs.

The Visible Human Project

http://www.nlm.nih.gov/extramural_research.dir/visible_human.html

This unappetizing project generated a lot of publicity on its launch, not just for itself but for the Internet's use as a visual teaching aid. What really caused the stir, yet isn't mentioned here, is that the 1878 CT scans came from the thinly sliced frozen body of an executed serial killer. Since then it's added the visible woman, interactive knee, and virtual colonoscopy to the menu.

KIDS' STUFF (MOSTLY)

Animal Information Database

http://www.bev.net/education/SeaWorld/homepage.html

Sea World USA/Busch Gardens' educational service for teachers and children has games, teaching guides, and quizzes about animals children love, such as whales, dolphins, dugongs, gorillas, lions, tigers, and walruses. Its interactivity attempts to inject some fun into biological science study.

The Asylum's Lite-Board

http://asylum.cid.com/lb/

This is fun. Insert colored pegs into a board, one color at a time, to create a pretty picture. After you've finished, you can title it and then submit it to the gallery for others to admire. Hours of gainful employment.

The Bug Club

http://www.ex.ac.uk/bugclub/

Creepy crawly fan club with e-pal page, newsletters, and pet care sheets on how to keep your newly bottled tarantulas, cockroaches, and stick insects alive.

Carlos' Colouring Book

http://www.ravenna.com/coloring/

Select a segment of a picture, choose a color and then shade it in. You don't need to be Leonardo.

Fractal Explorer

http://www.vis.colostate.edu/~user1209/fractals/

A fractal is a complex self-similar and chaotic mathematical
object that reveals more detail as you get closer. You can
explore a famous example, the Mandelbrot set, by zooming in
on the image and changing the color palette. Even if you
can't understand how this complex iteration works, you can
still generate funky graphics.

Graffiti Capital

http://darkwing.uoregon.edu/~econpeer/graffiti/graff.html

"Spray" your thoughts in HTML for all the Web to enjoy. Like
all graffiti, it'll get wiped off and sprayed over by someone
else sooner or later.

Kids Web

http://www.npac.syr.edu/textbook/kidsweb/

Choose from a range of 20 main educational subject
categories and explore a heap of stuff.

Make a Map

http://ellesmere.ccm.emr.ca/wnaismap/naismap.html

Tailor-make your own Canadian map. You can specify all
sorts of multiple constraints, layers, and relief projections,
like political boundaries, geological provinces, and even the
grizzly bear range.

Math Magic Activities
http://www.scri.fsu.edu/~dennisl/topics/math_magic.html

These card, rope, and calculation tricks require no mirrors or sleight of hand, just a basic understanding of mathematic principles.

Mr Edible Starchy Tuber Head
http://winnie.acsu.buffalo.edu/potatoe/

Create your own, customized Mr Potato Head.

The Yuckiest Site on the Internet
http://www.nj.com/yucky/

Crawl behind the walls with Rodney the Roach, get all the dirt from Wendell the Worm Reporter, mouth off in Strong Words, or kick with the New Jersey Youth soccer team.

White House for Kids
http://www.whitehouse.gov/WH/kids/html/kidshome.html

Follow Socks through the White House to uncover its previous inhabitants, including the kids and pets. Once done, you can write to Socks and get the goss on what goes down in DC after dark.

Yahooligans
http://www.yahooligans.com

Kid-friendly Web guide intuitively organized into subject groups like dinosaurs, hobbies, and homework answers. Like big brother Yahoo, but without the dodgy and heavy stuff.

LEGAL

Advertising Law
http://www.webcom.com/~lewrose/home.html

How far you can push your products has always been an iffy end of the law. And on the Internet, where any snake-oil merchant can set up shop for next to nothing, many business precedents are yet to be set. Here's help in finding the line between puffery and lies.

Bentham Archive of British Law

http://www-server.bcc.ac.uk/~uctlxjh/Bentham.html

Independent synopsis of Criminal, Roman, European, and property law, as well as a repository of UK legal threads and essential lawyer jokes. The criminal law section even gives advice on how to get away with it once you're caught.

The 'Lectric Law Library

http://www.lectlaw.com/

Maybe the Net's best-kept legal repository. Aimed at both laypeople and professionals, it archives reams of legal reference material plus guides to legal forms, phrases, software, law schools, business formalities, and professional bodies, as well as the latest case news.

West's US Legal Directory

http://www.westpub.com

Accused of grand theft, arson, or murder one? Then whip through this database of over half a million US lawyers who'd rather see you go free than go without their fee.

WWW Virtual Law Library

http://www.law.indiana.edu/law/v-law/lawindex.html

You'll never be short of free legal advice with this cornucopia of law resource links at your disposal.

MUSEUMS AND GALLERIES

A-Bomb WWWMuseum, Hiroshima

http://www.csi.ad.jp/ABOMB/index.html

Fiftieth anniversary commemoration project detailing the Hiroshima and Nagasaki bombs, interviews with survivors, and exhibits from the Hiroshima Peace Park and Museum.

The Exploratorium

http://www.exploratorium.edu

Museums generally haven't translated to the Web too successfully, but this showing from San Francisco's

Exploratorium is a notable exception. Some of its 650-odd interactive exhibits have adapted quite well, making it an engaging and educative experience, especially for children.

Expo Ticket Office
http://sunsite.unc.edu/expo/ticket_office.html

Jump aboard a virtual bus to tour exhibits of the Vatican, Soviet archives, European exploration of the Americas, Dead Sea Scrolls, Museum of Paleontology, and the city of Spalato. After all that, you're dropped off at the Expo Restaurant for a feed of French cuisine.

Field Museum of Natural History, Chicago
http://www.addressbook.com/Chicago/Gateways/Field.html

Page through the eras in the DNA to Dinosaurs exhibit, downloading movies and sound bites. Or explore Javanese masks, bats, and more. One for the kids.

Museum of Modern Art NY
http://www.moma.org

If you only ever visit one modern art museum, here's a sample of what to expect when you get there.

Museums Around The World

http://www.icom.org/vlmp/world.html

Directory of Web museums sorted by country.

The Natural History Museum

http://www.nhm.ac.uk/

London's Natural History Museum was one of the Web's
pioneering sites. It has a few science galleries that could be
classed as exhibits in their own right, but most of the
elaborate content simply teases. It won't save you a visit, but
it might convince you it's worth the trip.

UCMP Time Machine

http://ucmp1.berkeley.edu/timeform.html

Jump aboard the University of California's Museum of
Paleontology's time machine for a rocky ride through the
geological eras.

Vatican Library

http://www.ncsa.uiuc.edu/SDG/Experimental/vatican.exhibit/exhibit/
Main_Hall.html

Stroll though several virtual rooms in the Vatican each with
its own specialty such as literature, music, nature,
archeology, humanism, biology, and mathematics.

Andy Warhol Museum

http://www.warhol.org/warhol

Pittsburgh's Andy Warhol Museum hasn't put all the Pop
auteur's works online, but you can virtually tour its physical
gallery for a contents listing. Then order the book, postcard
set, and t-shirt to prove you've visited.

WebMuseum

http://mistral.enst.fr/~pioch/louvre/

Famous art from Gothic right through to Pop, classical
music samples, and special exhibitions of medieval art,
Cézanne and more to come, complete with commentary
courtesy of the Encyclopaedia Britannica. Used to be called
Le Louvre, until lawyers stepped in.

MUSIC

Music is one of the Web's biggest areas and fortunately well served by directories, the most encyclopedic of which is The Ever Expanding Web Music Listing (see below). Our selections below should be seen just as starter options. It's worth getting hold of Real Audio at: http://www.realaudio.com before visiting these sites, so you can hear music samples.

Addicted to Noise

http://www.addict.com

One of the longest-running and sharpest rock music magazines on the Web. Smart writing with a bias towards the Alternative end of the spectrum.

All Music Guide

http://www.allmusic.com

A massive guide to – as it says – all kinds of music, with good biographies and record reviews, and some rather odd classifications. A hugely impressive site, nonetheless, and with some useful built-in search engines.

Aus Music Guide

http://www.amws.com.au

A massive guide to all that's shakin' down under.

Bad Taste Records

http://www.siberia.is/badtaste/badhome.htm

The Sugarcubes, whose lead singer Björk rocketed to iconic
mainstream acceptance, have made a valiant attempt to bring
Iceland's underground talent to the world's attention through
their Bad Taste label. This may be your only chance to hear it.

Canonical List of Weird Band Names

http://204.254.248.7/~chelle/bandname.html

Directory of bands where, in many cases, more thought has
gone into the name than the sound. Amusing all the same.

CDnow!

http://cdnow.com/

CDnow! is everything you've ever wanted from an
entertainment megastore – but online. Alongside a vast
range of CDs, it has reviews, press clippings, and an
impressive selection of Real Audio new releases on the
Internet Jukebox, plus it sells movies, clothes, and
magazines, and accepts international orders, which, in some
cases, could work out cheaper than buying locally.

Cerberus Digital Jukebox

http://www.cdj.co.uk

To listen to any of the hundreds of independent-label music
tracks and samples available here, you first have to download
the CerCure sound player – and you sometimes have to pay.
The range varies from Bing Crosby to Funky Porcini, but not
much from the charts.

Classical Music on the Net

http://lmc.einet.net/galaxy/Leisure-and-Recreation/Music/
douglas-bell/Index.html

Got that address right? If so, you're in for a hefty, text-only
site providing informed links to pretty much every classical
music Net site.

Digital Dream

http://www.openworld.co.uk/staff/dd/

Hundreds of CD reviews conveniently searchable by genre,

rating, and title. Covers the overlapping spectrum of techno/ambient/drum'n'bassy stuff. Astound your too-cool disco pals with your new-found fluency in chill, ambient, trance, and trip hop, without ever having to buy an album.

Dirty Linen
http://kiwi.futuris.net/linen/

Online excerpts from the US folk, roots, and world music magazine. Features an excellent forthcoming gig guide, plus a host of related links.

dotmusic
http://www.dotmusic.com

Charts, goss, contacts, and profiles from industry rags *Music Week*, *Record Mirror*, *MBI*, and *Gavin*.

ECM
http://www.ecmrecords.com

Sound samples and online ordering from the German-based jazz and contemporary classical label, home to the likes of Keith Jarrett, Jan Garbarek, Pat Metheny, and Arvo Part.

The Ever Expanding Web Music Listing
http://www.columbia.edu/~hauben/music/web-music.html

Monolithic directory split into academic, non-academic, user-maintained, geographically local, and artist-specific sites. It comes close to the impossible task of completely indexing the Net's music content.

Firefly
http://www.agents-inc.com/

Rate and slate a hundred or so artists and have your tastebuds diagnosed. Once processed, it can then recommend selections of music you're likely to adore or abhor.

Folk Roots
http://www.cityscape.co.uk/froots/index.html

The UK's equivalent to Dirty Linen (see above) delivers on British and American folk roots, and Celtic music, and has a sublime ear for the best in global sounds.

Geffen/DGC

http://www.geffen.com/

The home of Nirvana, Teenage Fanclub, Herb Alpert and, more recently, Swervedriver, appears to have given up using this site to relaunch the Eighties. It now conventionally plugs its catalog through bios and clips.

Global Electronic Music Market

http://gemm.com

Commercial compilation of various music dealers' catalogs and secondhand music trading post. Once you've found what you want, you contact the vendor directly.

The Grateful Dead

http://www.cs.cmu.edu/~mleone/dead.html

The mother of all Dead pages, with lyrics, concert sets, tape trading guides, and links to just about every other Dead page on the Net. Thanks, Jerry – RIP.

HiFi on the Web

http://www.unik.no/~robert/hifi/hifi.html

If the news, reviews, and trade show reports housed on this site aren't enough to convince you that your hi-fi's crap, link to another site and find out that no matter how much you've spent, you're still insulting your ears.

Hyperreal

http://hyperreal.com/

One-stop shop for all your raving needs. Find out what's hip, where it's at, what's going down, and what to swallow.

Independent Underground Music Archive

http://www.iuma.com/

Get in touch with hundreds of unsigned and indie-label underground musicians. All bands provide samples, biographies, and contact details. You'll need to rummage around through loads of unfamiliar names, but it's often worth it.

Japanese Independent Music

http://www.atom.co.jp

Could the exploding underground Asian pop scene be the next big thing? Here's an offbeat selection to get you prepared.

Jazz Central Station

http://www.jazzcentralstation.com

Bulging global jazz multimedia digest in English or Japanese.

Juan Luis Guerra

http://www.math.fu-berlin.de/~stolting/JLG/jlg.html

Clips from the Latin superstar plus English and Spanish lyrics, FAQs, interviews, and links to other Merengue and Dominican Republic music pages.

Michael Jackson Internet Fan Club

http://www.fred.net/mjj/

All you want, and more than you need, to know about the little Mr Epaulettes and his troops.

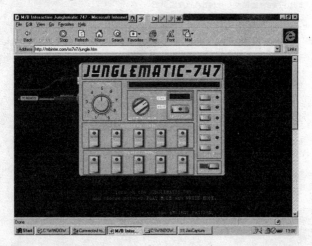

Junglematic 747

htttp://mbinter.com/ss7x7/jungle.htm

Mix your own Jungle tracks instantly with this astounding Shockwave toy.

Kraftwerk Infobahr

http://www.cs.umu.se/tsdf/kraftwerk

Demos, live out-takes, MIDI files, interviews, lyrics, and the discography of pioneering Krautrockers, Kraftwerk.

Lyrics Server

http://archive.uwp.edu/pub/music/lyrics/

Search a massive lyrics database by title, artist, or text. Everyone from Aaron Neville to 999.

MIDI Karaoke

http://www.teleport.com/~labrat/karsingles.shtml

Sing along to picks from an archive of MIDI instrumental files.

Mozart's Musical Dice

http://lecaine.music.mcgill.ca/~dawkins/html/waltz.html

Anyone can write music. Even you. Just by rolling a dice. Well that's what Mozart reckoned anyway. See for yourself. Or be like U2 and use a coin.

MTV

http://www.mtv.com/

After wrenching the domain name from ex-VJ Adam Curry in a protracted legal wrangle, MTV has finally got around to putting up some content. Mind you, if you can, you might prefer to switch on MTV itself, rather than download large, but low res, video clips.

MusicBase

http://www.musicbase.co.uk/

Home to such British labels as Deconstruction, Parlophone, Creation, Island, N-Gram William Orbit, and Perfecto records. Artists include Britpopsters Grid, Pet Shop Boys, Pulp, Blur, Oasis, Boo Radleys, and Paul Oakenfold.

NME

http://nme.com

On-the-pulse weekly reviews with soundclips, charts, features, news, gigs, demos, and archives from the world's most respected pop newspaper.

Offbeat

http://www.neosoft.com/~offbeat/

Monthly music news, dates, and jazzy sounds fresh out of Louisiana.

Polyester Records

http://www.polyester.com.au/PolyEster/index.html

Large indie selection for email order. It will ship internationally, but beware that Australia is one of the world's most expensive places to buy CDs.

The Residents

http://www.csd.uwo.ca/~tzoq/Residents/

The world's finest and weirdest neo-classical ensemble have performed anonymously, wearing giant eyeball heads, since the early 70s, so efficient at concealing their identities that even their most avid fans remain in the dark. Take this one for instance.

Resonance Records

http://www.netcreations.com/resonance/

Check into the listening booth and see what's hot in drum'n'bass. It will ship anywhere in the world.

Rolling Stones

http://www.stones.com

Originally set up to promote the Stones' Voodoo Lounge album, this official site has ongoing video feeds, loads of sound files, interviews, and pictures. It carved its place in history by hosting the first live Internet concert broadcast which, although not a critical success, was a turning point in the Net's evolution from research tool to lifestyle accessory.

The Rough Guide to Rock

http://www.roughguides.com/rock

The Rough Guide to Rock was developed as a work in progress on the Web prior to book publication, and this site has the full text (1100 band/artist biographies), plus Web links to find more on the artists. If you're a budding rock writer and spot a crucial missing entry (or one you could write a lot better), you can submit it for consideration. Rough Guides are in the process of posting text from their guides to World Music, Jazz, Reggae, Classical, and Opera.

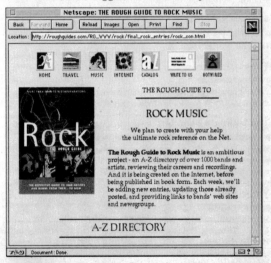

Sound Wire

http://soundwire.com/

Like most indie music shops, this one has lots of stuff similar to, but not necessarily exactly, what you're looking for. Relatively few albums have samples and cover shots, and none have track listings. All the same, it's well worth visiting the listening room to discover obscure gems.

Space Age Bachelor Pad Music

http://www.users.interport.net/~joholmes/

From garage sale bin to next big thing. Discerning hipsters say the Loungecore sounds of Esquival, Denny, Klaempert, and co. are more now than they were back then.

Stereolab

http://www.maths.monash.edu.au/people/rjh/stereolab

All the gas on the UK's front-runners in the Moog and strings revival.

Sub Pop Records

http://www.subpop.com

Try and buy grunge.

Timecast

http://www.timecast.com/

What's new on the Real Audio airwaves. Get a sound card, download Real Audio, and visit this site regularly.

The Ultimate Band List

http://american.recordings.com/wwwofmusic/ubl/ubl.shtml

Search for, or add, all your favorite pop ensemble's Internet presences. This is a massive resource that rock fans will want to bookmark right away and will keep referring to.

Virgin Records

http://www.vmg.co.uk

Prime multimedia tidbits from Chemical Brothers, Verve, FSOL, Auteurs, Rolling Stones, Lenny Kravitz, and the entire Hut Records catalog, plus gossip, and Virgin info.

WorldWide Music

http://worldiwidemusic.com/

This is perhaps the Web's most amazing record store – at least if you have a fast (and preferably direct) connection, so that you can make use of its stunning library of samples, which include at least six tracks from each disc in stock. The design is excellent, the range astonishing. Explore!

Yothu Yindi

http://www.yothuyindi.com/

Yothu Yindi's blend of tribal techno brought Aboriginal
music to the world's attention and won Mandawuy
Yunupingu nomination as Australian of the Year. This site
has Real Audio clips, videos, an art gallery, and passion for a
sunburnt country.

NATURE

Australian Botanical Gardens

http://155.187.10.12/anbg/anbg.html

All the gear on Canberra's Botanical Garden's projects, flora
and fauna. Like tourist guides, flowering calendars,
biodiversity studies, bird and frog call sound files, and even
the fire procedures. But it's a bit like stumbling into an office
and finding reams of papers strewn across the floor in
unrelated piles. In this case, substance certainly beats style.

British Trees

http://www.u-net.com/trees/home.htm

Apparently there are only 33 native British trees. You can
find out all about them here, but they would be easier to
recognize if the site included some pictures!

Canine Web Links

http://www.idyllmtn.com/acd/links.html

Link to sites devoted to individual dog breeds, pet products,
canine organizations, experiments, and all things poochish.

Dog World

http://www.houssennet.nb.ca/DogWorld.htm

Buy the training video or download the free manual. Either
way, Mr Fleabag will soon know who's boss.

The Electronic Zoo

http://netvet.wustl.edu/e-zoo.htm

This directory of fauna information will lead you way up the virtual garden path before you find what you're looking for. Despite its name, it's not a virtual zoo with animations and recordings of animal sounds. However, when one arrives, you'll be sure to find it here.

The EnviroWeb

http://envirolink.org

Claims to be the largest online environmental information service on the planet. It includes environmental links, forums, libraries, databases, and a green-friendly cybermall.

Natural History Bookshop

http://www.nhbs.co.uk

Browse or search the world's largest environmental bookshop.

NetVet

http://netvet.wustl.edu/vet.htm

If it's animal-oriented, you'll find a way to it from here. Choose from the NetVet Gopher, Electronic Zoo, Veterinary Medicine page of the WWW Virtual Library, or one of several specialist directories.

The Virtual Garden

http://pathfinder.com/vg/Welcome/welcome.html

This splendid horticultural digest is just a nibble of Time Warner's megalithic Pathfinder complex, yet provides the most fulsome online guide to gardening. It includes several plant society and gardening magazines, databases, book excerpts, plant directories, and an electronic encyclopedia which, among other things, can help you pick the best plants for your plot.

NEWS, NEWSPAPERS, AND MAGAZINES

Don't see your favorite rag below? Try one of the lists like AJR, MediaInfo, or Ecola's Newsstand – and don't forget to check our "Ezine" and "Music" listings.

AJR/Newslink

http://www.newslink.org

Features from the American Journalism Review and a well-stocked directory of newspapers, magazines, broadcasters' and journalists' resources.

Blender

http://www.blender.com

Web adjunct to the slick NY cyniculture CD-zine.

c/net

http://www.cnet.com/

First-class daily technology news and features (some in Real Audio), plus reviews, games updates and downloads, and schedules, transcripts, and related stories from c/net's broadcasting network.

Christian Science Monitor

http://www.csmonitor.com

Daily print news and opinion plus live and archived audio feeds from Monitor Radio.

Clarinet News

http://www.clarinet.com/

High-quality subscription news service providing newsgroup access to such big guns as Reuters, Associated Press and Newsbytes. A single-user subscription costs about $40 per month, or cheaper if shared across a site. If your access provider subscribes, you'll get the clari. series free in Usenet.

CNN

http://www.cnn.com

24-hour US and world news, weather, sports, showbiz, technology, food, and health updates.

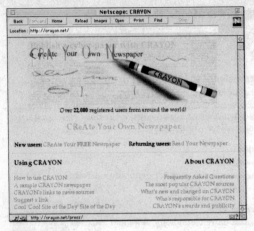

Crayon

http://crayon.net

This is a brilliant site that allows you to create your own custom newspaper from Web sources. It's entirely free and allows you to draw in a whole range of US and world publications, specifying your interests from politics to cartoons, sports to Internet developments. A must visit.

Ecola's Newsstand

http://www.ecola.com/news/

Only paper-printed newspapers or magazines with actively updated English-language content and free access qualify for this list. So far there's about 2000. Search, browse, or check what's new.

The Electronic Daily Telegraph

http://www.telegraph.co.uk

Generous up-to-date dose of the day's news, sports, finance, entertainment, and pictures. One of the bolder, pioneering mainstream newspaper electronic publishing ventures.

Electronic Journals

http://www.w3.org/hypertext/DataSources/bySubject/
Electronic_Journals.html

WWW Virtual Library listing of hundreds of magazine and periodical sites.

Electronic Newsstand

http://enews.com

Each publication "carried" by the Electronic Newsstand supplies a mission statement, subscription offer, current issue details including contents, and at least one complete article plus archives. There's also a separate Monster List with links to over 2000 magazines' home pages.

The Gate

http://www.sfgate.com

Two San Franciscan dailies, the *Chronicle* and *Examiner*, contribute daily news, archives, and oddities, plus a Bay Area entertainment guide, to this innovative free e-paper.

Go2: The Guardian Online

http://go2.guardian.co.uk/

Selections from the UK Guardian's Thursday Online liftout, snippets from the broadsheet, and bits that you won't find anywhere else. High quality but limited in extent.

The Hindu

http://www.webpage.com/hindu/

Daily online edition of India's national newspaper.

IGC Headline News

gopher://gopher.igc.apc.org/11/headlines

Ecologically aware news Gopher service from the Institute for Global Communications. Covers issues such as nuclear testing, refugees, corruption, racism, government policy changes, Third World crises, and Microsoft's world plan.

InfoSeek Personal

http://personal.infoseek.com

Live personalized news, stock quotes, comics, stars, weather, movie and TV updates. Specify which topics, companies, people, sports, etc, you want to monitor and it will look after the rest.

iWorld: Internet News and Resources

http://www.iworld.com

Daily Net-related news from Internet World and searchable archives from several other prime news sources such as *PC Magazine*, *HotWired*, *Interactive Age*, and *PC Week*.

MediaInfo

http://www.mediainfo.com/edpub/

Switched-on Net publishing news, commentary, and advice from *Editor & Publisher* magazine. It also maintains one of the best-kept online newspapers lists.

Multimedia Newsstand

http://mmnewsstand.com

Probably as good as anywhere to lodge subscriptions to any of over 500 popular magazines or to email order videos. However, only a few magazines, such as *Harper's Bazaar* and *Secret Agent X*, give previews, contents, or any details other than price.

New Scientist

http://www.newscientist.com/

Full features, daily bulletins, and scientific miscellany from the superlative science weekly.

New York Timesfax

http://nytimesfax.com

Previously fax-only eight-page daily condensed version of the *NY Times*. Needs Adobe Acrobat to read.

Newsdesk

www.newsdesk.co.uk

Multilingual online news and information service which provides journalists, consultants, and industry analysts with updates in the IT and telecomms industry.

NewsPage

http://www.newspage.com

Mostly free, daily business, sports, and weird news clippings
and press releases from over 600 sources.

PA NewsCentre

http://www.pa.press.net/

Live UK news, parliamentary proceedings, weather, sports,
and broadcast listings. A good place to get the latest cricket
scores.

Pathfinder

http://www.pathfinder.com

Whoah, this one from Time Warner's a monster, with
something for everyone. With publications like *Time, People,*
Sports Illustrated, Life, Money, Fortune, Entertainment
Weekly, and *Vibe,* plus CNN, to draw from, that's to be
expected. But it's not all rehashed features and samples. It's a
publishing venture in its own right and more like what you'd
expect from an Online Service.

PM Zone

http://popularmechanics.com/

Popular Mechanics has been showing us "the easy way to do
hard things" since the turn of the century. It provides a
generous selection of stories, retrospectives, movies, Web
tools, home improvement projects, and much more.

Skeptics Society

http://www.skeptic.com/

The Skeptics Society, a private organization of the
intellectually curious and the perennially unconvinced,
investigates the pseudosciences, paranormal, and claims of
fringe groups. At this site, you can subscribe to the
magazine, order books and tapes, read newsletters, and find
out what's new in the world of scientific enquiry.

South Polar Times

http://205.174.118.254/nspt/home.html

Includes the biweekly newsletter of the Amundsen-Scott

South Pole Station in the Antarctic, as well as links to other gateways to the Antarctic.

Sydney Morning Herald

http://www.smh.com.au

Streamlined news, columns, sports, computers, and the Metro, on the Net before the *Herald* hits the street. Plus Real Audio interviews and features, regular CU-SeeMe video conferences with newsworthy types, archives, and links to the *Financial Review* and Melbourne's *The Age*.

The Times

http://www.the-times.co.uk http://www.sunday-times.co.uk

Pretty close to the full *London Times* and *Sunday Times* newspapers, on the Net, before breakfast. An extremely impressive product – much easier to navigate than its rival, the *Daily Telegraph* – this is perhaps the nearest online has got to an acceptable alternative to print.

The Voice of America

gopher://ftp.voa.gov/1

Listen to audio clips of the day's news in various languages as you browse the staid megabroadcaster's other info.

PERSONAL

Lovelink

http://www.gold.net/lovelink/

Advertise or browse for a potential mate in the UK. To make
contact, you must phone a charge call service, enter a PIN
code, and leave a message.

Match.com

http://www.match.com

Browse for a perfect match. All entries come from the Net.

Single Search

http://nsns.com/single-search/

Don't stay at home alone playing on your computer. Just
submit your interests – beer, curry, Duke Nukem, footie,
engine numbers and speed metal, say – and sit back and wait.
Before long, you'll be Dukematching by candlelight.

Web Personals

http://www.webpersonals.com

Generally harmless free cyberdating and friendship service
with an anonymous remailer for the shy.

WWW Cemetery

http://www.io.org/cemetery/

Erect a memorial, leave flowers, or pay your respects in this
non-sectarian virtual cemetery.

POLITICS

Amnesty International

http://www.organic.com/Non.profits/Amnesty/index.html

"If you think virtual reality is interesting, try reality," says
Amnesty International, global crusaders for human rights.
Discover how you can help in its battles against militant
regimes and injustice.

Australian Political Parties

http://www.liberal.org.au   http://www.npa.org.au

http://www.alp.org.au   http://www.uq.edu.au/~e2gjenki/democrats.html

Liberal, National, Labour, and Democrat parties' sites respectively, with news, history, policies and contacts (although few by email). Expect a flurry of fresh content as elections loom.

Black Information Network

http://www.bin.com

This non-profit organization concerned with promoting educational, recreational, social, and supportive communication within the African-American community has produced a very pretty and polished but somewhat staid site.

Bosnia

http://www.cco.caltech.edu/~bosnia/bosnia.html

Details, pictures, and maps of the conflict in the former Yugoslavia from a Bosnia-Herzegovinan angle. Unsurprisingly, the list of war criminals and suspects are all Serbian, but if you pursue the provided links elsewhere, you'll get a more balanced view.

British Political Parties

http://www.poptel.org.uk/labour-party/

http://www.libdems.org.uk/

"New Labour" shows it's not techno-shy by offering its members cheap Net access via the Poptel BBS. While you can't actually join its ranks online (they need your signature), you can order the necessary form or print one from this page. The site also details who's who in the Party and the latest news and policies, such as its white paper on the, ahem, Information SuperHighway.

The Libdems' site is even more informative. You'll probably learn more about the Liberal Democrat Party from spending a few minutes here than from half-listening to years of hustings' static. Read its history, policies, and how it intends to reform Britain's place in the European union. But before you sign your life away online, why not email your gripes to Paddy Ashdown direct? And see what response you get.

Noam Chomsky Archive

http://www.lbbs.org/archive/index.htm

Oodles of highly controversial articles on, interviews with, lectures by, quotes from, and literary reviews of Noam Chomsky, Institute Professor of Linguistics at MIT and outspoken critic of US foreign policy. He can change the way you read the world.

DeathNet

http://www.islandnet.com/~deathnet/open.html

A side-effect of DeathNet's euthanasia campaign was the media's predictable focus on the Net as a medium for encouraging suicide. Consequently a large slab of this "right to die" library is dedicated to examples of the press's propensity to dramatize.

Feminist Activist Resources

http://www.igc.apc.org/women/feminist.html

Hundreds of links to feminist forums, articles, political action groups, legal documents, news items, women's organizations, counselling services, and spare-rib tickling humor.

Free Burma

http://freeburma.org/

A good example of the kind of international campaign that the Net can promulgate. And there are few better causes than this push against Burma's tyrannical military government.

Friends of the Earth

http://www.foe.co.uk/

Find out about Friends of the Earth's latest campaign, your nearest group, results of environment studies, or how to join forces. Plus plenty of links to other environmental resources and groups.

The Gallup Organization

http://www.gallup.com/

About 20% of Gallup's online visitors fill out the questionnaires and opinion polls. Not a bad response compared to say, Barclays' callers requesting credit card flyers. It also supplies results of past surveys, so you can keep up to date with trends and ratings such as the fickle swings of Slick Willy's popularity.

Gay and Lesbian Alliance Against Defamation

http://www.datalounge.com/glaad/glaad.html

Campaigning against homophobia in the media and beyond.

Greenpeace International

http://www.greenpeace.org/

Details of Greenpeace's various environmental campaigns and operations, plus links to like mindsets.

Intelligence Watch Report

http://www.awpi.com/IntelWeb

Brief updates on political disturbances, terrorism, and subterfuge worldwide, plus intelligence directories and jobs. And a mirror of the Secrecy and Government Bulletin, published by the Federation of American Scientists, which challenges excessive government secrecy in the US. But maybe it's just a diversion.

MIT Students for Free Expression

http://www.mit.edu:8001/activities/safe/home.html

According to these MIT students, the Net recognizes censorship as damage and routes around it. Find out what's being done to protect the Net's freedom of speech and link to controversial sites that certain groups would like to ban.

Newtwatch

http://www.newtwatch.org/

A full frontal assault on Newt Gingrich. And to keep it fair, links to supporters as well.

One World

http://www.oneworld.org

This is one of the best conceived sites on the Web – an umbrella for 60-plus non-governmental organizations and charities, who provide news stories (very different stories, oddly enough, to those you get in the newspapers) on areas of crisis, plus details on what they're doing to help. There is excellent archive material, too, from *New Internationalist* and *Index On Censorship*, and the site is building links with third-world partners and trying to address the problems of the Net's elitist access, while much of the world's population has no telephone or electricity.

Spunk Press

http://www.cwi.nl/cwi/people/Jack.Jansen/spunk/Spunk_Home.html

Spunk Press, an electronic publisher of anarchist literature, provides a fulsome index to anarchist resources around the Web. It's a little paradoxical to find anarchists so well organized and authoritative, but much of the writing here is either juvenile mischief or far left.

Trinity Atomic Test Site

http://www.environlink.org/issues/nuketesting/

Trinity, site of the first atomic test back in 1945, celebrated its 50th anniversary by opening its gates to the public. Here's where to find the photos, videos, maps, and details of all the action, plus links to archives of high-energy weapon testing, including commentary on French and Chinese efforts.

United Nations Development Programme

http://www.undp.org

Daily news of the United Nations' involvement in
international affairs.

US Party politics

http://www.digitals.org/digitals/

http://www.townhall.com

The Digital Democrats link to a couple of dozen senators, and
other party strands. You can't actually register to vote online,
but you can order the paperwork. The Republican Townhall –
the sassiest, dirtiest Republican site – is a pretty fascinating
meeting place for Newt's own party reptiles.

RADIO

Looking for net radio stations? Download Real Audio first at:
http://www.realaudio.com and check http://www.timecast.com for the
latest broadcast listings.

BBC

http://www.bbc.co.uk/

Inevitably this general information service on the BBC's
broadcasting schedules and activities will branch off into
separate sites as its various tentacles fulfil their Net
aspirations. Right now, it's a bit inconsistent, with some
departments appearing to lose their early enthusiasm.
Perhaps there are bigger things in the pipeline.

Phil's Old Radios

http://www.accessone.com/~philn/

If you've ever drifted to sleep bathed in the soft glow of a
crackling Bakelite wireless, Phil's collection of vacuum-era
portables may instantly flood you with childhood memories.

Radio Station WXYC

http://sunsite.unc.edu/wxyc/

Tune into alternative radio WXYC, the first real-time station
on the Net, through Maven, CU-SeeMe, or Streamworks. The

software is simple to configure and available for download here.

Real Time in Real Audio

http://www.cbcstereo.com/RealTime/soundz/realaudio/ra_menu.html

You'll need a sound card and Real Audio to listen to this Net radio's broadcasts on your PC or Mac. Unlike real radio, it's not quite live. Choose from a menu of pre-recorded specials.

Shortwave Radio Catalog

http://itre.uncecs.edu/radio/

If it's not on the Net, maybe it's crackling over the airwaves. Find out what's on what frequency, and get the latest station ID clips, maps, news, satellite info, propagation reports, sunspot readings, spy station sitings, and much more.

Virgin Radio

http://www.virginradio.co.uk

Tune into London's Virgin FM live via Real Audio.

REAL ESTATE

Estate Agent

http://nysernet.org/cyber/realestate/index.html

A vehicle for (mainly US) real estate agents to list their properties. It's a fairly convenient way to scout for land as it's quite detailed and usually includes pictures. However, once you make an enquiry, you still have to deal with a spieler.

Home Scout

http://www.homescout.com

Scan several US real estate databases at once.

International Real Estate Directory

http://www.ired.com/

There are rare times in your life when you'll actively seek the attentions of a real estate hawker. Wherever you live, this site will have you hooked up with one in no time.

Mortgage Calculator

http://www.nethomes.com/mortcalc.cgi/

Figure out your monthly payments or what you can afford.

UK Property Warehouse

http://www.uk-property.com/

Well-organized, searchable warehouse of (mostly) UK properties for sale or rent. Also links to mortgage companies, removal firms, and everything else for moving home.

Windermere Real Estate

http://windermere.com

Search for properties for sale in Washington, Oregon, Idaho, and British Columbia, or put your own on the market. Plus advice on how to beat the taxman, when to sell and various other tidbits to help you move your block.

REFERENCE

Acronyms

http://curia.ucc.ie/cgi-bin/acronym

Before you follow IBM, TNT, and HMV in initializing your company's name, make sure it doesn't stand for something blue by searching through these 12,000 acronyms.

alt.culture

http://www.altculture.com

A witty, digital A–Z of Nineties pop culture. Coupland meets Encyclopaedia Britannica. Fun to browse.

Alternative Dictionary

http://www.notam.uio.no/~hcholm/atlang/

Insult your foreign pals in their mother tongue.

AT&T's 1-800 Information

http://www.tollfree.att.net

Find those elusive 1-800 numbers and cut your phone bill. That is, if your online charges don't contra the savings.

Britannica Online

http://www.eb.com/

It might make sense to reference the massive Encyclopaedia Britannica online rather than pay for the whole bulky series. Especially when it goes out of date so quickly. You can try this impressive service free for seven days – after that you or your organization will have to fork out.

Computing Dictionary

http://wombat.doc.ic.ac.uk/

In theory, this concise glossary should help clarify many obscure computing terms and acronyms. However, these brief explanations may still leave you in doubt.

Globalink

http://www.globalink.com

Translate documents, including Web pages, between English and French, Spanish or German, in seconds. Run it back and forth a few times and you'll end up with something that wouldn't look out of place on a kitsch Japanese t-shirt.

Human Languages

http://www.willamette.edu/~tjones/Language-Page.html

An astoundingly rich digest of links to linguistic resources such as dictionaries, thesauruses, poetry, publications and more, in just about any language you can name, including Australian Aboriginal dialects, Esperanto, Hebrew, Manx Gaelic, Welsh, and Vietnamese.

Jeffrey's Japanese/English Dictionary Gateway

hhttp://www.wg.omron.co.jp/cgi-bin/j-e

Translate English to Japanese and vice versa. You can view the output in plain English text or in Japanese characters either as images or via the Japanese character enhanced version of Netscape. It takes a while to get started, but there's plenty of help along the way.

MIT Arab Student Organization

http://www.mit.edu:8001/activities/arab/homepage.html

If you've been looking for pointers to Arabic pages this is

your lucky day. This site links to Arabic software suppliers, student groups, cultural organizations, reference works, photo libraries, Middle Eastern servers, and other Arabic pages, sorted by country of origin.

NetGlos

http://wwli.com/translation/netglos/netglos.html

Multilingual, if fairly superficial, glossary of Internet terms.

Roget's Thesaurus

http://humanities.uchicago.edu/forms_unrest/ROGET.html

The bible of big words finds life anew in hypertext.

School Sucks

http://www.schoolsucks.com/

College plagiarist's paradise.

Skeptics Dictionary

http://wheel.ucdavis.edu/~btcarrol/skeptic/dictcont.html

You'll be able to blow holes through loads of popularly accepted superstitions and pseudo-sciences armed with this concise, practical, dinner party deflater. Yes, it's really here.

Websters

http://civil.colorado.edu/htbin/dictionary

Enter your mystery word and its definition will be promptly returned. It doesn't help out much with spelling errors and omits the crowd-pleasers you use when your computer crashes.

RELIGION

About Witchcraft

http://www.crc.ricoh.com/~rowanf/COG/iabout.html

The Covenant of the Goddess is a league of witch covens throughout North America. It intends to dispell some of the myths behind the persecution of witches over the centuries by creating public access to the rituals and practices of the craft. First you have to take them seriously.

Anglicans Online!

http://infomatch.com/~haibeck/anglican.html

The Anglican and Episcopalean churches seem more willing
than most sects to adapt to societal changes since the
scriptures were written. This independent site reflects such
concern by providing a friendly forum for debate and
concerns raised by Anglican youths. It also has links to
parishes all over the world.

Bhagvad Gita

http://www.cc.gatech.edu/gvu/people/Phd/Rakesh.Mullick/gita/gita.html

To view these PostScript Sanskrit pages of the Bhagvad Gita,
the most sacred of vedic literature, you'll need a program like
GhostScript or a PostScript printer. However, if your
Sanskrit is not up to scratch, you may find the English
summary and translation easier going.

The Bible Gateway

http://www.calvin.edu/cgi-bin/bible

Search the Bible as a database by textual references or
passage. Or turn scripture references into hyperlinks in your
own documents by referring to the gateway in your HTML
code.

Catholic Resources

http://www.cs.cmu.edu/Web/People/spok/catholic.html

Scripture, liturgy, early writings, Vatican documents, papal
encyclicals, pronouncements, books, and other Catholic
interests.

Hell – The Online Guide

http://www.marshall.edu/~allen12/

Let's face it, this lot have never enjoyed good press. On the
rare occasions they're taken seriously it's only to accuse them
of some heinous crime against humanity, like backmasking
racy slogans into heavy metal tracks, inciting suicide as a
fashion statement, and killing the Czar and his ministers.
According to this site, Satanism is a bona fide religion whose
followers do not worship the devil, but follow their
Darwinian urges to disinherit the meek of the earth.

Hindunet

http://www.hindunet.org

The most comprehensive site covering Hindu dharma – the philosophy, culture and customs.

Homosexuals and the Church

http://www.qrd.com/QRD/religion/

Pointers to many documents reflecting the church's attitude to sexuality.

Islamic Resources

http://latif.com/

Links to Islamic FAQs, announcements, conferences and social events, Qu'ran teachings, Arabic news, and the Cyber Muslim guide.

Magick

http://www.student.nada.kth.se/~nv91-asa/magick.html

You won't find card tricks, Uri Geller, or hatfulls of bunnies here, this is the Aleister Crowley version, spelt with a 'k'. What you will find is an immense stash of links to alternative spiritualist groups, strange orders, superstitions, soothsayers, and mystical literature. It's all stuff you should know better than to believe in, but it still makes compulsive reading. There are gateways to the Freemasons, Rosicrucians, Temple of the Psychic Youth, and Builders of the Atydium, as well as works on Voodooism, Druidism, divination, astrology, alchemy, and so much more it casts an eerie light on the human condition.

Network for Jewish Youth

http://www.ort.org/anjy/anjy.htm

Drop-in centre for UK Jewish youths with info, activities, and the biggest directory of Jewish/Israeli links on the Net.

Religious and Multifaith Sites

http://www.crc.ricoh.com/~rowanf/religion.html

Whether you're looking for Christian, Islamic, Pagan, or Onanist presences, this page will show the way.

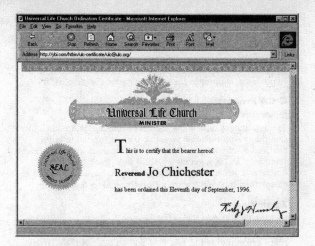

Universal Life Church

http://ulc.org/ulc/

You're already a member, just not aware of it yet. Ordain yourself within seconds online and print out the certificate to frame for your bedroom wall.

SCIENCE AND SPACE

Cabot Science Library

http://www.fas.harvard.edu/~cabref/

Harvard University library is an ideal jumpstation for scientific research. Apart from information about the library's catalog and policies, it has links to several Harvard scientific publications, external databases, and useful journals.

Chicago University Philosophy

http://csmaclab-www.uchicago.edu/philosophyProject/philos.html

Scholarly discussion of philosophical works. You can join in and voice your opinions on such vital subjects as Nelson Goodman's theory of metaphor, the language of thought hypothesis, counterfactuals, and Kripke. Go on, bluff it.

CICA Projects

http://www.cica.indiana.edu/projects/index.html

Details, images, and some results of the Center for Innovative Computer Applications' projects. It's not limited to any particular scientific strain, with experiments in linguistics, feminism, biology, geometry, fluid flow, geology, 3D, basketball, kinesiology, and more. If you have an enquiring scientific mind, you'll surely find something fascinating.

Earth Viewer

http://www.fourmilab.ch/earthview/vplanet.html

View the Earth in space and time via this nifty simulator. Maps are generated in real time so you can see the current positioning, lighting, and shadows.

EarthView

http://www.ldeo.columbia.edu/EV/EarthViewHome.html

Find out where it's quaking in the USA or link to other seismological stations around the world.

Entomology Image Gallery

http://www.ent.iastate.edu/imagegallery

If images of lice, ticks, mosquitoes, and potato beetles turn you on, you'll leave this area feeling very aroused.

Interactive Frog Dissection

http://curry.edschool.virginia.edu/~insttech/frog

This step-by-step frog disembowelment is one of the Web's most popular and talked about sites. It might be because it's educational, interactive, and finely detailed, but more likely because it's so gruesome. All you have to do is pin down a frog, grab your scalpel, and follow the pictures. That's all very well, but then what are you going to do – eat it?

Jungian Personality Test

http://sunsite.unc.edu/jembin/mb.pl

Confirm what a beast you really are. Skeptics insist it's simply a psychological parlor game.

Known Nuclear Explosions

gopher://wealaka.okgeosurvey1.gov/

Technical details, coordinates, and records of the use and testing of nuclear devices, plus seismological data.

NASA

http://www.nasa.gov/

The top level of NASA's mighty presence on the Web. Details of its projects, databases, policies, missions, and discoveries are scattered all over the Net, but you can find them all from here, if you persist. If you saw the first moon missions in the late 60s, it's sure to bring back vivid memories of mankind's greatest step.

Net Telescopes

http://deepspace.physics.ucsb.edu

http://www.telescope.org/rti

http://inferno.physics.uiowa.edu

Probe deep space by sending observation requests to remote telescopes.

Northern Lights – Aurora Borealis

http://www.uit.no/npt/homepage-npt.en.html

If you're ever lucky enough to see the aurora borealis during a solar storm, you'll never be able to look skyward with the same nonchalance again. It will challenge your paradigm of the visible universe and its relative stasis. This Norwegian planetarium does a commendable job in explaining a polar phenomenon that very few people understand.

Space Calendar

http://newproducts.jpl.nasa.gov/calendar/calendar.html

A guide to upcoming anniversaries, rocket launches, meteor showers, eclipses, asteroid and planet viewings, occultations, and happenings in the intergalactic calendar.

Space Environment Laboratory

http://www.sel.bldrdoc.gov

If you've been involved in long-distance wireless communication or aviation, you're probably aware of solar activity's effects. Otherwise, you may be baffled by the significance of this research. The Space Environment Agency provides current space weather, sunspot levels, solar images, research information, and a brief explanation of its purpose that won't leave you too much wiser.

Stars and Galaxies

http://www.eia.brad.ac.uk/btl/

Take a multimedia tour through the stars. Find out how they behave, how they generate energy, where they come from, and why they burn out.

The Magellan Mission to Venus

http://www.jpl.nasa.gov/magellan/

News releases and historical footage taken from the first planetary spacecraft launched from a space shuttle. There are enough images, animations, and technical documents on Venus and the project itself to satisfy even the most ardent astrophile. However, don't bother if you're looking for evidence of extraterrestrial life forms. Apparently those photos are kept in a secret vault called the X-files.

Volcano World

http://volcano.und.nodak.edu/

Monitor the latest eruptions, see photos of every major volcano in the world, virtually tour a Hawaiian smoky, or shop in a Volcano Mall.

Web-Elements

http://www.cchem.berkeley.edu/Table/index.html

Click on an element in the periodic table and find out more about its properties. Plus links to a fairly useless element percentage calculator and an entirely useless isotope pattern calculator.

Weird Science

http://www.eskimo.com/~billb/weird.html

Free energy, Tesla, anti-gravity, aura, cold fusion, parapsychology, and other strange scientific projects and theories.

SHOPPING

The Web is full of shopping possibilities, and this is just a selection of the more useful, established, or offbeat. See also our sections on "Music" (for CDs) and "Books" (for books!).

Barclay Square

http://www.itl.net/barclaysquare/

With Barclay's Bank behind it, and UK high-street names like Argos, Toys 'R' Us, Sainsbury's, Blackwells, Debenham, and Eurostar in the aisles, this mall might just be able to convince British shoppers that the Net is officially open for trading.

Catalog Mart

http://catalog.savvy.com/

Rather than have to hunt through lists of catalogs and contact the firms individually, Catalog Mart contacts them free on your behalf. Just choose the product areas you're interested in, supply your details, and it looks after the rest.

Catalog Select

http://pathfinder.com/CatalogSelect

Another catalog service, this time courtesy of Time Warner.

CatalogSite

http://www.catalogsite.com/

This catalog directory does a smart job of listing and reviewing major US mail order houses. In some cases you can link to a Web site and order, or request a catalog, online.

CompUSA

http://www.compusa.com/

Order from this US computer megastore's online catalog. They'll ship anywhere and international buyers might find the prices particularly cheap.

Condom Country

http://www.ag.com/Condom/Country

The mail order condoms, sex aids, books, and jokes are pretty harmless, but the mere mention of the penis size ready reckoner may prove disquieting to some.

Downtown Anywhere

http://www.awa.com

Handy directory of online shops, galleries, libraries, museums, sports sites, and more.

Gadgets

http://www.netcreations.com/gadget/index.html

Email order assorted novelty gadgets and useful knick-knacks. While this one's not so impressive, there are enough links to all sorts of engaging gizmoteers and oddities to make it well worth the drive-by.

Hall of Malls

http://www.nsns.com/MouseTracks/HallofMalls.html

All cashed up and nowhere to go? Step into any of these cybermarkets for quick relief.

Highland Trail

http://www.highlandtrail.co.uk/highlandtrail/

Enjoy fine Scottish produce such as malt whiskies, smoked salmon, kippers, oysters, and smoked venison delivered to your doorstep. Although several merchants are represented, you can order via credit card from one secure form.

Internet Mall

http://www.internet-mall.com

With well over 12,000 stores, Meckler Media's mall directory is as close to definitive as you're likely to find. Each entry includes a brief review.

Jarred's Wonderful World of Free Stuff

http://www.oberlin.edu/~jmcadams

Here's that magic word again. Stuff your mailbox for life.

Khazana

http://www.winternet.com/~khazana/

Indian and Nepalese collectibles purchased direct from the artisans and artists, with a "fair trade" policy of payment.

Lakeside Products

http://virtumall.com/Lakeside/Lakeside.html

Order the gags and novelties you could never afford when you really needed them. They're all here. Whoopee cushions, xray specs, itching powder, joke buzzers, and coffin piggy banks, ripped straight from the pages of your childhood comics. And it's still the same company selling them.

London Mall

http://www.londonmall.co.uk/

There's no need to click through the individual pages of this
prominent UK cybermall. Just take the hands-free automatic
tour and let Netscape's server-push technology turn the
pages for you. You'll find employment and travel agents,
bookies, tailors, campaigns, entertainment directories,
computer dealers, financial services, and various retailers.

MarketNet

http://mkn.co.uk

Shop for flowers, insurance, chocolate, books, shares, travel
and legal services, and more via a secure link to this
nonsense-free UK cybermall.

Marrakesh Express

http://uslink.net/ddavis/

Come my friend – I'll show you something special. If you've
been pestered to the end of your tether by Moroccan carpet
dealers, this site will breathe new life into those rugs you
tried to avoid. Susan Davis, a Californian anthropologist, has
presented this online souk in such an educative manner that
it might tempt you to buy a carpet or kilim online.

Mind Gear

http://www.mind-gear.com

There's a theory that if you bombard yourself with light and
sound of a certain frequency you'll be bludgeoned into a
higher state of consciousness. Mind Gear sells various such
devices, tapes, and potions to fine-tune your mind.

Mondo-tronics Robot Store

http://www.robotstore.com

Build machines that do exactly what they're told.
Exterminate, exterminate!

New and Kewl

http://www.new-kewl.com

Jump site for new and nifty gadgets on sale around the Net.

Online Yacht Brokerage
http://www.aladdin.co.uk/cpy/

Scan through the list of yachts on offer, find something in
your price range, and then access a staggeringly detailed
description complete with pictures of the craft. Once you've
narrowed it down to two or three, you can email or phone to
arrange a viewing. Theoretically, it can arrange delivery
anywhere in the world.

The Shopping Expressway
http://shopex.com/

Ever wondered where else you can get those revolutionary
products advertised on TV, usually late at night when you're
most receptive to hypnotic gesturing? Wonder no more,
because a large section of this exploding cybermall has been
cordoned off for all those money-back guaranteed miracles
that were designed to be sold rather than used.

Speak to Me
http://www.clickshop.com/speak/

Want a swearing keychain, sneezing salt shaker, flirting
birthday candle, rapping Christmas tree, or some other
talking novelty? Order it, or preview the sound files, here.

UK Internet Florist
http://mkn.co.uk/help/flower/info

Enter your credit card number, apology, and delivery details
into the provided form, and be back in the good books before
you get home.

Used Software Exchange
http://www.hyperion.com/usx/index.html

Search for used software by type, price, currency, and
platform. When you find something you want, just contact
the vendor by email to arrange the trade.

WFMU's Catalog of Curiosities
http://www.wmfu.org/Catalog/catalog.html

Try and buy eccentric music and literature.

SPORT

Abdominal Training

http://www.dstc.edu.au/TU/staff/timbomb/ab/

Get "abs like ravioli."

Aladdin Sailing Index

http://www.aladdin.co.uk:80/sihe/

The Web's main hub for sailors. Link to pages from the likes of the Royal Yachting Association, Royal Ocean Racing Club, Royal Southampton Yacht Club, US Coast Guard, or catch up on racing news, promotions, and product launches.

Australian Rugby League

http://www.arl.org.au   http://ww2.eis.net.au/~chrisc/bronco.htm

First, the official ARL page with results, news, tipping, and anti-Super-League sentiments. Second, the unofficial home of the very wonderful Brisbane Broncos.

Cric Info

http://www.cricket.org

Don't despair at the domination of American sports on the Internet. Frolic here and be assured there'll always be an England. Someone's got to defend the bottom of the international cricket ladder.

Cybernude

http://www.cybernude.com

Struggling to keep up with fashion? Then join the growing ranks of the nude. All undressed and nowhere to go? Fret not, here's advice, news, and a roundup of spots to hang out with other naked fun seekers.

ESPN Sportzone

http://espnet.sportszone.com/

Current news, statistics, and commentary on major US sports.

Faith Sloan's Bodybuilding Site

http://www.frsa.com/bbpage.shtml

Galleries of proud pictures of the human form pushed to near-illogical extremes, as well as competition results, videos, fan mail addresses, workout advice, and links to individual bodybuilders' pages.

Golf.com

http://www.golf.com/

When it comes to golf, this one has the lot. Like international course maps, pro-golf schedules, golf tips, golf publications, golf merchandise, golf properties, golf travel, golf weather, golf, golf, and, uhh, more golf.

International Rugby League

http://www.brad.ac.uk/~cgrussel/

Read how 26 men bash themselves senseless, push each other's faces into the dirt as they're trying to stand up, and then meet for a drink afterwards.

Internet Disc Shoppe

http://www.digimark.net/disc/

Why risk your fingernails in a rough sport like rugby or strain your back over a croquet stick when you can fling one of these blighters back and forth? They're totally foolproof and available where all good ice cream is sold.

NBA.com

http://www.nba.com

Official NBA site with loads of pro basketball news, picks, player profiles, analyses, results, schedules, and highlight videos.

Red Devils Unofficial Home Page

http://www.iol.ie/~mmurphy/red-devils/mufc.htm

Manchester United – the world's most popular and most sublime football team – have more Web pages than any other club. This is perhaps the best of the unofficial sites, updated daily, with match reports, comments from the manager, and lots of detail on Eric and the boys.

Sky Sports

http://www.sky.co.uk/sports/

Regular soccer, cricket, and rugby scores and updates.

SnoWeb

http://www.snoweb.com/

Satellite photos, snow reports, resort cams, ski gear, accommodation, and coming events in resorts across the world.

Soccer Pages

http://www.atm.ch.cam.ac.uk/sports/webs.html

Links to most of the English and European, US, Brazilian, and Japanese clubs. Plus tables, fixtures, results, news, and all sorts of soccer chat.

Sport Virtual Library

http://www.atm.ch.cam.ac.uk/sports/sports.html

This wing of the WWW Virtual Library has probably the

most extensive set of links to sports information on the Internet. And it's not all baseball, grid iron, and basketball. Whatever you play, it should be here. If not, start your own page and let them know.

Sportsline

http://www.sportsline.com

US sports news, scores, gossip, and fixtures, including live play-by-play baseball action.

Stockdog Server

http://worm.biosci.arizona.edu/Stockdog/Stockdog.html

Here's a way to keep up with who's who in the stockdog trials. This is where the only two mammals with any mutual affection collaborate to corner a very stupid animal into an enclosure. The ambush is appraised by the dominant species while the subordinates inspect each others' equipment. Also includes sturdy shots of startled sheep, if that's your scene.

SurfLink

http://www.surflink.com

Regionally sorted links to the sort of dude stuff that real surfers live for. Like how to forecast waves, where El Nino's at, surfboard shops, Dick Dale riffs, and surfcams. And keeping in mind that tough guys don't read in public, there's also a stonking great gallery of cracking breakers to call up if a Kombi pulls up in the driveway unexpectedly.

The Virtual Flyshop

http://www.flyshop.com/

A meeting point to trade tips and generally exaggerate about aquatic bloodsports. Don't let this one get away.

WagerNet

http://www.vegas.com/wagernet/

Punt on sporting results online via a proprietary secure link to Belize. While these offshore ventures can be a way around local prohibitions, chances are you're still breaking the law.

Weight Training

http://www.cs.unc.edu/~wilsonk/weights.html

Links to fitness newsgroups, weightlifting FAQs, competitive lifting rules, workout software, dieting advice, routines, and fetching snaps of grimacing men.

SUPPORT

Missing Kids Database

http://www.missingkids.org/

Potentially an indispensable tool in the search for missing children. However, the interface seriously limits its usefulness. To identify a missing child, you pick a region, scan through a long list of names, choose one, and then retrieve the picture. Fine if you have their real name, not an alias, but if you only have a face it's next to impossible. Plus advice on how to prevent it from happening in your family.

Precious in His Sight

http://www.adoption.com/

Disturbing photos and descriptions of children from all over the world seeking adoption.

Psychological Self-Help Resources

http://www.gasou.edu/psychweb/resource/selfhelp.htm

Many psychological disorders can be self-cured. For some, it's the only solution. The answer usually comes through finding others who've overcome the same anxieties or neuroses and taking their advice. The Net is the perfect medium for this sort of interaction as it's easy to make contact and still maintain your privacy. This site lists hundreds of resources for such support.

Queer Resources Directory

http://www.qrd.org/qrd/

AIDS, legal news, attitude trends, clubs, publications, broadcasts, images, political action, community groups, and assorted gay links.

Silent Witness

http://www.getnet.com/silent/

Become a bounty hunter for the Phoenix police department.
Just take the brief, get on the case, find your quarry, and call
the toll-free number to claim your booty.

Vietnam Veterans

http://www.vietvet.org/

Lest we forget.

TELECOMMUNICATIONS

See also "Search Tools and Directories" (p.158) for phone
directories.

Free Fax Service

http://www.tpc.int

Transmit faxes anywhere in the world via the Internet for the
price of your connection. In practice, coverage is limited and
subject to delays. But give it a shot anyway.

Page Mart – Wireless Email

http://www.pic.net/pagemart/pagemart.html

Pagemart's service sends your email messages straight to
your pager, notebook computer, or pocket organizer,
anywhere in the US.

World Time

http://www.whitepages.com.au/v2-0/time.htm

International dialing info from anywhere to anywhere,
including current times and area codes.

TIME

Cuckoo's Clock

http://asylum.cid.com/clock/

This one gives you the current time in California along with
a suitable sound accompaniment.

Greenwich Mean Time

http://www.cs.yale.edu/cgi-bin/saytime.au

Enter this address and you'll hear a time, hopefully the right one, played back through your PC speaker.

Time Zone Converter

http://www.cilea.it/MBone/timezones.html

Link to either of two time zone converters. One is simple – you just click on a region to find its time. The other converts from one time zone to another at any time and date, not just the present.

28 hour Day

http://www.kaplan.com/bosh/index.html

Living by a 28-hour day, 6-day week regime has a number of benefits, according to Mr Mike Biamonte. No more Mondays for one.

TRANSPORT

Aircraft Shopper

http://aso.solid.com/

Troubled by traffic? Rise above it, with something from this range of new, used, and charter aircraft. And if you can't fly, then sign up for training or flight simulation.

DealerNet

http://www.dealernet.com

Locate, browse, compare specs, and read reviews of the latest new and used cars, boats, and specialty vehicles from trusty US dealers.

European Railways Server

http://mercurio.iet.unipi.it/home.html

Timetables, news, and groovy liveries created by ardent loco locos. Some are faithful reproductions depicting national color schemes, while others are fantasy sketches conjuring up futuristic engines.

Exchange and Mart

http://www.ExchangeAndMart.co.uk

Choose from over 50,000 used British bangers. As you can
filter it down by locality, make, model, price, color, and more,
it's actually superior to the print edition.

Goodyear Tires

http://www.goodyear.com

Find where to get the best tires for your buggy, or attend the
Tire School for a Masters in rubber technology. Plus driving
tips, troubleshooting lessons, and nurturing pointers for
your vulcanized masterpieces.

Paramotor

http://cyberactive-1.com/paramotor/

According to this source, paramotors are the among the
smallest, yet safest, aircraft. They require no licence, weigh
less than 65 pounds, can be lugged about in a backpack,
assembled in under five minutes, and can soar to heights of
10,000 feet at up to 500 feet per minute. At only $10,000,
what are you waiting for?

Pickup Trucks

http://www.rtd.com/~mlevine/pickup.html

How could anyone not be charmed by this installation of
lovingly photographed sporting supertrucks?

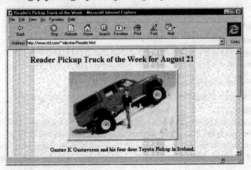

Railroad Internet Resources

http://www-cse.ucsd.edu/users/bowdidge/railroad/rail-home.html

Locophilial banquet of railroad maps, databases, mailing lists, transit details, and hundreds of shunts all over the Net.

RailServer

http://rail.rz.uni-karlsruhe.de/rail/english.html

European railroad schedules, pictures, prices, and discounts, plus hints and links.

Vespa

http://www.vespa.com

Vespa scooter adulation and links to other brands.

TRAVEL

Abandoned Missile Base

http://www.xvt.com/users/kevink/silo/

Missile bases aren't generally the sort of places to open to the public. Consequently your best and safest chance to see inside one is through this surreptitious photo tour.

Adventurous Traveler Bookstore

http://www.gorp.com/atbook.htm

No matter how far you're heading off the track, this store has the guides, maps, and videos to help you on your way.

AESU

http://www.aesu.com/

Discount airfare specialist with online quote and reservation system.

Air Traveler's Handbook

http://www.cis.ohio-state.edu/hypertext/faq/usenet/travel/air/handbook/top.html

Now that this FAQ-style travel cookbook has been converted to hypertext, it's quite easy to find your way around. It aims to wise you up to the tricks of the travel trade, help you beat the system, save you money, and get you home in one piece.

Arab Net

http://www.arab.net

A bulging omniscient resource of rare detail comprising
thousands of pages on North Africa and the Middle East,
their peoples, geography, economy, history, culture, and, of
course, camels.

Asia Online

http://www.asia-online.com.sg/

Jump on this digital silk route for Asian travel, news,
entertainment, shopping, business, and investment
information.

Asia World

http://www.asiaworld.co.uk

This UK-based publisher puts its entire brochure online, and
does it well. Lots of very tempting ideas.

Automap

http://www.microsoft.com/automap/

Key in two US cities to get directions on how to get from one
to the other.

Bermuda Triangle

http://tigger.cc.uic.edu/~toby-g/tri.html

Dispels myths about the infamous Caribbean vortex.

British Foreign Office Travel Advice

http://www.fco.gov.uk/

Use this service in conjunction with the US travel warnings
when planning your next holiday in Afghanistan or Chad –
though it's often hopelessly brief or out of date, and tends to
recommend that you contact the local consul.

CIA World Factbook

http://www.odci.gov/cia/publications/pubs.html

Encyclopedic summary of every country's essential statistics
and details. Disputed zones such as the Gaza Strip and West
Bank are recognized as separate political entities. It covers
geographical boundaries, international disputes, climate,

geography, economy, demographics, government, communications, and defense. Which makes it perfect for a school project but not quite enough for a military takeover.

City.Net

http://www.city.net/

Regionally sorted digest of links to community, geopolitical, and tourist information from all around the globe. Choose a locality directly or zoom in from a larger region.

Currency Converter

http://bin.gnn.com/cgi-bin/gnn/currency

This nifty program makes currency conversion a doddle. By clicking on any of nearly 60 weekly updated currencies you can create a new list, with your selection as the basis.

GNN Travel

http://nearnet.gnn.com/gnn/wic/wics/trav.new.thml

AOL-owned GNN is an outstanding directory of travel-related links. All sites are briefly reviewed and the links seem to be kept up to date. Interesting features, too.

Hospex

http://hospex.icm.edu.pl/~hospex/

Help out foreign tourists by offering a free place to crash for a few days. And while you're at it, see if someone can do the same for you.

Hotel Net

http://www.u-net.com/hotelnet/

Find, appraise, and reserve European hotels. There aren't that many choices but what it does cover is well documented.

How far is it?

http://www.indo.com/distance/

Calculate the distance between any two cities.

Interactive Map of the UK and Ireland

http://www.cs.ucl.ac.uk/misc/uk/intro.html

Click on the part of the British Isles you're interested in. Or, if you're not so hot with a mouse, choose from the menu to summon news, weather, statistics, entertainment and broadcast listings, transport routes, and travel times, interactive rail and city maps, guided tours, and Web servers in your locale of choice. It can only grow from here, maybe with your help.

Internet Travel Services

http://www.itsnet.co.uk

UK travel cybermall gathering info from 28 operators. A useful feature is its late-booking search. Click on "Lates" and you can see what flights are still available from the UK.

International Student Travel Confederation

http://www.istc.org

Find out where to get an international student identity card and what it's good for.

Japan – NTT

http://www.ntt.jp/

Tokyo's Nippon Telegraph and Telephone Corp takes a back seat in this bundle of Japanese links and tourist aids. Weather, music, customs, image maps, working, travel tips, audio language lessons, yellow pages, legal matters, sports, and how to get your browser to read Japanese script.

The Jerusalem Mosaic

http://www1.huji.ac.il/jeru/jerusalem.html

After you've taken this pleasant tour through the old city of Jerusalem, scout around the rest of Israel by selecting each region from a contact-sensitive map.

London Calling

http://www.demon.co.uk/london-calling/

Guide to what's on and where it's at in London for those more into the arts and markets than package tours.

London Club Guide

http://secure.londonmall.co.uk/londonclubguide/

London life after dark.

London Pubs Reviewed

http://www.cs.ucl.ac.uk/misc/uk/london/pubs/index.html

Find out why Londoners practically live in their locals. You
can even add your own, if it's not already there.

Lonely Planet Guidebooks

http://www.lonelyplanet.com.au

Lonely Planet's own content here consists of summaries of
every country in its series along with basic info and health
precautions. But where it scores is in the wealth of first-hand
tales posted by backpacking survivors. The bulletin board
and postcard sections make ideal complements to the rec.travel
groups when looking for travel partners, advice, and ideas
for your next stint away from the keyboard.

MapBlast!

http://www.mapblast.com

Key in addresses or domain names to get local maps.

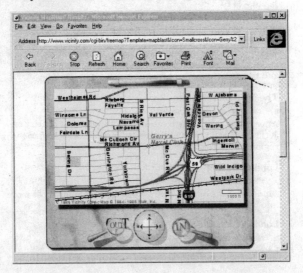

Map Browser

http://pubweb.parc.xerox.com/

Xerox PARC brought the world GUIs (Graphical User
Interfaces) and Ethernet. This site provides, among other
things, a way to build maps showing rivers, roads, rail lines,
borders, and other information, by specifying a location.

MCW International Travelers Clinic

http://www.intmed.mcw.edu/ITC/Health.html

Although there's only token information about the diseases
travelers are likely to encounter, the links should fill in the
gaps. These include the American Society of Tropical
Medicine, the AMSTMH directory of Travel Clinics &
Physicians, and the International Society of Travel Medicine.
Like the consular warnings, it's all bad news, so be prepared
for the worst.

Moon city

http://www.euro.net/5thworld/mooncity/moon.html

This virtual tour of Amsterdam is a veritable labyrinth, not
unlike tulip town itself. It's likewise frank, graphic, and
entertaining and might make you yearn for its freewheeling
lifestyle. But it's not all cannabis capers and erotica, there's
food, music, art, history, attractions, cinema, bookstores,
famous coffee-shops, and much more. If you can't make it in
person, at least visit here.

Moon Travel Guides

http://www.moon.com/

Moon has been on the Net longer than most and this well-
designed site provides some fine tasters of its guides – which
major on US states and Mexico. There's a particularly
graphic tour of Big Island Of Hawaii – clunky but pretty.
Take a look, too, at Moon's "Travel Matters" newsletter, which
is full of interesting snippets from the road, and doesn't just
boast its own (admirable) line of books.

Outside Online

http://outside.starwave.com

Current and back issues of *Outside* magazine, covering all
kinds of outdoor activities from cycling to whale watching.

Paddynet

http://www.paddynet.com/

Here's the place for all things Irish – from business contacts
to folklore. It's split into three major areas: Green Pages, a
Yahoo-like directory of Irish sites; Island, a discovery tour
through Irish culture and legends; and Virtual Blarney, a
real-time chat room.

Paris

http://www.paris.org/

Feel like a trip to Paris? Here's a virtual tour of popular
museums, cafés, monuments, shops, rail systems,
educational institutions, and many other attractions. It's
posted both in English and, if you want to punish yourself,
French.

PCTravel

http://www.pctravel.com/

Check timetables and book flights with over 500 airlines
through the Apollo reservation system. Tickets can be
Fedexed anywhere in the world.

Rough Guides

http://hotwired.com/rough   http://roughguides.com/

Okay – we're
clearly
biased, but
these are
pioneering
sites. The
first address
will take
you to
Rough
Guides on
HotWired
and into a
menu
offering the
full text of

our guides to the USA, Canada, Mexico, Northern Europe, and more to follow. These are free to access, searchable, hypertext linked within their body, and gradually building in links to sites and establishments reviewed in the pages, from small jazz clubs to hotels.

On Rough Guides' own home pages, you'll find details of all the print titles, along with excerpts from books such as our *Women Travel* special, plus readers' updates, menu decoders, and more.

Terraquest

http://www.terraquest.com

One of the Web's most stylish travel magazines, with an emphasis on expeditionary destinations (Antarctica, Galapagos) and a mass of links to strong background information on the subjects. Strong green bias, too.

Time Out

http://www.timeout.co.uk

Dig into *Time Out*, London's weekly listing guide's site, and you'll find no excuse to stay at home in not just London, but also Amsterdam, Berlin, Edinburgh, Madrid, New York, Paris, Prague, Rome, San Francisco, Sydney, and Tokyo. It has fortnightly updated tourist guides to each city, classifieds, postcard stores, city maps, sample features and, of course, the highlights of what's on.

Tourism Offices Worldwide

http://www.mbnet.mb.ca/lucas/travel/tourism-offices.html

Locate tourist offices around the world, and if there's a Web presence, link to it. It's a pretty low-fi affair, so it's unlikely it's up to date. But it's another place to look.

Traffic and Road Conditions

http://www.accutraffic.com

Live traffic updates in various US cities.

Travelmag

http://www.travelmag.co.uk/travelmag/

Excellent monthly adventurer's ezine with bold features and regular health, trade, crime, and publishing news.

TravelWeb

http://www.travelweb.com

Reserve accommodation in thousands of swanky hotels worldwide. The choices are oriented mainly to business travel, but vacationers may find this a useful resource for scoring weekend and summer deals.

US Travel Warnings

http://www.stolaf.edu/network/travel-advisories.html

Essential information if you're planning to visit a potential hot spot, but not necessarily a definitive guide to safety. It only takes an isolated incident with a foreign tourist to start panic, but it can take years to settle the fear. Don't ignore these bulletins, but seek a second opinion before postponing your adventure.

The Virtual Tourist

http://wings.buffalo.edu/world/

Click on the atlas interface to zoom into the region of your choice. Once you're down to country level, choose between a resource map, resource list, or general country information. This could ultimately link you with any server in the region.

The World Traveler Books & Maps

http://www.travelbookshop.com

Order from a wide range of travel literature, online.

World's Largest Subway Map

http://metro.jussieu.fr:10001/

Pick from a selection of major cities, and choose a starting and finishing destination to estimate the traveling time. It's relatively entertaining but not really practical – after all, how many rail networks run this smoothly?

Yahoo Travel

http://www.yahoo.com/Recreation/Travel/

Yahoo's travel section is one of its best stacked areas, with links to thousands of travel and regional sites. Most have one-liners, rather than reviews, but they'll give you some idea of what to expect. It's broad, but uncritical.

WEATHER

Interactive Weather Browser
http://rs560.cl.msu.edu/weather/interactive.html

Interactive temperature map of the USA giving detailed hourly updated weather reports.

National Severe Storms Laboratory
http://www.nssl.uoknor.edu/

If tornadoes, blizzards, flash floods, thunderstorms, hurricanes, cyclones, lightning, and severe storms are just your bag, step in here. These guys are not put off by a bit of drizzle spoiling their cricket, they're out whipping up lightning rods on mountain peaks, trying to attract the big stuff. If you're a thunder buff, read the advice on responsible storm chasing. It may just temper that Pavlovian frenzy for the car keys the next time a distant rumble snaps you from your post-prandial stupor.

The Daily Planet
http://www.atmos.uiuc.edu/

Meteorological maps, satellite images, and pointers to sources of climatic data, courtesy of the University of Illinois Department of Atmospheric Sciences.

Weather
http://www.cs.ucl.ac.uk/misc/weather/weather.html

Of the many good reasons to live in the UK, here's evidence that the weather isn't one.

Weather Information
http://web.nexor.co.uk/users/jpo/weather/weather.html

Regularly updated weather and satellite images from all over the world, particularly Europe and the UK.

World Meteorological Organisation
http://www.wmo.ch

Division of U.N. responsible for monitoring global climate. Link to national bureaus worldwide.

WEIRD

The Aetherius Society

http://www.rain.org/~brianck/aetherius.html

When the
Cosmic Masters
from the
Interplanetary
Council need to
give their
message to
Earth, Sir
George King,
their chosen
Primary
Terrestrial
Mental
Channel, must
enter a Positive
Yogic Samadhic
Trance. Sort of
like when
Ramjet takes
his protein
pills.

Amazing Clickable Beavis

http://web.nmsu.edu/~jlillibr/ClickableBeavis/

Click on Beavis for a suitable reaction.

Active Most Wanted and Criminal Investigations

http://www.gunnyrag.com/crimes.htm

Compendium of fugitive listings including the FBI's Top Ten
Most Wanted, the US State Department's Anti-Terrorism Unit,
and a war criminal directory.

Anders Main Page

http://www.student.nada.kth.se/~nv91-asa/

Anders Sandberg has put together an immense, diverse
digest of extreme oddity. His primary focus is on the

occultish side of spirituality, but there's also plenty on transhumanism, mad science, discordia, illumination, and magick.

Astral Projection
http://www.lava.net/~goodin/astral.html

Don't go out of your mind, go out of your body. Here's how to do it, and land back on your feet.

Bacon Worship Page
http://ithaca.gateways.com/homepages/pmb/announce.html

One man's meat.

Blue Dog Can Count
http://hp8.ini.cmu.edu:5550/bdf.html

Give the blue dog an equation and hear her bark the answer.

The Butt Page
http://www.well.com/www/cynsa/newbutt.html

Highlights from Surgery Magazine, complete with X-rays, confirming the danger of having too much fun in the privacy of your own home.

Church of the Subgenius
http://sunsite.unc.edu/subgenius/

Pipe-puffing Bob's three-fisted surreal preaching. Beyond description.

Exploding Heads
http://www.mit.edu:8001/people/mkgray/head-explode.html

Worried that your head might explode? These tips will help you identify early symptoms.

Faking UFOs
http://www.strw.leidenuniv.nl/~vdmeulen/Articles/UFOfake.html

Create your own crop circles to amuse new-agers and the press.

Fortean Times

http://forteana.mic.dundee.ac.uk/ft/

Fans of strange, unexplained, and improbable phenomena will relish every entry in this taste of the UK monthly *Fortean Times*. Read about spontaneous combustion, alien sex-beasts, flying saucers, zombies, Uri Geller, and surfing to the stars on warped space. Highlights of the last 20 years include bizarre photographs, such as the "magnetic man" and the "kitten with wings." You'll surely want more.

Gallery of the Absurd

http://omni.cc.purdue.edu/~royald/gallery.htm

Strange ways to sell strange stuff.

Backpackable Portable
Goose Decoy Blind
- Backpackable
- 2 minute setup
- Monster Mag Shell
- Ultimate Concealment!

Huge size pulls in wary birds from long distances. Comfortable to hunt from 10 feet long overall. 7½"L x 31"H x 42"W blind cavity provides excellent concealment. Pin-hinged wings open for entry and shooting. 2 mesh windows and opening in lower neck area let you see out and call through. Made of reinforced fiberglass. Snap hasps and hinge pins for fast setup and take-down. Comes with backpack. Ship Wt. 43 lbs.
#6120-H448 - ~~$399.99~~ Sale $379.99

Geek Site of the Day

http://www.owlnet.rice.edu/~indigo/gsotd/

Further proof that geek is tres hip. Each day, a new obsessive. Always entertaining.

George Goble's Page

http://ghg.ecn.purdue.edu

Engineer George demonstrates the power user way to light a BBQ.

Glenfiddich's Guide to the Weird and Wonderful

http://www.glenfiddich.co.uk

Twice-weekly-updated links to the weird and wonderful site listings in the UK Net rag, *The Web*.

Hutt River Province

http://www.wps.com.au/hutriver/hut1.htm

Leonard Casley got such a raw deal on his 1969 wheat quota that he officially seceded his 18,500-acre property from West Australia. The whole thing got so tied up in colonial red tape that, to this day, no-one has marched in to reclaim the territory. Consequently HRH Prince Leonard thinks it's a quite a lark to hand out passports, driver's licences and honors to anyone who asks. Just fill out the forms.

Hyper-Weirdness

http://phenom.physics.wisc.edu/~shalizi/hyper-weird/

Signposts the highway to some of the Web's most impassioned wells of weirdness. You name it: UFOs, cults, political action groups, extropians, fringe science, fantasy, and drugs. Water always seems to find its own level.

Infamous Exploding Whale

http://www.xmission.com/~grue/whale/

Easy. Take one beached whale carcass, add half a ton of dynamite, turn on the video and run. In this case not all went as planned.

Klingon Language Institute

http://www.kli.org/klihome.html

With multimedia language tutorials like this, it's a wonder Klingon isn't more widely spoken. In fact, if Captain James T. Kirk had a better grip on it perhaps the Enterprise would be still in one piece. Oh, and don't miss Hamlet restored to the Bard's native tongue.

Mrs Silk's Cross Dressing Magazine

http://www.cityscape.co.uk/users/av73/

Mrs Silk can furnish you with a variety of products to ensure that when you do step out of the closet, it's with style.

News of the Weird

http://nine.org/notw

> Chuck Shepard's syndicated column of bizarre news. Get it here, or subscribe to have it delivered direct to your mailbox, weekly.

Ranjit's Lunch

http://moonmilk.volcano.org/miscellany/old-lunch.html

> Fascinating itemization of Ranjit Bhatnager's diet, with links to Sho Kuwamoto's, Ben Cox's, and other crucial lunchers.

Steps in Overcoming Urges

http://www.tezcat.com/~kritikal/masturbation.html

> Having trouble leaving it alone? Here's timely advice.

Strawberry Poptart Blow Torches

http://www.cbi.tamucc.edu/~pmichaud/toast/

> Insert Poptart, depress lever, aim, fire! This innovative experiment turns an innocent kitchen appliance into a deadly incendiary device. As long as you adhere to strict laboratory procedures, no-one need get hurt.

Toilet-train Your Cat

http://www.sff.net/people/
karawynn/cat/toiletcat.htp

> How to point pusskins at the porcelain. Literally.

Tango

http://www.tango.co.uk

> Subliminal inducements to drink orange Tango embedded in pages and pages of entertaining nonsense.

Tasty Insect Recipes

http://www.ent.iastate.edu/
Misc/InsectsAsFood.html

> Dig in to such delights as

Bug Blox, Banana Worm Bread, Rootworm Beetle Dip, and
Chocolate Chirpie Chip Cookies (with crickets).

Virtual Presents

http://www.virtualpresents.com

Why waste money on real gifts when, after all, it's only the
thought that counts?

Vomitus Maximus Museum

http://www.primenet.com/vomitus/

Take heed. Steve Connett's gallery of surreal sadism is not in
particularly good taste. It's one of the most popular galleries
on the Net, and the one most likely to invoke a strong
reaction. Don't say you weren't warned.

WearCam

http://www-white.media.mit.edu/~steve/netcam.html

Steve has a Netcam fixed to his head. You see what he sees.
But that won't stop him having fun.

What Miles is Watching

http://www.csua.berkeley.edu/~milesm/ontv.html

So what is Miles watching on TV? Tune in to see the current
screen shots. But shouldn't you be out making some friends?

Weird World

http://monkey.hooked.net/m/chuck/

If you like what you see, you're in luck because Chuck's keen
to sell it off. But what exactly will you do with the likes of
David Koresh's business card or copies of Pee Wee Herman's
arrest report? And for the most disturbing real-life horror
story you'll ever read, try the ill-fated Shuttle Challenger's
final transcript.

Why Cats Paint

http://www.netlink.co.nz/~monpa/

New paintings by emerging feline artists, how to spot fakes,
updates from the Museum of Non-primate Art, moggy
masters caught on video, and merchandise including, and
inspired by, the best-selling book of the same name.

A Guide to Newsgroups

Whatever you're into – hobbies, sports, politics, music, philosophy, business, and a thousand other pursuits – there's sure to be a Usenet Newsgroup devoted to it. In fact, you might be surprised to discover how many other people share your interests. Usenet Newsgroups provide a forum to meet like-minded people, exchange views, and pose those perplexing questions that have been bugging you for years. And the groups are as much yours as anyone's, so once you've got the feel of what a group's about, don't hold back on participating.

We cover the practical stuff in the section beginning on p.79. The following pages are brief directories covering about 700 of the most interesting Newsgroups on Usenet, with the addresses to reach them. That figure of 700 might seem a lot, but it's in fact only around three percent of the total number of Newsgroups. Not that anyone knows exactly how many Newsgroups there are, as many are only propagated within a local area and new groups are added every day.

Excluded from our directories are the Newsgroups devoted to "adult interests" – sex, mainly, either talking about it or looking at it. If that's your bag, you don't need our help to browse the alt.sex and alt.binaries.pictures series (or such as your Internet Provider supplies on its newsfeed), or the alt.personals hierarchy. If you do browse the murkier areas of sex Newsgroups – or the rackets discussed in the pirate software (.warez and .cracks), phone tampering (.2600), or other mischief-making groups – be aware that just because this stuff is readily available on the Net doesn't make it legal. So don't put anything on your hard drive that you wouldn't like to defend in front of a jury. And be aware, too, that downloading pirate programs can leave nasty viruses . . .

NEWSGROUPS DIRECTORY

For ease of reference, we've broken down Newsgroups into the following categories:

Arts, Architecture, and Graphics

ART

ARCHITECTURE

GRAPHICS AND LAYOUT

Authors and Books

REFERENCE

DISCUSSION

Business and Finance

BUSINESS

FINANCE

misc.invest.stocks	Stock market tips
misc.invest.technical	Predicting trends
sci.econ	Economic science
uk.finance	UK financial issues

Buying and Selling

alt.cdworld.marketplace	Trading compact discs
alt.co-ops	Collaborative buying
alt.forsale	Step right up
ba.market.misc	Bay Area trading post
demon.adverts	UK network's classifieds
la.forsale	Los Angeles trading
misc.forsale	Trading hierarchy
rec.arts.books.marketplace	Online books trading
rec.arts.sf.marketplace	Science fiction trading
rec.arts.comics.marketplace	Buy and sell comics
rec.audio.marketplace	Low price hi-fi
rec.autos.marketplace	Trade your dream machine
rec.bicycles.marketplace	Buying and selling bikes
rec.music.makers.marketplace	Instrument trading
rec.music.marketplace	Record and CD trading
rec.photo.marketplace	Camera trading
rec.radio.swap	Trading radios
uk.forsale	UK trading post

Comedy and Jokes

alt.adjective.noun.verb.verb.verb	Usenet wordplay
alt.binaries.pictures.tasteless	Spoil your appetite
alt.comedy.british	Best of British chuckles
alt.comedy.slapstick.3-stooges	Pick three
alt.comedy.standup	Comedy industry gossip
alt.devilbunnies	They're cute, but want our planet
alt.fan.monty-python	Cleese and chums
alt.flame	Insults and abuse

Comics

Computer games

Computer technology

MISCELLANEOUS

COMPUTER HARDWARE

comp.sys.laptops	Portable computing
comp.sys.mac.hardware	Macintosh computers
comp.sys.powerpc	RISC processor-driven computers
comp.sys.sgi.misc	Silicon Graphics forum
comp.sys.sun.misc	Sun Microsystems forum

COMPUTER SECURITY

alt.comp.virus	Computer vaccines
alt.security	Keeping hackers out
alt.security.espionage	Cyberspies
alt.security.pgp	Pretty good privacy encryption
comp.society.privacy	Technology and privacy
comp.virus	Virus alerts and solutions
sci.crypt	Data encryption methods

COMPUTER SOFTWARE

alt.comp.shareware	Try before you buy software
biz.comp.software	Commercial software postings
comp.binaries.ibm.pc	PC software postings
comp.binaries.ibm.pc.wanted	Requests for PC programs
comp.binaries.mac	Macintosh programs
comp.binaries.ms-windows	Microsoft Windows programs
comp.binaries.newton	Apple Newton files
comp.binaries.os2	OS/2 programs
comp.databases	Data management
comp.sys.mac.apps	Macintosh software
comp.os.ms-windows.apps.comm	Windows comms software
comp.os.ms-windows.apps.misc	Windows software
comp.sources.sun	Sun workstation software
comp.sources.wanted	Software and fixes

NETWORKING AND EMAIL

alt.winsock	PC TCP/IP stacks
alt.winsock.trumpet	Tuning Trumpet Winsock
comp.dcom.lans.misc	Local area networking

OPERATING SYSTEMS

Crafts, Gardening, and Hobbies

CRAFTS

GARDENING

HOBBIES

Dance and Theater

Drugs

Education

Employment

Fashion

Food

Health and Medicine

History, Archeology, and Anthropology

```
sci.archaeology ................................................ Can you dig it?
soc.history ................................................ Looking backwards
```

International culture

Almost every culture/ethnic group has a soc.culture and/or an alt.culture group. If yours doesn't, start one!

```
alt.chinese.text ........................... Chinese character discussion
alt.culture .......................................... Cultural forum hierarchy
alt.culture.saudi ......................................... Arabian might
alt.culture.us.asian-indian ................... Native American culture
soc.culture .......................................... Cultural forum hierarchy
soc.culture.african.american ................... Afro-American affairs
soc.culture.yugoslavia ........................... All ex-Yugoslav factions
uk.misc ................................................ All things British
```

Internet Stuff

BBS LISTINGS

```
alt.bbs ................................................ Bulletin board systems
alt.bbs.internet ....................... BBSs hooked up to the Internet
alt.bbs.lists ................................ Regional BBS listings
```

CYBERSPACE

```
alt.cybercafes ......................................... New café announcements
alt.cyberpunk ........................................... High-tech low-life
alt.cyberpunk.tech ........................... Cyberpunk technology
alt.cyberspace ........................................... The final frontier
sci.virtual-worlds ........................................... Virtual reality
```

IRC

```
alt.irc ........................... Internet Relay Chat material
alt.irc.questions ................................ Solving IRC queries
```

NEWSGROUPS

SERVICE PROVIDERS

WORLD WIDE WEB

Legal

Movies and TV

rec.arts.disney	Taking the Mickey.
rec.arts.drwho	Help conquer the Daleks
rec.arts.movies	Movies and movie-making hierarchy
rec.arts.movies.reviews	Films reviewed
rec.arts.sf.movies	Science fiction movies
rec.arts.sf.tv.babylon5	Babylon 5 discussion
rec.arts.startrek.current	New Star Trek shows
rec.arts.startrek.fandom	Trek conventions and trinkets
rec.arts.tv	Television talk
rec.arts.tv.soaps	Parallel lives hierarchy
rec.arts.tv.uk	UK television talk
rec.video.production	Making home movies

Music

There are hundreds more specialist groups under the alt.music and rec.music hierarchies.

GENERAL

alt.cd-rom.reviews	Read before you buy
rec.music.info	Music resources on the Net
rec.music.misc	Music to any ears
rec.music.reviews	General music criticism
rec.music.video	Budding Beavis and Buttheads

POP

alt.elvis.sighting	Keep looking
alt.exotic-music	Strange moods
alt.fan.frank-zappa	The late Bohemian cultural minister
alt.fan.rolf-harris	King of the stylophone
alt.gothic	Dying fashion
alt.music.bootlegs	Illicit recordings
alt.music.brian-eno	Eno's worldly activities
alt.music.hardcore	Head banging
alt.music.kylie-minogue	Is she Elvis?

alt.music.lyrics	Spreading the words
alt.music.peter-gabriel	From Genesis to the Real World
alt.music.prince	The artist formerly named after a dog
alt.music.progressive	Almost modern music
alt.rock-n-roll	Counterpart to alt.sex and alt.drugs
alt.rock-n-roll.metal	Heavy, man
alt.rock-n-roll.oldies	The golden years
rec.music.dylan	Rolling Stone cover model
rec.music.gdead	Jerry lives on

INDIE AND DANCE

alt.music.alternative	Indie talk
alt.music.alternative.female	Indie women
alt.music.canada	Canadian indie scene
alt.music.independent	Alternative pop
alt.music.dance	Water? E? Okay, let's go
alt.music.hardcore	Serious punks
alt.music.house	Hip hop to the grocery shop
alt.music.synthpop	Keyboard capers
alt.music.techno	Repetitive beats
alt.punk	The attitude and the music
alt.rave	Late-night loonies
rec.music.ambient	Soundscapes
rec.music.industrial	Metal machine music

RAP

alt.rap	Tuneful nattering
alt.rap.sucks	Fans of singing

WORLD MUSIC AND FOLK

alt.music.jewish	Klezmer developments
alt.music.world	Tango to Tuvan throatsinging
rec.music.afro-latin	African, Latin, and more
rec.music.celtic	Irish music mostly
rec.music.folk	Folk/world music/singer-songwriters

rec.music.indian.classical .... Raga sagas
rec.music.reggae .... Rasta nation

COUNTRY

rec.music.country.western .... Both types, C & W

JAZZ

rec.music.bluenote .... Jazz and the blues

CLASSICAL

rec.music.classical .... Classical music
rec.music.early .... Early music

MUSIC MAKING

alt.guitar .... You axed for it
alt.music.makers.electronic .... Electric friends
rec.music.makers.guitar .... Six string along
rec.music.makers.synth .... Synthesize your mind

HI-FI AND RECORDING

rec.audio.high-end .... Audiophile equipment
rec.audio.opinion .... Hi-fi reviews
rec.audio.pro .... Professional sound recording

MUSIC UTILITIES

alt.binaries.multimedia .... Sound and vision files
alt.binaries.sounds.midi .... Music making files
alt.binaries.sounds.music .... Music files
alt.binaries.sounds.utilities .... Sound programs

Mysticism and Philosophy

alt.astrology .... Soothsaying by starlight
alt.chinese.fengshui .... Mystical interior design
alt.consciousness .... Philosophical discourse

Pets

Politics and Media

CURRENT AFFAIRS/POLITICAL ACTION

POLITICAL THEORY

talk.politics.misc .... Get your piece of the action

SEXUAL POLITICS

alt.abortion.inequity .... Whose choice?
alt.culture.riot-grrrls .... Angry femmes
alt.dads-rights .... Custody battles
alt.fan.camille-paglia .... Flamboyant feminist
alt.feminazis .... Feminist flames
alt.feminism .... Sisters for sisters
alt.politics.homosexuality .... Gay power
soc.feminism .... Gender war zone
soc.men .... Men wanting more
soc.women .... Women wanting more

US PARTY POLITICS

alt.impeach.clinton .... Presidential peeves
alt.politics.democrats .... Democrat party discussion
alt.politics.usa.congress .... US congressional affairs
alt.politics.usa.republican .... Republican party reptiles
alt.president.clinton .... Spotlight on Clinton

MEDIA

alt.fan.noam-chomsky .... Media watchdogs
alt.journalism .... Hack chat
alt.journalism.freelance .... Unemployed lines
alt.news-media .... Don't believe the hype
alt.quotations .... The things people say
bit.listserv.words-l .... English language mailing list
biz.clarinet .... ClariNet newsfeed news
biz.clarinet.sample .... ClariNet news samples
uk.media .... UK media issues

Psychological support

For more support groups, see also "Health."

GENERAL PSYCHOLOGY

alt.psychology.nlp .... Neurolinguistic programming
alt.sci.sociology .... Human watching
sci.psychology.misc .... Troubleshooting behavior
sci.psychology.personality .... Why you are you

SUPPORT AND EXPLORATION

alt.adoption .... Matching parents and children
alt.child-support .... Coping with split families
alt.cuddle .... Drop in for a hug
alt.good.morning .... Big sister of alt.cuddle
alt.homosexual .... Talk to other gays
alt.infertility .... Difficulty conceiving
alt.lefthanders .... Gaucherie
alt.life.sucks .... Pessimism
alt.love .... Mushy stuff
alt.med.cfs .... Chronic fatigue syndrome
alt.med.fibromyalgia .... Coping with fibromyalgia
alt.missing-kids .... Locating missing children
alt.parenting.solutions .... Dealing with kids
alt.recovery.aa .... Sobering up
alt.romance .... Love, exciting and new
alt.sexual.abuse.recovery .... Support for sexual trauma
alt.support .... Dealing with crisis
alt.support.anxiety-panic .... Coping with panic attacks
alt.support.arthritis .... Easing joint pain
alt.support.asthma .... Breathe easier
alt.support.attn-deficit .... Attention deficit disorder
alt.support.big-folks .... Big is better
alt.support.cancer .... Cancer news and support
alt.support.depression .... Serious cheering-up

Radio and Telecommunications

Religion

Science

GENERAL

ELECTRONICS

ENERGY AND ENVIRONMENT

alt.energy.renewable .... Alternative fuels
sci.bio.ecology .... The balance of nature
sci.energy .... Fuel for talk
sci.environment .... Ecological science
talk.environment .... Not paving the earth
uk.environment .... British ecological action

ENGINEERING

sci.engr .... Engineering sciences
sci.engr.biomed .... Biomedical engineering
sci.engr.chem .... Chemical engineering
sci.engr.mech .... Mechanical engineering

GEOLOGY

sci.geo.geology .... Earth science
sci.geo.meteorology .... Weather or not
sci.geo.satellite-nav .... Satellite navigation systems

Space and Aliens

alt.alien.research .... Identifying flying objects
alt.alien.visitors .... Here come the marchin' martians
sci.astro .... Staring into space
sci.space.news .... Announcements from the final frontier
sci.space.policy .... Ruling the cosmos
sci.space.shuttle .... Space research news

Sports

alt.fishing .... Advice and tall tales
alt.sports.baseball .... Baseball hierarchy split by clubs
alt.sports.basketball .... Basketball hierarchy split by clubs
alt.sports.darts .... Pub sport
alt.sports.football .... Gridiron hierarchy split by clubs

Transport

Travel

Software
Roundup

There's no better place to find the latest Net software than on the Net itself. This chapter lists a selection of the most popular and essential programs, which will get you started – and then some – on a PC or Mac. Most of them are shareware, often with superior commercial versions. As the Net is constantly evolving, it's worth checking in often to keep up to date.

How to find the software files

We've given **Web locations** (when available) for files to download, so you can read about the program first to decide if it's what you want and make sure you get the latest version. If addresses specified prove invalid (they change frequently), run the program's name through a search engine to see if you can trace it – see p.110. Of course, you'll have to get a Web browser first to do this, and if you haven't been supplied with one, that should be the first thing you download.

FTP addresses are given in **URL format** so they can also be entered into your browser. On stand-alone FTP clients, leave off the ftp:// and separate the host name from the directory path. We've omitted filenames, as being mostly betas, they'll change.

When you log in, look around the directory for a README.txt, INDEX.txt, or similar file. Click on it to find what's in the directory and if the file you're after isn't there, try other directories. When you've identifed the file, double-click to download it, making sure you've chosen "binary transfer." Once you've received it, transfer it to a temporary directory or folder ready for **decompression**. Unless it's a self-extracting file (.exe or .sea), you'll need an archiving program such as WinZip or Stuffit (see p.75). When you've extracted the file, read accompanying text files for instructions on how to install the program. It's usually a matter of clicking on install.exe or setup.exe in Windows File Manager, or on an install icon on the Mac.

Most programs are now being released in **16-bit and 32-bit versions**. If you're running Windows 95, NT, OS/2, or a PowerMac, go for the faster 32-bit versions. These programs will not work with 16-bit operating systems like Windows 3.x or earlier Macs, nor 16-bit TCP/IP stacks like Trumpet Winsock and many of the ones that ISPs and Online Services provide. Check first, and if you need to do so, it's better to upgrade the stack rather than download more 16-bit software.

Software programs in the pages following have been graded as: ★ Recommended   ★★ Essential

---

Chat

CU-SEEME .... PC, MAC

http://www.cu-seeme.com
Video/audio conferencing via the Net. Better at high
bandwidths.

★★ HOMER .... MAC

http://mrcnext.cso.uiuc.edu/pub/info-mac/comm/MacTCP
Groovy IRC client with inbuilt text-to-voice converter.

★ INTERNET PHONE .... PC

http://www.vocaltec.com/
Real-time Internet telephony over IRC.

IRCLE .... MAC

http://www.xs4all.nl/~ircle/
Audio-capable IRC client with handy common phrase
shortcuts.

NETPHONE .... MAC

http://www.emagic.com
Internet telephone for the Mac.

★★ NETMEETING .... PC

http://www.microsoft.com/ie/conf/
Real-time voice, applications-sharing, and multi-user
whiteboard.

NETSCAPE CHAT .... PC, MAC

http://home.netscape.com/comprod/netscape_products.html
Netscape's simple IRC add-on.

PIRCH .... PC

http://www.bcpl.lib.md.us/~frappa/pirch.html
Snazzy IRC client with built-in multimedia player.

SPEAK FREELY .... PC

http://www.fourmilab.ch/speakfree/windows/

Internet telephone with encryption and show-your-face feature.

★ **THE PALACE** .... PC, MAC

http://mansion.thepalace.com/downloads.html

Chat and frolic in interactive animated rooms.

★ **VDOPHONE** .... PC

http://www.vdolive.com/vdophone/

Full-colour video telephony even over a modem.

★ **VISUAL IRC** .... PC

http://apollo3.com/~acable/virc.html

Audio/visual/text IRC client with features to boot.

★★ **WEBPHONE** .... PC

http://www.itelco.com/

Polished point-to-point Net telephony with encryption and smart online directory.

★★ **WORLDS CHAT/ALPHA WORLD/JUMANJI** .... PC

http://www.worlds.net/

Join and build 3-D Net colonies.

★★ **WS-IRC/WS-IRC VIDEO** .... PC

ftp://papa.indstate.edu/winsock-l/winirc/

Solid IRC client with added audiovisual capacity.

Combination Suites

All-in-one packages are rapidly becoming more acceptable alternatives to the eternal Net software chase. CyberJack and Emissary, for example, can be automatically upgraded online. All are better than nothing, but none beat the best mix-and-match combinations.

CYBERDOG .... MAC

http://cyberdog.apple.com

Apple's me-too browser, newsreader, FTP, email,
Telnet package.

★ CYBERJACK .... PC

http://www.cyberjack.com/

All-you-can-eat Win95 bundle, complete with wizards
and registry tampering.

★ EMISSARY .... PC

http://www.twg.com/

An often amazing feature-chocked bundle muddled
together. Worth downloading as a puzzle.

★ TURNPIKE .... PC

http://www.turnpike.com

Demon's simple, but adequate, turnkey dial-up pack.
You source the browser.

File Transfer and Handling

ANARCHIE .... MAC

http://ftp.share.com/pub/peterlewis/

Multitasking file searches, FTP-ready results.

★★ CUTEFTP .... PC

http://papa.indstate.edu:8888/CuteFTP/

Constantly improving file transfer client.

★★ DISINFECTANT .... MAC

http://ftp.acns.nwu.edu/pub/disinfectant/

Anti-virus scanner.

★★ FETCH .... MAC

http://www.dartmouth.edu/pages/softdev/fetch.html

Multiple connection, drag-and-drop file transfer with automatic decoding.

★★ STUFFIT EXPANDER/DROPSTUFF .... PC, MAC
ftp://ftp.scruz.net/users/aladdin/public/
http://www.aladdinsys.com/
Essential drag-and-drop decoding/archiving tool for Mac/PC.

UULITE .... MAC
http://ftp.hiwaay.net/pub/mac/utils/
Convert UUencoded files into binaries.

★★ VIRUSCAN .... PC
http://www.mcafee.com
McAfee's top-notch virus scanner.

★★ WINZIP .... PC
http://www.winzip.com/
Must-have PC file compression/decompression utility.

WS ARCHIE .... PC
http://dspace.dial.pipex.com/town/square/cc83/
Preconfigured with Archie addresses. Needs separate FTP client.

★ WS-FTP .... PC
http://www.csra.net/junodj/
Popular file transfer client.

HTML Editors

When checking out HTML editing programs, don't forget that Netscape's Gold Series has its own built-in. It's not perfect but it works – a comment that can be applied to most of the specialized programs below. Microsoft's home page (http://www.microsoft.com) has several tools and add-ons for viewing and converting its applications.

AUTOWEB .... MAC
http://www.hotwired.com/userland/autohome.html
Automatically creates a Web site from folders of text.

★★ BB EDIT.. MAC
http://www.barebones.com
A fine hands-on HTML editor for Macs, with an array
of features. It's not WISYWYG but gets around it with
a useful preview function. Good T-shirt, too.

★★ HOTDOG/PRO .... PC
ftp://ftp.sausage.com/pub/
The best HTML editor for PCs, though it's still really
a cut and paste affair.

★★ HOTMETAL/PRO .... PC, MAC
http://www.sq.com/
Improving commercial WYSIWYG HTML editor.

INTERNET PUBLISHER .... PC
http://wp.novell.com/elecpub/fawpip.htm
Add HTML capabilities to WordPerfect.

★ MAP THIS! .... PC
http://galadriel.ecaetc.ohio-state.edu/tc/mt/
Image map editor.

★ PAGEMILL .... PC, MAC
http://www.adobe.com/prodindex/pagemill/main.html
As WYSIWYG as HTML editors get.

THE WEB MEDIA PUBLISHER .... PC
ftp://ftp.wbmedia.com/
Features include basic Java, Shockwave and Internet
Explorer support.

★ **WEBFORMS** .... PC
  http://www.q-d.com/
  Friendly Web form creation tool.

★ **WEBIMAGE/GRAPHX VIEWER** .... PC
  http://www.group42.com/
  Graphic tool aimed at Web page designers.

Mail

People who use **Eudora** swear by it – as do those who
use **Pegasus** and **Microsoft Exchange/Internet Mail and
News**. We prefer the commercial version of Eudora,
which is quick, reliable, simple to use, and lets you
know what's happening. **Netscape's** email program
works fine, too, but like Exchange gives little progress
feedback and isn't suited to heavy use.

★★ **EUDORA/EUDORA LIGHT** .... PC, MAC
  http://www.qualcomm.com/
  Reliable mail client, and one that's perhaps even
  worth the commercial upgrade.

★ **MAIL-CHECK** .... PC
  http://www.starbase21.com/winsock.html
  Background checks multiple mail accounts.

★★ **MICROSOFT MAIL & NEWS** .... PC
  http://www.microsoft.com/
  Upgrade clunky old Exchange to handle Internet
  mail or use the excellent and improving Internet Mail
  and News (which also comes bundles with Internet
  Explorer). Check this site regularly for patches, fixes,
  and add-ons.

★ PEGASUS MAIL .... PC, MAC
http://www.cuslm.ca/pegasus/
Feature-packed, supports PGP, and comes free. A
little unintuitive but worth considering.

★ PGP ENCRYPTOR INTERFACE .... PC
ftp://ftp.aimnet.com/pub/users/jnavas/winpmail/
Send secret messages via Pegasus mail.

VOICE EMAIL .... PC
http://www.bonzi.com/
Add voicemail capabilities to your mail client.

Newsreaders

You can get away with Netscape as a Newsreader for
Usenet, but it's cranky, and you'll have less frustration
with a tailor-made program. Microsoft's Internet Mail
and News, which comes with Internet Explorer, is pretty
good. Others to pick from include . . .

★★ AGENT/FREE AGENT .... PC
http://www.forteinc.com/forte/agent/agent.htm
Queues multiple articles and auto-decode binaries.
Unrivaled.

NEWSHOPPER .... MAC
http://www.demon.co.uk/sw15/
Offline commercial newsreader with superior
filtering.

★ NEWSWATCHER .... MAC
http://ftp.acns.nwu.edu/pub/newswatcher
Free automatic binary-decoding newsreader.

NEWS XPRESS .... PC
http://www.malch.com/nxfaq.html
Fast, but single-threaded, newsreader with smart
filtering and decoding.

NUNTIUS .... MAC
http://guru.med.cornell.edu/~aaron/nuntius/nuntius.html
Free multitasking newsreader.

SMART NEWSREADER .... PC
http://www.intel.com/iaweb/aplets/newsread.htm
Slow reader with highly advanced search, filter, and
kill capabilities.

Plug-ins

Plug-ins are meant to extend your browser's capacities.
Most are designed to be used with **Netscape**, but should
work with **Internet Explorer** and a few other browsers
as well. Some, like the increasingly essential **Real Audio**,
also have stand-alone versions that are useful when you
don't have the system resources to open a browser. This
list is only a small sample. For close to the full range,
see: http://www.browserwatch.com

★ ACROBAT AMBER .... PC, MAC
http://www.adobe.com/Amber/
View PDF files within Netscape. This was big news
for a while (it seems to be becoming redundant) and
browsing the Web you may come across rich text
pages posted in this format.

CARBON COPY .... PC, MAC
http://www.microcom.com/cc/ccdnload.htm
Remote control another computer via the Net.

COOLFUSION — MAC

http://webber.iterated.com/coolfusn/download/cf-loadp.htm

Inline streaming multimedia player.

EARTHTIME — PC

http://www.starfishsoftware.com/

World time clock within Netscape.

ENVOY — MAC

http://www.twcorp.com/plugin.htm

View Envoy documents from Netscape on or offline.

★ HISTORYTREE — PC

http://www.smartbrowser.com

A useful alternative to Netscape's flawed history files.

KEYVIEW — PC

http://www.ftp.com/mkt_info/evals/kv_dl.html

Convert, view, and print about 200 different file
formats.

LISTENUP — MAC

http://snow.cit.cornell.edu/noon/ListenUp.html

Use Apple's PlainTalk to activate Web commands by
speech.

LOOK@ME — PC, MAC

http://collaborate.farallon.com/www/look/ldownload.html

View another online computer's desktop.

★★ REAL AUDIO — PC, MAC

http://www.realaudio.com/

Essential real-time sound add-on or stand-alone to
listen to sound samples or Internet radio.

★★ SHOCKWAVE .... PC, MAC

http://www.macromedia.com/Tools/Shockwave/

View inline Macromedia Director movies.

VIZSCAPE

http://www.superscape.com/

Explore high-res 3D worlds.

TALKER .... MAC

http://www.albany.net/~wtudor/

Reads Web pages aloud via Apple's text-to-speech
conversion.

★★ VDOLIVE .... PC, MAC

http://www.VDOLive.com/newplug.htm

Impressive live video viewer, but no threat to TV yet.

★★ WIRL .... PC, MAC

http://www.vream.com/3wirl.html

View and create virtual worlds.

Servers

Setting up a server using your own PC or Mac is easy
with the right software. Just read the help files.

ALIBABA .... PC

http://www.csm.co.at/csm/alibaba.htm

Easy-to-install Web server.

★ FTP SERV-U .... PC

http://CatSoft.dorm.duke.edu/features.htm

Set up your own desktop FTP server within minutes.

MACHTTP .... MAC

http://www.biap.com/machttp/machttp_software.html

Mac Web server.

NETPRESENZ .... MAC

    http://ftp.share.com//pub/peterlewis/
    FTP, Gopher, and Web server.

SLMAIL/WINSMTP .... PC

    http://www.seattlelab.com/prodsmtp.html/
    SMTP/POP3 mail server with auto-responders and
    mailing lists.

★ **WEBSITE** .... PC

    http://website.ora.com/
    Well-regarded, undaunting, 32-bit Web server.

★ **WFTPD** .... PC

    ftp://ftp.coast.net/SimTel/win95/winsock/
    An excellent FTP server.

Sound and Vision

It's useful to keep an armory of audio, graphics, and
video players that activate when you click on the file.
Netscape and Explorer can play most multimedia types,
but dedicated programs provide more options. See also
under "plug-ins."

★★ **ACDSEE** .... PC

    http://vvv.com:80/acd/
    Extraordinarily fast graphics file viewer.

INTERNET WAVE .... PC

    http://www.vocaltec.com/iwave.htm
    Real-time audio from the makers of Internet Phone.

JASCAPTURE .... PC

    http://www.jasc.com/pcs.html
    Take screen snapshots.

JPEGVIEW — MAC
http://ftp.luth.se:/pub/mac/graphics/graphicsutil/
View most image file formats.

LVIEW PRO — PC
http://world.std.com/~mmedia/lviewp.html
Basic image editor and simple, but slow, viewer.

MEDIAWRANGLER — PC
http://www.altavista.com/
Versatile multimedia design tool. Includes image-mapping HTML.

MIDI GATE — PC
http://www.prs.net/midigate.html
MIDI music file player.

★ NET TOOB — PC
ftp://duplexx.com/pub/duplexx/
Versatile viewer for MPEG, AVI, and QuickTime movie files.

★ PAINT SHOP PRO — PC
http://www.jasc.com/psp.html
For heavy-duty graphics manipulation.

★★ QUICKTIME — PC, MAC
http://quicktime.apple.com/
Play QuickTime (.MOV) movie files.

★★ QUICKTIME VR — PC, MAC
http://qtvr3.quicktime.apple.com/toys/WinOS/
View 360-degree images.

SOUND APP — MAC
http://ftp.utexas.edu/pub/mac/sound/
Play most sound file formats.

★ SPARKLE .... MAC

http://www.znet.com/mac/sparkle.html

Play QuickTime and MPEG movies.

★★ STREAMWORKS .... PC

http://204.62.160.251/sw-winclient/software/

Real-time audio and MPEG video on demand.

★ TRUESPEECH .... PC

http://www.dspg.com/

Streaming audio comparable to Real Audio. Uses
encoded WAV files.

VIDEO FOR WINDOWS .... PC

ftp://ftp.microsoft.com/Softlib/MSLFILES/

AVI playing driver for Windows 3.x Media Player.

★ VUEPRINT .... PC

http://www.hamrick.com/

Manipulate oodles of image file types, even zipped,
coded, and video files.

TCP/IP, Timers, and Dialers

AUTOWINNET .... PC

http://www.computek.net:80/physics/

Automates FTP, news, mail, and Web tasks.

CRAIG'S CONNECT MONITOR .... PC

ftp://ftp.enterprise.net/pub/mirror/winsock-l/time_log/

Monitors time spent online.

INTERNET CONFIG .... MAC

http://ftp.tidbits.com/pub/tidbits/tisk/tcp/

Configure your Net preferences centrally.

INTERSLIP
MAC

http://ftp.intercon.com/intercon/sales/InterSLIP/
SLIP enabler and dialer.

MACPPP
MAC

ftp://ftp.merit.edu/internet.tools/ppp/mac/
http://macsolutions.interstate.net/macppphelp.html
Use in conjunction with MacTCP to enable PPP
connectivity.

MACPPP TIMER
MAC

http://ftp.tidbits.com/pub/tidbits/tisk/tcp/
Track online charges.

MACTCP UPDATERS
MAC

http://www.info.apple.com/
Update MacTCP to the latest version.

MACTCP WATCHER
MAC

http://redback.cs.uwa.edu.au/Others/PeterLewis
TCP/IP testing tools such as Ping and DNS lookup.

★ RAS PLUS
PC

http://www.lambsoftware.com/
Win95 launchpad and time monitor.

TRUMPET WINSOCK
PC

http://www.trumpet.com.au/wsk/winsock.htm
Reliable TCP/IP socket for Windows. Includes Ping,
TCPMeter, and Hop.

★WS-WATCH
PC

ftp://papa.indstate.edu/winsock-l/Misc-Winsock/
Network monitor plus Ping, Trace, Whois, Finger,
FTP, and more.

Telnet

Telnet is a powerful tool that enables you to **log into a remote computer** via the Net to run programs or access local data on UNIX servers (common in universities). Although its technology is useful, there's less and less call for it, as services move on to the Web and more tasks become automated – and that's a blessing, as it requires learning a few UNIX commands.

Browsers need to be configured to launch a separate Telnet client in order for Telnet Web links to work. To log on to a remote server, enter the server's address, and then follow the prompts. It may require a log-in and password, which you should presumably have. If you don't, try hitting return instead. If that doesn't work, you'll have to go back to where you got the address and get the log-in details.

COMET .... MAC
http://ftp.cit.cornell.edu/pub/mac/comm/
Efficient, feature-packed Telnet client.

CRT .... PC
http://www.vandyke.com/vandyke/crt/
Combined Rlogin and Telnet.

★ NETTERM .... PC
http://starbase.neosoft.com/~zkrr01/netterm.html
Supports remote host file editing, Zmodem, and Kermit.

Web Browsers

The best advice in choosing a browser is to get the latest **Netscape** and **Internet Explorer** betas and stick with whichever you prefer. If downloading huge upgrade files each time Netscape expires gets to you, try buying an official release; it may not have as many features, but it may be more stable. For a full list of browsers see http://www.browserwatch.com

★★ MICROSOFT INTERNET EXPLORER .... PC, MAC
ftp://ftp.microsoft.com
http://www.microsoft.com/ie/
The Microsoft browser is getting better with every release, even in its Mac version.

★★ NETSCAPE NAVIGATOR/ATLAS/GOLD .... PC, MAC
ftp://ftp20.netscape.com/
http://home.netscape.com
The state-of-the-art browser. Download the latest beta immediately.

ORACLE POWERBROWSER .... PC
ftp://www-1.us.oracle.com/pub/www/powerBrowser/
http://www.oracle.com/products/websystem/powerbrowser/
Includes built-in server capability.

★ QUARTERDECK MOSAIC .... PC
ftp://ftp.qdeck.com/pub/demo/
http://www.qdeck.com/beta/
The fastest Mosaic, with caching that works.

Various other Tools

★ BLUE SKIES .... PC, MAC
http://groundhog.sprl.umich.edu/WUnderground/
Hook into The Weather Underground.

INFOMARKET NEWSTICKER .... PC
http://www.infomkt.ibm.com/ht2/ticker.htm

Live news highlights via a scrolling ticker bar. Click to download in full.

★ MACWEATHER .... MAC
http://ftp.utexas.edu/pub/mac/tcpip/
Install a global weather station on your desktop.

NETSCAPE POWERPACK .... PC, MAC
http://home.netscape.com/comprod/power_pack_summary.thml
Navigator, Chat, SmartMarks, Antivirus, Cyberspell, and more.

NETSTOCK .... PC
http://jax.jaxnet.com/~henrik/pages/splitcycle.html
Exportable delayed stock quotes and statistics.

NETWORK TIME .... MAC
http://mirrors.aol.com/pub/info-mac/comm/tcp/
Synchronize your Mac clock across the Net.

NSMED .... PC
http://www.lamplight.com/lamplight/index.html
Netscape bookmark editor.

★★ THE POINTCAST NETWORK .... PC
http://www.pointcast.com/
Stocks, sports, weather, news, stars, and more delivered live. Amazing.

★ REMOTELY POSSIBLE .... PC
http://www.avalan.com
Control a Win95 machine over the Net.

★ SURFBOT/WEBWATCH .... PC
http://www.specter.com/products.html
Track URL changes.

★★ TARDIS .... PC

http://tucows.phx.cox.com/files/

Synchronize your PC time online.

★ WEB COMPASS .... PC

http://arachnid.qdeck.com/qdeck/demosoft/

Customize and automate your Web searches.

★ WEBSPACE .... PC, MAC

http://www.sd.tgs.com/~template/WebSpace/

Silcon Graphics VRML browser.

★ WEBWHACKER .... PC

http://www.ffg.com/whacker.html

Auto-retrieves and stores Web pages – even images
and secondary links.

★ WETSOCK .... PC

http://vanbc.wimsey.com/~atekant/wetsock.htm

Delivers current US weather data to your Win95
system tray.

★ WINWEATHER .... PC

http://www.webcom.com/igs/

Up-to-date international weather reports, forecasts,
and images via the Net.

WS-FINGER .... PC

http://www.biddeford.com/~jobrien/

Get information from UNIX "plan" files.

But that's not all

For more, see the Software guides section of our Web
Guide's **Search Tools and Directories** (p.158).

PART THREE

---

contexts

A Brief History
of the Internet

The Internet may be an overnight media sensation, but it's hardly new. In fact, as a concept, it's actually older than most of its users; it was born in the 60s – a long time before anyone coined the buzzword "Information SuperHighway." Of course, there's no question that the Internet deserves its current level of attention. It's a quantum leap in global communications. But, right now, it's more prototype than finished product. While Microsoft's Bill Gates and US Vice President Al Gore rhapsodize about such household services as video-on-demand, most Net users would be happy with a system fast enough to view stills-on-demand. Nonetheless, it's getting there. The medium is moving so fast that there's always something new promising to revolution-ize the Net and maybe even our lifestyles.

THE ONLINE BOMB SHELTER

The concept of the Net might not have been hatched in Microsoft's cabinet war rooms, but it did play a role in a previous contest for world domination. It was 1957, at the height of the Cold War. The Soviets had just launched the first Sputnik, thus beating the USA into space. The race was on. In response, the US Department of Defense formed the Advanced Research Projects Agency (ARPA) to bump up its technological prowess. Twelve years later, this spawned **ARPAnet** – a project to develop a military research network, or specifically, the world's first decentralized computer network.

In those days, no-one had PCs. The computer world was based on mainframe computers and dumb terminals. These usually involved a gigantic, fragile box in a climate-controlled room, which acted as a hub, with a mass of cables spoking out to keyboard/monitor terminal ensembles. The concept of independent intelligent processors pooling resources through a network was brave new territory that would require the development of new hardware, software, and connectivity methods. The driving force behind decentralization, ironically, was the bomb-proofing factor. Nuke a mainframe and the system goes down. But bombing a network would, at worst, only remove a few nodes. The remainder could route around it unharmed.

WIRING THE WORLD

Over the next decade, an increasing number of **research agencies** and **universities** joined the network. US institutions such as UCLA, MIT, Stanford, and Harvard led the way, and in 1973, the network crossed the Atlantic to include University College London and Norway's Royal Radar Establishment.

The 70s also saw the introduction of **electronic mail**, **FTP**, **Telnet**, and what would become the **Usenet newsgroups**. The early 80s brought **TCP/IP**, the **Domain Name System**, **Network News Transfer Protocol**, and the European networks **EUnet** (European UNIX Network), **MiniTel** (the widely adopted French consumer network), and **JANET** (Joint Academic Network), as well as the Japanese **UNIX** Network. ARPA evolved to handle the research traffic, while a second network, MILnet, took over the US military intelligence.

An important development took place in 1986, when the US National Science Foundation established **NSFnet** by linking five university super-computers at a back-bone speed of 56 kbps. This opened the gateway for external universities to tap in to superior processing power and share resources. In the three years between 1984 and 1988, the number of host computers on the **Internet** (as it was now being called) grew from about 1000 to over 60,000. NSFnet, meanwhile, increased its capacity to T1 (1544 kbps). Over the next few years, more and more countries joined the network, creating a truly global structure from Australia and New Zealand, to Iceland, Israel, Brazil, India, and Argentina.

It was at this time, too, that **Internet Relay Chat** – which had just been released – enjoyed its moment of glory, as an alternative to CNN's incessant, but censored, coverage of the Gulf War. By this stage, the Net had grown far beyond its original charter. Although ARPA had succeeded in creating the basis for decentralized computing, whether it was actually a military success was debatable. It might have been bomb-proof, but on the other hand, it had opened new doors for espionage. It was never particularly secure and it is suspected that Soviet agents routinely hacked in to forage for research data. In 1990, ARPAnet folded, and NSFnet took over administering the Net.

COMING IN FROM THE COLD

Global electronic communication was far too useful and versatile to stay confined to academia. Big business was starting to take an interest with the Cold War apparent-ly over and world economies regaining confidence after the 1987 stock market savaging. Market trading moved from the pits and blackboards onto computer screens. The financial sector expected fingertip real-time data and that feeling was spreading. The world was ready for a people's network. Since the foundation of the Net was already in place, and funded by taxpayers, there was really no excuse not to open it to the public.

In 1991, the NSF lifted its restrictions on commercial usage. During the Net's early years, its **"Acceptable Use Policy"** specifically prohibited using the network for profit. Changing that policy irreversibly opened the door to business.

However, before anyone could connect to the Net, someone had to sell them a connection. The **Commercial Internet eXchange (CIX)**, a network of major commercial access providers, was formed to create a commercial backbone and divert traffic from the NSFnet, and before long, dozens of budding access providers were rigging up points of presence in their bedrooms. Meanwhile, NSFnet upgraded its backbone to T3 (44,736 kbps).

The Net had established itself as a viable medium for transferring data, but it was nearly impossible to find anything. The next few years saw an explosion in navigation protocols, such as **WAIS**, **Gopher**, **Veronica**, and, most importantly, the **World Wide Web**, which emerged into the public domain in 1992.

THE GOLD RUSH BEGINS

In 1989, Tim Berners-Lee of **CERN**, the Swiss Particle Physics institute, proposed the basis for the World Wide Web, initially as a means of sharing physics research. His goal was to design a seamless network in which information from any source could be accessed in a consistent and simple way using one program, on any platform. The Web did this, encompassing all existing infosystems, such as FTP, Gopher, and Usenet, without alteration. It was an unqualified success.

As the number of Internet hosts exceeded one million, the **Internet Society** was formed to brainstorm protocols and attempt to coordinate and direct the Net's escalating expansion. **Mosaic** – the first **graphical Web browser** – was released, and declared to be the "killer application of the 90s." It made navigating the Internet as simple as pointing and clicking, and took away the need to know UNIX. The Web's traffic increased by 2500 percent in the year up to June 1994, and domain names for commercial organizations (.com) began to outnumber those of educational institutions (.edu).

As the Web grew, so too did the global village. The media was starting to notice, slowly realizing that the Internet was something that went way beyond propeller heads and students. They couldn't miss it, actually, with almost every country in the world connected or in the process. Even the White House was online.

Of course, as word of a captive market got around, entrepreneurial brains went into overdrive. Canter & Seigel, an Arizona law firm, set a precedent by continuously **"spamming"** Usenet with advertisements for the US green card lottery. Although the Net was tentatively open for business, crossposting advertisements to every newsgroup was decidedly bad form. Such was the ensuing wrath that C&S had no chance of filtering out genuine responses from the server-breaking level of hate mail. A precedent was thus established for how not to do **business on the Net**. Pizza Hut, by contrast, showed how to do it subtly by setting up a trial service on the Web. Although it generated wads of positive publicity, it too was doomed by impracticalities. Nevertheless, the ball was beginning to roll.

THE HOMESTEADERS

As individuals arrived to stake out Web territory, businesses followed. Most had no idea what to do once they got their brand on the Net. Too many arrived with a bang, only to peter out in a perpetuity of "still under construction signs." Soon business cards not only sported email addresses, but Web addresses as well. And rather than send a CV and stiff letter, job applicants could now send a brief email accompanied with a "just see my Web page for more."

The Internet moved out of the realm of luxury into an elite necessity, verging toward a commodity. Some of the early business sites gathered such a following that by 1995 they were able to charge high rates for advertising banners. A few, like the search engines **InfoSeek** and **Yahoo**, even made it to the Stock Exchange boards, while others, like **GNN**, attracted buyers.

But it wasn't all success stories. Copyright lawyers arrived in droves. Well meaning devotees, cheeky opportunists, and info-terrorists alike felt the iron fists of the likes of Lego, McDonald's, MTV, the Louvre, and the Church of Scientology clamp down on their "unofficial web sites" or newsgroups. It wasn't usually a case of corporate right but of might, as small players couldn't foot the expenses to test **new legal boundaries**. The honeymoon was officially over.

POINT OF NO RETURN

By the onset of 1995, the Net was well and truly within the public realm. It was impossible to escape. The media was already becoming bored with extolling its virtues, so it turned to **sensationalism**. The Net reached the status of an Oprah Winfrey issue. New tales of hacking, pornography, terrorist literature, and sexual harassment were beginning to tarnish the Internet's iconic position as the great international equalizer. But that didn't stop businesses, schools, banks, government bodies, politicians, and consumers from swarming online, nor the major **Online Services** – such as CompuServe, Prodigy, and America Online, which had been developing in parallel since the late 80s – from adding Internet access as a sideline to their existing private networks.

As 1995 progressed, Mosaic, the previous year's killer application, lost its footing to a superior browser, **Netscape**. Not such big news, you might imagine, but after a half-year of rigorous beta-testing, Netscape went public with the third largest ever NASDAQ IPO share value – around $2.4bn.

Meanwhile, **Microsoft**, which had formerly disregarded the Internet, released **Windows 95**, a new PC operating platform incorporating access to the controversial **Microsoft Network**. Although **IBM** had done a similar thing six months earlier with **OS/2 Warp** and its IBM Global Network, Microsoft's was an altogether different scheme. It offered full Net access, but its real product was its own separate network, which many people feared might supersede the Net, giving Microsoft the sort of reign over information that Coke has over tooth decay. But that never happened. Within months, Microsoft, smarting from bad press, and finding the Net a larger animal even than itself, about-turned and declared a full commitment to furthering the Internet.

BROWSER WARS

As Microsoft appeared on the horizon, Netscape continued pushing the envelope, driving the Web into new territory with each beta release. New enhancements arrived at such a rate that competitors began to drop out as quickly as they appeared. This was the era of "This page looks best if viewed with Netscape." Of course, it wasn't just Netscape, much of the new activity stemmed from the innovative products of third party developers like **MacroMedia** (**ShockWave**), **Progressive Networks** (**Real Audio**), **Apple** (**QuickTime**), and **Sun** (**Java**). The Web began to spring to life with animations, music, and all sorts of new tricks.

While Netscape's market dominance gave developers the confidence to accept it as the de facto standard, treating it as a kind of Internet operating system into which to "plug" their products, Microsoft, an old hand at taking possession of cleared territory, began to launch a whole series of free Net applications. These included **Internet Explorer**, a browser with enhancements of its own, including **ActiveX**, a Web-centric programming environment more powerful than the much lauded Java, but without the same platform independence, and clearly geared to toward progressing Microsoft's software dominance. Not only was Internet Explorer suddenly the only other browser in the race, many were rating it as the better product, crediting Microsoft with a broader vision of the Net's direction.

FOUND ON THE INTERNET

Skipping back to late 95, the **backlash against Internet freedom** had moved into full flight. The expression **"found on the Internet,"** became the news tag of the minute, depicting the Net as the source of everything evil from bomb recipes to child pornography. Editors and commentators, often with little direct experience of the Net, urged that "Children" be protected, while the Net's own media and opinion shakers urged the ultimate importance of freedom of speech. It was – is – a skewed debate, with many of the Net's proselytizers suspicious that the real debate lies elsewhere, in the relationship between the Net and **democracy** in the light of a new, digitally empowered generation of self-publishers.

At first politicians didn't take much notice. Few could even grasp the concept of what the Net was about, let alone figure out a way to regulate its activities. Action seemed to be called for, however, and the easiest – indeed the most pressing – area was pornography, whose presence on the Net had mirrored all too closely its dominance in "real life." In Europe and North America, through 1995 and 1996, there were raids on hundreds of private pornographic bulletin boards and a few much publicized convictions for the possession of paedophile material. BBSs were an easy target, being mostly self-contained and run by someone who could be prosecuted. Net activists, however, feared that the primary objective was to send a ripple of fear through a Net community that believed it was bigger than the law, and to soften the public to the notion that the Internet as it stood posed a threat to national wellbeing.

In December 95, at the request of the German authorities, CompuServe cut its newsfeed to exclude the bulk of newsgroups carrying sexual material. But the groups cut weren't just pornographers, they also included groups covering gay and abortion issues. This brought to light the difficulty in drawing the lines of obscenity, and the problems with publishing across foreign boundaries. Next came the **US Communications Decency Act**, a proposed legislation to forbid the publication of "obscene" material. It was poorly conceived, however, and, following opposition from a very broad range of groups (including such mainstream bodies as the American Libraries Association), was overturned, and at time of writing lies dormant.

Outside the US, meanwhile, more authorities reacted. In France, chiefs of three major access providers were temporarily jailed for supplying obscene newsgroups. Australian police prosecuted several users for downloading child pornography. The NSW courts introduced legislation banning obscene material with such loose wording that the Internet itself could be deemed illegal – if the law is ever tested. In Britain, in mid-1996, the police tried a "voluntary" approach, identifying newsgroups that carried pornography beyond the pale, and requesting that Providers remove them from their feed. Most complied but there was unease among many in the Internet business that this was the wrong approach, and that closing down Newsgroup access only led the groups to "migrate" elsewhere – creating potentially greater dangers.

But the debate is about far more than pornography, despite the huffing and puffing. For Net fundamentalists, the issue is about holding ground against any compromises in liberty, and retaining the **global village** as a political force – potentially capable of bringing down governments and large corporations. Indeed, Net fundies would argue that these battles over publishing freedom have shown governments to be out of touch with both technology and the social undercurrent, and that in the long run the balance of power will shift toward the people, toward a new democracy.

WIRETAPPING

The other popular Net story of the mid-90s has been about **hackers**, who are depicted gaining control of networks, stealing money, and creating havoc. While such activities made great news items, the reality was less alarming. Although the US Department of Defense reported hundreds of thousands of break-ins to computer networks, there was little evident damage beyond the odd credit card file going missing. In fact, by and large, for an online population greater than the combined size of New York, Moscow, London, and Tokyo, there were surprisingly few noteworthy crimes. Yet the perception was – and still is – that the Net is too unsafe for the exchange of sensitive information like payment details.

Libertarians raged at the US Government's refusal to lift export bans on crack-proof **encryption algorithms**. But cryptography, the science of message coding, has traditionally been classified as a weapon and thus export of encryption falls under the Arms Control acts.

Encryption requires a secret key to open the contents of a message and often another public key to code the message. These keys can be generated for regular use by individuals or, in the case of Web transactions, simply for one session upon agreement between the server and client. Several governments proposed to employ official escrow authorities to keep a register of all secret keys, to be surrendered upon warrant – an unpopular proposal, to put it mildly, among a Net community who regard **invasion of privacy** as an issue equal in importance to censorship, and government monitors as instruments of repression. However, authorities were so used to being able to tap phones, intercept mail, and install listening devices to aid investigations, that they didn't relish giving up their freedom either. Government officials made a lot of noise about needing to monitor data to protect national security, but the real motives probably involve monitoring internal insurgence and catching tax cheats – stuff they're not really supposed to do, but we put up with anyway because if we're law-abiding it's mostly in our best interests.

The implications of this obstinacy go far beyond personal privacy. Net commerce awaits browsers that can talk to commerce servers using totally snooper-proof encryption. That technology has been available for use within the USA for years, but until restrictions are lifted, online business will continue to flounder. With big shots like Microsoft's Bill Gates lobbying Congress, it can only be a matter of time before bans are lifted and digital trading gets the green light.

INTO THE FUTURE

Such debates might seem a little academic to many Internet users, whose chief concerns, at time of writing, are likely to be that the whole system is **way too slow**. Even with a high bandwidth connection you're at the mercy of whatever the backbone can carry and, right now, that's nowhere near enough.

In the short term things will likely get worse. The Internet population will continue to grow, Web demands will rise, and bandwidth-hungry technologies like Real Audio, PointCast, and Internet telephony will prosper, but the wires that carry the data will not expand quickly enough to meet capacity. Something will give before too long and it's likely to come through those who own the major cables – and effectively control the Internet. Over the next few years, the big guns of global telecommunications will probably manage to starve the small players out of the market, and – before the new millennium, at least in the West – Internet access will be bundled with household services like telephone and cable TV.

The telcos realize that even the fastest modems are already becoming inadequate for Web use, and ISDN is only marginally better, so they aren't devoting much effort to promoting it or making it practical. It's up to the cable companies, telcos, and access providers to come up with a long-term solution and settle on a standard that will pay off the investment.

In this scenario early adopters pay a high premium for the risk. Telcos like **AT&T** are ready to roll out **ADSL**

into homes and offices, which can supply up to 10 Mbps downstream and 640 kbps upstream over normal phone lines – ample for Web surfing, and maybe even for video on demand. However, to do so would require fitting out an enormous amount of exchange side hardware. Meanwhile, cable and satellite companies have equally powerful solutions, possibly requiring less expenditure. Naturally, this increase in user bandwidth will either require a commensurate increase in the backbone, or heavy content like real-time video will have to relocate closer to demand. In the latter case, that will mean Access/Cable providers may become closer to our present Online Services model.

In the interim, 1997 will see the introduction of the **network PC** and **PC TV** – low-cost devices ready-made to plug into the Net, perhaps using remote software. Many aren't convinced it will work, including Microsoft and Forrester Research, but it won't be for the lack of money thrown at it by the likes of Apple, Oracle, IBM, and Akai, plus a list of companies that reads like a who's who in multimedia.

And despite this doom and gloom, what we have now may be slow and stifled by limitations, but it's still miles ahead of where we were even a year ago. The problem with rapid improvement is that our expectations likewise grow to meet it.

Net Language

The Internet hasn't always been a public thoroughfare: it used to be a clique inhabited by students and researchers nurtured on a diet of UNIX programming language, scientific nomenclature, and in-jokes. Meanwhile, in a parallel world, thousands of low-speed modem jockeys logged into independent bulletin board networks to trade files, post messages, and chat in public forums. These groups were largely responsible for the development of an exclusively online language consisting of acronyms, emoticons (smileys and such), and tagged text. The popularizing of the Internet brought these groups together along with, more recently, the less digitally versed general public.

Low online speed, poor typing skills, and the need for quick responses were among the pioneers' justifications for keeping things brief. But, using Net lingo was also a way of showing you were in the know. These days, it's not so prevalent, but you're sure to encounter Netty terms in **Internet Relay Chat** (IRC) and, to a lesser extent, in **Usenet Newsgroup** postings. Since IRC is a snappy medium, and line space at a premium, acronyms and the like can actually be useful – as long as they're understood.

Shorthand: Net acronyms

It doesn't take long in IRC to realize that Net acronyms are peppered with the F-initial. It's your choice whether you add to this situation, but if you don't tell people to "f*** right off" in ordinary speech or letters, then FRO is hardly appropriate on the Net, and nor is adding F as emphasis. However, you may at least want to know what's being said. And, BTW (by the way), the odd bit of Net shorthand may be useful and/or vaguely amusing – although hardly likely to make you ROFL (roll on the floor laughing).

AFK	Away from keyboard
AOL	America Online
BAK	Back at keyboard
BBL	Be back later
BD or BFD	Big deal
BFN	Bye for now
BRB	Be right back
BTW	By the way
CUL8R or L8R	See you later
FB	Furrowed brow
FUBAR	F***ed up beyond all recognition
GAL	Get a life
GDM8	G'day mate
GRD	Grinning, running, and ducking
GR8	Great
GTRM	Going to read mail
HTH	Hope this helps
IMO	In my opinion
IMHO	In my humble opinion
IYSWIM	If you see what I mean
IAE	In any event
IOW	In other words
LOL	Laughing out loud
NRN	No reply necessary
NW or NFW	No way
OIC	Oh I see

OTOH	On the other hand
PBT	Pay back time
RTM or RTFM	Read the manual
SOL	Sooner or later
TTYL	Talk to you later
YL/YM	Young lady/young man
|LY| & +LY	Absolutely and positively

Smileys and emoticons

Back in the old days, it was common in Usenet postings to temper a potentially contentious remark with <grins> tacked on to the end in much the same way that a dog wags its tail to show it's harmless. But that wasn't enough for the Californian E-generation, whose trademark smiley icon became the 80s peace sign. From the same honed minds that discovered 71077345 inverted spelled Greenpeace's bête noire, came the **ASCII smiley**. This time, instead of turning it upside-down, you had to look at it sideways to see a smiling face. An expression that words, supposedly, fail to convey. Well, at least in such limited space. Inevitably this grew into a whole family of **emoticons** (emotional icons).

The odd smiley undoubtedly has its place in diffusing barbs, but how many of the other emoticons you use, and how often you use them, is up to your perception of the line between cute and dorky. All the same, don't lose sight of the fact that they're only meant to be fun :-) Here's just a few:

:-)	Smiling
:-D	Laughing
:-o	Shock
:-(	Frowning
:'-)	Crying

;-)	Winking
X=	Fingers crossed
: =)	Little Hitler
{}	Hugging
:*	Kissing
$-)	Greedy
X-)	I see nothing
:-X	I'll say nothing
:-L~~	Drooling
:-P	Sticking out tongue
(hmm)Ooo.. :-)	Thinking happy thoughts
(hmm)Ooo.. :-(	Thinking sad thoughts
0:-)	Angel
}:>	Devil
(_)]	Beer
\V/	Vulcan salute
\0/	Hallelujah
@—`;———	A rose

Emphasis

Another way of expressing actions or emotions is by adding commentary within < **these signs** >.

For example: <flushed> I've just escaped the clutches of frenzied train-spotters < removes conductor's cap, wipes brow >. Some also use asterisks in email to *emphasize* words, in place of bolds and italics. You simply *wrap* the appropriate word: Hey everyone look at *me*.

Misspellings and intracaps

Some clowns pointedly overuse **phonetic spellings**, puns, or plain misspellings (kewl, windoze, macintrash, etc) And wannabe crackers like to **intracapitalize**, LiKe tHis. You can safely assume they're either very young and trying to make an impression, total plonkers, or both.

Glossary

A

Access Provider Company that sells Internet connection. Known variously as Internet Access or Service Providers (IAPs or ISPs).

ActiveX Microsoft's standard that allows software components to interact with one another in a networked environment regardless of the language they were created in.

ADSL Asynchronous Digital Subscriber Line. High-speed copper wire connections at up to 6 Mbps downstream and 640 kbps up.

Anonymous FTP server A remote computer, with a publicly accessible file archive, that accepts "anonymous" as the log-in name and an email address as the password.

Altavista Free Web and Usenet search service at: http://www.altavista.digital.com

AOL America Online. Presently, the world's most populous Online Service.

Archie A program that searches Internet FTP archives by filename.

ASCII The American Standard Code for Information Interchange. A text format readable by all computers. Also called "plain text."

Attachment   A file included with email.

B

Bandwidth   The size of the data pipeline. The higher the bandwidth, the faster data can flow.

Baud rate   The number of times a modem's signal changes per second when transmitting data. Not to be confused with bps.

BBS   Bulletin Board System. A computer system accessible by modem. Members can dial in and leave messages, send email, play games, and trade files with other users.

Binary file   All non-plain text files are binaries, including programs, word processor documents, images, sound clips, and compressed files.

Binary newsgroup   Usenet group that's specifically meant for posting the above files.

Binhex   A method of encoding, commonly used by Macs.

Bookmarks   A Web browser file used to store URLs.

Bounced mail   Email returned to sender.

Bps   Bits per second. The rate that data is transferred between two modems. A bit is the basic unit of data.

Browser   A program, such as Netscape, that allows you to download and display Web documents.

C

Client   A program that accesses information across a network, such as a Web browser or newsreader.

Crack   To break a program's security, integrity, or registration system, or fake a user ID.

Crash When a program or operating system fails to respond or causes other programs to malfunction.

Cyberspace A term coined by science fiction writer William Gibson, referring to the virtual world that exists within the marriage of computers, telecommunication networks, and digital media.

D

Direct connection A connection, such as SLIP or PPP, whereby your computer becomes a live part of the Internet. Also called full IP access.

DNS Domain Name System. The system that locates the numerical IP address corresponding to a host name.

Domain Part of the DNS name that specifies details about the host, such as its location and whether it is part of a commercial (.com), government (.gov), or educational (.edu) entity.

Download Transfer of a file from one computer to another.

E

Email Electronic mail carried on the Net.

Email address The unique private Internet address to which your email is sent. Takes the form user@host

Eudora Popular email program for Mac and PC.

F

FAQ Frequently Asked Questions. Document that answers the most commonly asked questions on a particular subject. Every newsgroup has at least one.

File Anything stored on a computer, such as a program, image, or document.

Finger A program that can return stored data on UNIX users or other information such as weather updates. Often disabled for security reasons.

Firewall A network security system used to restrict external traffic.

Flame Abusive attack on someone posting in Usenet.

Frag Network gaming term meaning to destroy or fragment. Came from DOOM.

FTP File Transfer Protocol. The standard method of transferring files over the Internet.

G

GIF Graphic Image File format. A compressed graphics format commonly used on the Net.

Gopher A menu-based system for retrieving Internet archives, usually organized by subject.

GUI Graphic User Interface. A method of driving software through the use of windows, icons, menus, buttons, and other graphic devices.

H

Hacker Computer enthusiast who derives joy from discovering ways to circumvent limitations. A criminal hacker's called a cracker.

Home page Either the first page loaded by your browser at start-up, or the main Web document for a particular group, organization, or person.

Host A computer that can allow you to connect to another computer.

HTML HyperText Markup Language. The language used to create Web documents.

HyperText links The "clickable" links or "hotspots" that connect pages on the Web to each other.

I

Image map A Web image that contains multiple links. Which link you take depends on where you click.

Infoseek Web and Usenet search service at: http://www.infoseek.com

Internet A cooperatively run global collection of computer networks with a common addressing scheme.

Internet shortcut Microsoft's terminology for a URL.

IP Internet Protocol. The most important protocol on which the Internet is based. It defines how packets of data get from source to destination.

IP address Every computer connected to the Internet has an IP address (written in dotted numerical notation), which corresponds to its domain name. Domain Name Servers convert one to the other.

IRC Internet Relay Chat. An Internet system where you can chat in text, or audio, to others in real time, like an online version of CB radio.

ISDN Integrated Services Digital Network. An international standard for digital communications over telephone lines, which allows for the transmission of data at 64 or 128 kbps.

ISP Internet Service Provider. A company that sells access to the Internet.

J

Java Platform independent programming language designed by Sun Microsystems. http://www.sun.com

JPEG A graphic file format that is preferred by Net users because its high compression reduces file size, and thus the time it takes to transfer.

K

Kill file A newsreader file into which you can enter keywords and email addresses to stop unwanted articles.

L

Leased line A dedicated telecommunications connection between two points.

Lycos Free Web search service at: http://www.lycos.com/

M

MIME Multipurpose Internet Mail Extensions. A recent standard for the transfer of binary email attachments.

Mirror A replica FTP or Web site set up to share traffic.

Modem MOdulator/DEModulator. A device that allows a computer to communicate with another over a standard telephone line, by converting the digital data into analog signals and vice versa.

Mosaic The first point-and-click Web browser, created by NCSA, now (largely) superseded by Netscape.

MPEG A compressed video file format.

Multithreaded Able to process to multiple requests simultaneously.

N

Name server A host that translates domain names into IP addresses.

The Net The Internet.

Netscape The most popular Web browser – and the company that produces it.

Newbie A newcomer to the Net, discussion, or area.

Newsgroup The Usenet message areas, or discussion groups, organized by subject hierarchies.

NNTP Network News Transfer Protocol. The standard for the exchange of Usenet articles across the Internet.

Node Any device connected to a network.

P

Packet A unit of data. In data transfer, information is broken into packets, which then travel independently through the Net. An Internet packet contains the source and destination addresses, an identifier, and the data segment.

Packet loss Failure to transfer units of data between network nodes. A high percentage makes transfer slow or impossible.

Phreaker Person who hacks telephone systems.

Ping A program that sends an echo-like trace to test if a host is available.

Platform Computer operating system, like Mac System 7.0, Windows 95, or UNIX.

Plug-in Program that fits into another.

POP3 Post Office Protocol. An email protocol that allows you to pick up your mail from anywhere on the

Net, even if you're connected through someone else's account.

POPs Points of Presence. An access provider's range of local dial-in points.

Post To send a public message to a Usenet newsgroup.

PPP Point to Point Protocol. This allows your computer to join the Internet via a modem. Each time you log in, you're allocated a temporary IP address.

Protocol An agreed way for two network devices to talk to each other.

R

Robot A program that automates Net tasks like collating search engine databases. Also called a Bot.

S

Server A computer that makes services available on a network.

Signature file A self-designed footer that can be automatically attached to email and Usenet postings.

SLIP Serial Line Internet Protocol. A protocol that allows your computer to join the Internet via a modem and requires that you have a pre-allocated fixed IP address configured in your TCP/IP setup. It's slowly being replaced by PPP.

SMTP Simple Mail Transfer Protocol. The Internet protocol for transporting mail.

Spam Inappropriately post the same message to multiple newsgroups.

Streaming Delivered in real time instead of waiting for the whole file to arrive, eg, Real Audio.

Stuffit A common Macintosh file compression format and program.

Surf To skip from page to page around the Web by following links.

T

TCP/IP Transmission Control Protocol/Internet Protocol. The protocols that drive the Internet.

Telnet An Internet protocol that allows you to log on to a remote computer and act as a dumb terminal.

Trumpet-Winsock A Windows program that provides a dial-up SLIP or PPP connection to the Net.

U

UNIX An operating system used by most service providers and universities. So long as you stick to graphic programs, you'll never notice it.

URL Uniform Resource Locator. The addressing system for the World Wide Web.

Usenet User's Network. A collection of networks and computer systems that exchange messages, organized by subject into Newsgroups.

UUencode A method of encoding binary files into text so that they can be attached to mail or posted to Usenet. They have to be UUdecoded to convert them back. The better mail and news programs do this automatically.

W

Warez Software, usually pirated.

Web The World Wide Web or WWW. Graphic and text documents on the Internet that are interconnected through clickable "hypertext" links.

Web authoring Designing and publishing Web pages using HTML.

World Wide Web See Web, above.

WYSIWYG What You See Is What You Get. What you type is the way it comes out.

Y

Yahoo The Web's most popular directory at:
http://www.yahoo.com

Z

Zip PC file compression format that creates files with the extension .zip using PKZip or WinZip software. Commonly used to reduce file size for transfer or storage on floppy disks.

Zmodem A file transfer protocol that, among other things, offers the advantage of being able to pick up where you left off after transmission failure.

Further Reading

The best way to find out more about the Net is to get online and crank up a search engine, but sometimes it's more convenient – and maybe more enjoyable – to read about it in a book or magazine. Among Internet mags, good reads include the US-based *Internet World* and cyber-style bible *Wired*, the British-based *Internet* and *.net*, and the Australian *Internet.au*.

Net books are harder to recommend as they date so quickly – it's hardly worth opening one that's more than a year old – and for practical guidance, this book should be more than enough to get you started. However, the techie manuals can be handy when you need to check specifics, and don't feel like trawling the Net for them. Following are a few volumes that might prove useful, plus a selection of Net-related tales and discussions.

Techie manuals

Barron, Ellsworth, Savetz et al *The Internet Unleashed,* (SAMS, US). Quality doorstopper of a techie manual, covering most Internet aspects in reasonable depth.
Adam Engst *The Internet Starter Kit* (Hayden, US). Step-by-step guidance, plus software. For Mac/Windows.

Web-site design

Mary Jo Fahey *Web Publisher's Design Guide* (Coriolis, US). Visual, step-by-step guide to Internet multimedia design tools, on the Mac.

Laura Lemay and Charles Perkins *Teach Yourself Java in 21 Days* (SAMS, US). Hardly a three-week vacation but the clearest guide to date on Java.

Bruce Morris *HTML in Action* (Microsoft Press, US). Useful coverage of Microsoft Web authoring technology like ActiveX.

Scott Zimmerman and Christopher Brown *Web Site Construction Kit for Windows 95* (SAMS, US). Building Web presences using HTML, Java, Perl, etc, on PCs.

Special interests

Vince Emery *How to Grow Your Business on the Internet* (Coriolis, US). How to market on the Net. Not that anyone really seems to know.

Jim Jubak *The Worth Guide to Digital Investing* (Harper Business, US). Using the Net to trade and monitor the markets.

Thomas Mandel and Gerard Van der Leun *Rules of the Net* (Hyperion, US). As if. Despite the oxymoronic title, it's packed with sound advice.

John Vacca *Internet Security Secrets* (IDG, US). How to keep hackers out of your network.

Peter Wayner *Digital Cash* (AP Professional, UK). New payment methods.

Web directories

Maloni, Greenman, Miller, and Hearn *NetGuide* (Michael Wolff & Co., US). This is the general volume in a six-plus book series that offers concise, informed reviews of Web sites. Other specific volumes include Travel, Music, Games, Chat, Money, and Star Trek.

Rositano, Rositano, and Stafford *Que's Mega Web Directory* (Que. US). Over 18,000 Web sites by subject.

Net culture

Joshua Bagby *Throbbing Modems* (Index, US). Online dating advice.

Michael Hyman *PC Roadkill* (IDG, US). Humorous exposé of computer industry warfare.

Katie Hafner and Mathew Lyon *Where Wizards Stay Up Late* (Simon & Schuster, US). The origins of the Net.

Jonathan Littman *The Fugitive Game* (Little, Brown, US). Catching super-hacker Kevin Mitnick.

Nicholas Negroponte *Being Digital* (Knopf, US/ Hodder, UK). MIT luminary and *Wired* columnist sets out what's in store for the future.

John Plunkett and Louis Rossetto *Mind Grenades* (HardWired, US). Subtitled "Manifestos From The Future", this is a thought-provoking collection from the founder of *Wired* magazine.

Clifford Stoll *Silicon Snake Oil* (Doubleday, US/Macmillan, UK). Stoll reckons it was better back in the old days. Ever heard that before?

Brad Wieners and David Pescovitz *Reality Check* (HardWired, US). A take on the digital culture from hundreds of digerati.

Still want more?

Well, the Net, of course, has its own directories of books about itself. The best is:

The Unofficial Internet Booklist at:
http://www.northcoast.com/savetz/booklist/

PART FOUR

directories

Internet Service Providers

The directories following cover major Internet Service Providers (ISPs or IAPs) in North America, Britain, Europe, Australia, New Zealand, Asia, and beyond. They are by no means complete lists and concentrate on larger ISPs with multiple access points: ie a range of phone numbers to use to dial in for access. There are, in addition, many hundreds of local access providers, catering for individual cities and states.

Your first priority is to find a provider with local call access, preferably without paying a higher tariff for the convenience. If you can't find one from our lists, ask around locally, or sign up temporarily, get online, and consult one of these **lists on the Net**:

  http://www.the-list.com (global)
  http://www.best.be/iap.html (global)
  http://www.cs.monash.edu.au/~zik/netfaq.html (Australia)
  http://www.limitless.co.uk/inetuk (UK)

or try the newsgroup: alt.internet.services. Each of these provide extensive listings by region, but do not recommend one provider above another.

For something more subjective, check out your local computer/Internet publications. For example, in the UK, *Internet* magazine runs monthly performance charts.

INTERNATIONAL ISPs

Most providers only operate in one country (or the US and Canada). For truly **international access**, which may be a priority if you plan to use the Net on your travels, consider one of the following (for more on which – and phone numbers for US, UK, and Australia – see our "Online Services" section, p.39).

Provider Points of Presence	Web address
AOL North America, Europe, Japan	http://www.aol.com
CompuServe/SpryNet Worldwide	http://www.compuserve.com
IBM Global Net Worldwide	http://www.ibm.net
Microsoft Network Worldwide	http://www.msn.com
Netcom North America, UK	http://www.netcom.com
UUNet Pipex Worldwide	http://www.uunet.pipex.com

If you travel within widely within the **Pacific Rim**, you may also want to check out Aimnet (http://www.aimnet.com), a joint venture between several of the region's providers.

NORTH AMERICA

Provider ✉ Email	
✆ Phone	Points of Presence
ACM	✉ account-info@acm.org
✆ 817 776 6876	USA
ANS	✉ info@ans.net
✆ 800 456 8267	USA
ARInternet	✉ info@ari.net
✆ 800 459 7175	USA, SprintNet
AT&T Worldnet	✉ worldnet@attmail.com
✆ 800 WORLDNET	USA, may expand
BBN Planet	✉ net-info@bbnplanet.com
✆ 800 472 4565	USA
Circle Net	✉ info@circle.net
✆ 704 254 9500	USA
Cogent Software	✉ info@cogsoft.com
✆ 800 733 3380	USA
Concentric Networks	✉ info@concentric.net
✆ 800 939 4262	USA, Canada
Delphi Internet	✉ service@delphi.com
✆ 800 695 4005	USA, Canada
Diamond Net	✉ info@dmnd.net
✆ 314 727 5596	USA
EarthLink Network	✉ info@earthlink.net
✆ 800 395 8425	USA, Canada
General Internet	✉ info@general.net
✆ 818 760 5011	USA

Global Enterprise Services	✉ market@jvnc.net
☎ 800 358 4437	USA

Global Internet	✉ info@gi.net
☎ 800 682 5550	USA

Greenlake	✉ greenlak@cris.com
☎ 810 540 9380	USA

HoloNet	✉ support@holonet.net
☎ 510 704 0160	USA

Hookup	✉ info@hookup.net
☎ 800 363 0400	Canada

IPSnet	✉ ingram@ipsnet.net
☎ 407 426 8782	USA

Liberty	✉ info@liberty.com
☎ 800 218 5157	USA

Netcom	✉ info@netcom.com
☎ 800 501 8649	USA, Canada

Portal	✉ info@portal.com
☎ 800 433 6444	USA

PowerNet	✉ www@pwrnet.com
☎ 214 488 8295	USA, Canada

PSINet	✉ info@psi.com
☎ 800 82PSI82	USA, Canada, Japan, Netherlands, UK, South Korea

Solgate	✉ info@solgate.com
☎ 800 419 4484	USA

SpryNet	✉ info161@sprynet.com
☎ 800 SPRYNET	Worldwide through CompuServe

| Sympatico | ✉ assistance@sympatico.ca |
| ☎ 800 773 2121 | Canada |

| Team | ✉ info@teamnet.net |
| ☎ 800 728 8326 | USA, Canada |

| The OnRamp | ✉ info@onramp.net |
| ☎ 800 603 2721 | USA, Canada |

| The WELL | ✉ info@well.com |
| ☎ 415 332 9200 | USA, Canada |

| UUNet | ✉ info@uu.net |
| ☎ 800 4UUNET4 | USA, Canada |

| WebSpinners Inc | ✉ sales@webspinnersinc.com |
| ☎ 800 909 SPIN | USA |

| YPN | ✉ info@ypn.com |
| ☎ 800 NET 1133 | USA |

BRITAIN AND IRELAND

| Provider | ✉ Email |
☎ Phone	Points of Presence
BTnet	✉ info@bt.net
☎ 01442 295 828	UK
Connect Ireland	✉ info@connect.ie
☎ 01 671 1687	Ireland
Demon	✉ sales@demon.net
☎ 0181 371 1234	UK
Direct Connection	✉ helpdesk@dircon.co.uk
☎ 0181 297 2200	UK

| Easynet | ✉ admin@easynet.co.uk |
| ✆ 0171 209 0990 | UK, France |

| Enterprise | ✉ sales@enterprise.net |
| ✆ 0800 269 146 | UK |

| Frontier Internet | ✉ info@ftech.net |
| ✆ 0171 243 3383 | UK |

| Global Internet | ✉ info@globalnet.co.uk |
| ✆ 0181 957 1008 | UK |

| Internet Central | ✉ sales@netcentral.co.uk |
| ✆ 01270 611 000 | UK |

| Ireland Online | ✉ sales@iol.ie |
| ✆ 01 855 1739 | Ireland |

| Net Direct | ✉ info@ndirect.co.uk |
| ✆ 0171 732 3000 | UK |

| Netcom | ✉ info@netcom.com |
| ✆ 0800 973 001 | UK, North America |

| Nethead | ✉ sales@nethead.co.uk |
| ✆ 0171 207 1100 | UK |

| Nildram | ✉ sales@nidram.co.uk |
| ✆ 01442 891 331 | UK |

| Onyx | ✉ onyx-support@octagon.co.uk |
| ✆ 01642 210 087 | UK |

| Planet Internet | ✉ info@uk.pi.net |
| ✆ 0171 345 4040 | UK |

| RedNet | ✉ info@red.net |
| ✆ 01494 513 333 | UK |

| U-Net | ✉ hi@u-net.com |
| ✆ 01925 633 144 | UK |

UK Online	✉ sales@ukonline.co.uk
✆ 0645 000 011	UK

UUNet Pipex	✉ sales@pipex.com
✆ 01223 250 120	Worldwide

EUROPE

Provider	✉ Email
✆ Phone	Points of Presence
Access Net	✉ info@accessnet.nl
✆ 0528 269 260	Netherlands
AquaNet Israel	✉ webmaster@aquanet.co.il
✆ 3 536 6503	Israel
Bahnhof	✉ bahnhof-info@bahnhof.se
✆ 18 100 899	Sweden
bitMailer Online	✉ ventas@bitmailer.com
✆ 1 402 1551	Spain
Clinet	✉ clinet@clinet.fi
✆ 437 5209	Finland
Easynet	✉ info@easynet.fr
✆ 1 44 545 333	France, UK
EUnet	✉ http://www.eu.net/
✆ (31) 20 623 3803	Europe, North Africa
Imaginet	✉ info@imaginet.fr
✆ 1 43 381 024	France

| ISnet | ✉ isnet-info@isnet.is |
| © 525 4747 | Iceland |

| Nacamar | ✉ info@nacamar.net |
| © 610 399 010 | Germany |

| Netlab | ✉ info@netlab.it |
| © 81 578 7439 | Italy |

| Online Store | ✉ info@onlinestore.com |
| © (41) 75 373 6677 | Germany, Switzerland, Liechtenstein |

| OsloNet | ✉ oslonett@oslonett.no |
| © 22 461 099 | Norway |

| PeterLink | ✉ webmaster@peterlink.ru |
| © 812 166 0648 | Russia |

| Ping | ✉ info@ping.de |
| © 231 979 10 | Germany |

| Switch | ✉ postmaster@switch.ch |
| © 1 268 1515 | Switzerland |

| Telepac | ✉ info@telepac.pt |
| © 1 790 7000 | Portugal |

| Worldnet | ✉ info@worldnet.net |
| © 1 40 379 090 | France |

| Xs4all | ✉ helpdesk@xs4all.nl |
| © 20 622 2753 | Netherlands |

AUSTRALIA

Provider ✆ Phone	✉ Email / Points of Presence
Access One ✆ 1800 818 391	✉ info@aone.net.au Capitals, Gold Coast, Sunshine Coast, Cairns, Townsville, Bundaberg, Mackay, Newcastle, Rockhampton, Toowoomba, Townsville, LatrobeValley, Whyalla
Apana ✆ 02 635 1751	✉ propaganda@apana.org.au Capitals, limited regional
Ausnet ✆ 02 241 5888	✉ sales@world.net Capitals except Hobart, Auckland
Dialix ✆ 1902 292 004	✉ info@DIALix.com Capitals except Darwin and Hobart
Enternet ✆ 1800 642 067	✉ info@enternet.com.au Capitals except Darwin and Hobart
Opennet ✆ 02 373 2701	✉ interface@opennet.net.au Australia-wide
Ozemail ✆ 1800 805 874	✉ sales@ozemail.com.au Capitals, Alice, Cairns, Gold Coast, Gosford, Newcastle, Sunshine Coast, Townsville, Woolongong
Pegasus ✆ 07 257 1111	✉ support@peg.apc.org Capitals except Darwin and Hobart

NEW ZEALAND

Provider / Phone	Email / Points of Presence
Internet Co of NZ / 09 358 1186	ikuo@iconz.co.nz / New Zealand
Lynx / 03 3790 568	info@lynx.co.nz / New Zealand
Wave / 0800 809 283	info@wave.co.nz / New Zealand

ASIA

Provider / Phone	Email / Points of Presence
Brain Net / 42 783 2039	info@brain.net.pk / Pakistan
DataCom / 1 312 063	support@magicnet.mn / Mongolia
Global OnLine / 3 5341 8000	Japansales@gol.com / Japan, USA, Canada
Hinet / 2 344 3143	nisc@hntp2.hinet.net / Taiwan
Indonet / 21 470 2889	sales@indo.net.id / Indonesia
Jaring / 254 9601	info@jaring.my / Malaysia

| KSC | ✉ iru@ksc.net.th |
| ✆ 02 719 1948 | Thailand |

| Pacific Internet | ✉ info@pacific.net.sg |
| ✆ 1800 872 1455 | Singapore |

| Status Indiagate | ✉ more@indigate.lod.com |
| ✆ 11 698 5111 | India |

| Supernet | ✉ info@hk.super.net |
| ✆ 2358 7924 | Hong Kong |

REST OF THE WORLD

| Provider | ✉ Email |
✆ Phone	Points of Presence
Africa Online	✉ info@africaonline.co.ke
✆ 2 243 775	Kenya
Classe A Internet	✉ classea@classea.com.br
✆ 79 224 9403	Brazil
Gulfnet	✉ info@kuwait.net
✆ 242 6728	Kuwait
Internet Africa	✉ info@iafrica.com
✆ 0800 020 003	South Africa
Networks Mexico	✉ info@netmex.com
✆ 5 259 8181	Mexico
Pipex SA	✉ andrew@pipex-sa.net
✆ 11 233 3200	South Africa, Worldwide
SatLink S.A.	✉ soporte@satlink.com
✆ 1 474 4512	Argentina

Cybercafés

The easiest way to test drive the Internet or to pick up mail on the road is by visiting a cybercafé. As well as coffee and snacks, they provide casual Internet access. You'll get to try all the latest Internet software, there's usually someone to lend a hand, and all you pay is an hourly fee for the time you spend online. Terminals are also finding their way into libraries, bookstores, computer stores, and even the odd bar or pub, and we've included a selection of these in the following listings.

To pack in as many places as possible, we've printed phone numbers only, so you'll need to call for addresses; you could even ask if they know of any closer to home – cybercafés are a growth industry. For fullest listings, you should, as ever, consult the Net, and view Mark Dziecielewski's superb guide at:

http://www.cyberiacafe.net/cyberia/guide/ccafe.htm

or consult the newsgroup: alt.cybercafes

Argentina

Buenos Aires .... American CyberCafe 1 775 9440

Australia

Adelaide .... Café on Net 05 359 2662
Adelaide .... Cyberscene 08 223 3066
Adelaide .... Cyber Net Space 08 376 3755

Blacktown	Hard Net Café	02 672 4725
Brisbane	Interactive Web	07 3368 3190
Brisbane	The Hub	07 3229 1119
Brisbane	Grand Orbit	07 236 1384
Broadbeach	Internet Quest	075 570 2322
Canberra	National Library Internet Café	06 262 1489
Fremantle	Café Aria	09 335 3215
Fremantle	Net Trek Café	09 336 4446
Glebe	Well Connected	02 566 2655
Melbourne	CyberNet Café	03 9818 1288
Melbourne	Virtual Access Café	03 9879 8777
Newcastle	Planet Access	049 623 862
Sydney	Earthlink	02 482 7606
Sydney	The Internet Café	02 261 5666

Austria

Graz	WIFI Motivation Center	316 602 691
Vienna	Café Stein	1 319 7241

Bahrain

Gudabiya	The Idea Gallery	(973) 778 392

Belgium

Auderghem	The 1101	2 646 0364
Brussels	CyberAccess	2 640 7158
Diepenbeek	SurfCity	11 351 010
Ghent	CyberK@fee	9 233 7928
Herentals	The Kick	14 210 907
Koersel-Beringen	Jeugdhuis Club 9	11 42 625
Liège	Le Pot-Au-Lait	41 220 584
Louvain-La-Neuve	Interweb	10 452 211
Mortsel	Smiley	3 449 8181
St. Niklaas	Netscafé	3 760 1512

Bosnia Herzegovina

Sarajevo .... The Avatar 71 668447

Brazil

Rio de Janeiro .... Inter.Net.B@R 21 287 5996

Britain

Aberdeen .... Netropolis Café 01224 595 223
Ashington .... Oasis 01760 521 702
Bath .... The Hub InterC@fé 01225 427 441
Bedford .... Cyber 01234 349 990
Birmingham .... Cyber Pizza 0121 459 7560
Birmingham .... Café Surf 0121 622 4010
Birmingham .... Sputnik 0121 643 0426
Birmingham .... Custard Factory 0121 604 7777
Bournemouth .... Cyberw@y 01202 292 933
Brighton .... The Sanctuary Cybercafé .. 01273 888 424
Bristol .... Intercafé Telecall 0117 907 7771
Cambridge .... The Six Bells 01223 566 056
Cambridge .... CB1 .... 01223 576 306
Cardiff .... Grassroots Cyber Café 01222 235 757
Crawley .... Internet Café 01293 619 925
Dundee .... Cyberbyte 01382 204 672
Ealing .... Cyberia 0181 840 3131
Edinburgh .... WEB13 .... 0131 229 8883
Edinburgh .... Cyberia 0131 220 4403
Edinburgh .... electricFROG 0131 226 1505
Exeter .... Internet Express Web Café .. 01392 201 544
Greenock .... Café Roslin 01475 631 223
Harrow .... The Edge 0181 910 4680
Hastings .... Internet Café 01424 714 524
Huddersfield .... Window on the World 01484 431 289
Hull .... Net21 .... 01482 322 488

Ipswich	Global Net-Café	01473 215 225
Kingston upon Thames	Cyberia	0181 974 9650
Leeds	Planet Connect	0113 297 0040
Leicester	Cyber Café @ The Ark	0116 233 9660
Liverpool	The Acorn Gallery	0151 709 5423
Liverpool	Café Internet	0151 255 1112
London	Buzz Bar	0171 727 7898
London	Cyberia	0171 209 0982
London	Cyberspy	0171 287 2242
London	Dillons CyberStation	0171 636 1577
London	Network City	0171 224 4400
London	North London Net Centre	0171 209 0898
London	SpiderCafé	0171 229 2990
London	The World C@fé	0171 833 3222
Luton	The Hard Drive Café	01582 485 621
Manchester	Wet	0161 236 5920
Manchester	Cyberia	0161 236 6300
Manchester	brain café	0161 907 3123
Marlborough	Internet Shop	016872 511 388
Northampton	Fried Green Tomatoes	01604 232 388
Norwich	Jumpin Jak's	01603 764 035
Nottingham	Cyberpub	01159 475 394
Orpington	Electr@NET	01689 877 878
Romford	Global Net Café	01708 728 139
Sheffield	Elektra The InterNet Café	0114 270 1171
Sheffield	Punters Cyber Café	0114 276 2668
Southampton	The Cyberscone	01703 635 429
Stockport	Peak Art Cybercafé	01663 747 770
Victoria	Café Internet	0171 233 5786
Wolverhampton	The Molineux CyberB@r	01902 651 111
York	Brubakers	01904 612 159

Canada

Calgary .... Global Net Café 403 250 5462
Fredericton .... Whitney Coffee Company ... 506 454 2233
Kamloops .... Cup and Easel 604 376 5642
Kelowna .... The Mind Grind 604 860 5363
Kingston .... Internet Café 613 546 5824
La Pocatière .... Café Bistro L'Exhaust 418 856 2952
Montréal .... Cybermind 514 875 7956
Montréal .... Café Electronique 514 849 1612
Montréal .... Le Café Mondial d'Internet 514 343 4736
Morin-Heights .... La Cuisson de ma mère ... 514 226 5420
Ottawa .... CyberPerk 613 789 7873
Prince George .... The Internet Café 604 563 4583
Québec .... Chez Ulysse et Pénélope 418 653 9344
Toronto .... eRendezvous 416 483 4784
Trail .... Java Junction .... 604 368 JAVA
Vancouver .... Coffee Café 604 948 1477
Winnipeg .... Zine's Infocafé 204 475 5515

Chile

Santiago .... Internet Café 2 243 3753

Denmark

Copenhagen .... Babel 33 339 338
Copenhagen .... C@fé Internet 31 427 202

Finland

Helsinki .... CompuCafé Helsinki 90 685 2976

France

Agde Hérault .... InterneThé 6721 4905
Besançon .... Le Web 8181 2846

Grenoble	CyberForum	7615 3737
Marseille	Cyb.Estami.Net	9111 4243
Montpellier	Cyber Forum	6706 5014
Nice	La Douche Cyber Café	9392 3434
Paris	Cyberia	4454 5333
Paris	Net Coffee	4336 7046
Paris	Café Orbital	4020 0514
Paris	Riva Multimedia	4260 4081
Paris	Le Shop Internet Café	4233 5289
Paris	Web Café	4272 6655
Paris	UGC WorldNet Café	4013 0545
Paris	Virgin Megastore	4953 5000

Germany

Berlin	Virtuality Café	30 327 5143
Duisburg	Dorfschenke	206 547 270
Frankfurt	Cyber's	69 9193 9984
Frankfurt	CyberRyder	69 9208 4010
Fürth	Falken's Maze	911 708 635
Köln	Internet-Café	221 257 3079
München	Internet-Café	89 129 47 44
Neustadt	ConCept Net-C@fe	632 139 360

Iceland

Reykjavík	SÍBERÍA Netc@fe	551 6003

Ireland

Belfast	Bytes	01232 242 050
Belfast	Revelations	01232 320 337
Dublin	Internet Exchange Café	1 475 8788

Italy

Milano	Cyber Café	2 2730 4426
Milano	Jenner68	2 3322 0287
Padova	Osteria alla Ventura	49 663 023
Torino	Virtualia	11 606 3070

Japan

| Tokyo | Café des Près | 3 3448 0039 |

Malaysia

| Kuala Lumpur | POEM | 3 284 1977 |

Mexico

| Mexico City | Club Internet | 5 360 4121 |
| Mexico City | Internet Café | 5 245 0330 |

Netherlands

Amsterdam	MySTèR 2000	20 620 2970
Eindhoven	Trafalgar Pub	40 244 8820
Rotterdam	Café De Unie	10 4117394

New Zealand

Auckland	Comm-Unity Cybercafé	09 379 2779
Auckland	Cyba Café	09 379 6282
Wellington	CyberSpace Internet Café	04 499 8560

Poland

| Lodz | Cyber Café | 42 302 194 |
| Warsaw | Cyber Café | 22 622 6611 |

Portugal

Lisbon .... Cyberbica 1 342 1707

Russia

St Petersburg .... Tetris 812 164 6785

Singapore

Singapore .... café@boatquay 230 0140
Singapore .... CyberNet Café 324 4361

South Africa

Cape Town .... iCafé 021 246 576
Durban .... Im@giNet Cyber Café 031 368 153
Johannesburg .... Milky Way Internet Café 011 487 3608
Port Elizabeth .... Cyber Joe's Internet Café 083 226 2181

South Korea

Seoul .... NET Café 2 733 7973

Spain

Barcelona .... El Café de Internet 3 412 1915
Madrid .... La Ciberteca 1 556 6773
Pamplona .... iturNet 48 252 820

Sweden

Linköping .... BerZyber 013 207 422
Malmö .... Kajplats 305 .... 040 342 574
Stenungsund .... Internet Café 0303 69 648
Stockholm .... aswellas coffee 08 241 782
Stockholm .... Café Access 08 700 0153

Switzerland

Basel	@LOUNGE	13 207 422
Fribourg	Scottish Bar Pub	37 268 202
Geneva	Global Café	22 328 2619
Lausanne	Club Internet	21 691 2593
Lucerne	Café Parterre	41 210 4093

Taiwan

Taipei	Human Space CyberTe@	2 396 1920

USA

Anchorage, AK	H2Espresso	907 344 4480
Flagstaff, AZ	CyberCafé	520 774 0005
Phoenix, AZ	Congo Internet Café	602 946 5944
Fullerton, CA	Al Cappuccino Coffee House	714 870 7588
La Verne, CA	Connected Café	909 593 1188
Ashland, OR	Garo's Java House	503 482 2261
Costa Mesa, CA	DP's Coffee House	714 722 9673
Long Beach, CA	Almost Paradise Café	310 429 2066
Los Angeles, CA	Buzz Coffee	213 650 7742
Los Angeles, CA	Captgo	310 824 2277
Los Angeles, CA	Congo Square	310 395 5606
Los Angeles, CA	Equator	818 564 8656
Los Angeles, CA	Grounds Zero	818 567 4257
Los Angeles, CA	Highland Grounds	213 466 1507
Los Angeles, CA	Horse Shoe Coffee House	818 986 4262
Los Angeles, CA	ICON Byte Bar & Grill	861 BYTE 2983
Los Angeles, CA	StageLeft Coffee House	818 551 9791
Los Angeles, CA	The Abbey	310 289 8410
Los Gatos, CA	Los Gatos Coffee Roasting	800 877 7718
San Diego, CA	Café Renaissance	619 297 2700
San Francisco, CA	Brewed Awakenings	255 1928
San Francisco, CA	Café Abir	567 7654

San Francisco, CA	Café Babar	282 6789
San Francisco, CA	Coffee Zone	863 2443
San Francisco, CA	Green Tortoise Hotel	834 1000
San Francisco, CA	Horse Shoe	626 8852
San Francisco, CA	ICON Byte Bar & Grill	861 BYTE 2983
San Francisco, CA	Jammin Java	566 5282
San Francisco, CA	Java Beach	665 5282
San Francisco, CA	Java Bound	664 3154
San Francisco, CA	Jumpin Java	431 5282
San Francisco, CA	Muddy Waters	621 2233
San Francisco, CA	Muddy's	647 7994
San Francisco, CA	Royal Ground	567 8822
San Francisco, CA	SF Net Cafés	695 9824
San Francisco, CA	Simple Pleasures	387 4022
San Francisco, CA	Source	387 8025
San Francisco, CA	Yakety Yak	885 6908
Santa Barbara, CA	eCafé	805 897 3335
Santa Cruz, CA	Coffeetopia	408 338 1940
Santa Monica, CA	The World Café	310 399 6964
Venice, CA	Cyber Java	310 581 1300
Ventura, CA	SurfNet Café	805 658 1287
Boulder, CO	Caffé Mars	303 938 1750
Denver, CO	Jitters Internet Café	303 298 8490
Denver, CO	Majordomo's Net Café	303 830 0442
Dillon, CO	Caroline's Coffeehouse	970 468 8332
Boca Raton, FL	Planet Internet	305 570 3263
Fort Lauderdale, FL	Cybernation	954 630 0223
Sarasota, FL	Café Kaldi	941 366 2326
Tampa, FL	Infohaus	813 878 2233
Temple Tce, FL	Cybercup	813 980 0860
Atlanta, GA	Red Light Café	404 874 7828
Honolulu, HI	Coffee Haven	808 732 2090
Honolulu, HI	The Internet C@fe	808 735 JAVA
Twin Falls, ID	Metropolis Bakery Café	208 734 4457
Chicago, IL	Interactive Bean	312 528 2881

Chicago, IL	The 3rd Coast Café	312 664 7225
Chicago, IL	Urbus Orbis	312 252 4446
Bloomington, IN	Original Kona Koffee Co.	812 334 1233
Des Moines, IO	The Internet Café	515 279 9357
Louisville, KY	The Internet C@fe	502 456 0912
Boston, MA	Designs for Living	617 536 6150
Cambridge, MA	Cybersmith	617 547 8588
Nantucket Island, MA	InterNet Café	508 228 6777
Sheffield, MA	Sheffield Pub	413 229 7770
Detroit, MI	Big Surf Cyber Café	810 433 3744
Detroit, MI	Caffe' Bravo	810 344 0220
Grand Haven, MI	The Coffee Grounds	616 847 3078
Grand Rapids, MI	4 Friends CyberLounge	616 456 5356
Mankato, MN	Techno Village	507 FUN COOL
St Paul, MN	Cahoots Coffee Bar	612 644 6778
St Louis, MO	The Grind	314 454 0202
Chapel Hill, NC	Caffe Driade	919 933 4161
Jacksonville, NC	ESCape	910 347 2800
Raleigh, NC	Cup@Joe	919 828 9886
Hoboken, NJ	Hoboken Coffee Warehouse	201 792 0707
Las Vegas, NV	Cyber City Café	702 732 2001
New York, NY	alt.coffee	212 529 2233
New York, NY	@Café	212 979 5439
New York, NY	Internet Café	212 614 0747
New York, NY	Cyber Café	212 334 5140
White Plains, NY	Cybersmith	914 686 3570
Norman, OK	Main Street CyberHall	405 364 0071
Oklahoma City, OK	InterEarth	405 840 0502
Eugene, OR	Sip n' Surf Cybercafé	541 302 1581
Portland, OR	The Habit	503 235 5321
Camp Hill, PA	Cornerstone Coffeehouse	717 737 5026
Erie, PA	Chacona's	814 835 2233
Philadelphia, PA	Cyber Loft	215 564 4380
Scranton, PA	Internet Café	717 344 1969
Nashville, TN	Bean Central	615 321 8530

Amarillo, TX	inter@ctive Caffe	806 467 1515
Austin, TX	Discovery Incubator	512 495 9448
Austin, TX	WWW Café	512 495 1880
Corpus Christi, TX	Raven & Sparrow Café	512 887 7778
Houston, TX	PJ's Coffee & Tea	713 521 2002
Plano, TX	Java Island Coffee Roasters	214 491 1695
San Antonio, TX	The Coffee Gallery	210 226 5123
Blacksburg,VA	Bogen's	703 953 2233
Charlottesville, VA	Mudhouse	804 984 MUDD
Norfolk, VA	C@fe.net	804 625 5483
Richmond, VA	Cyber House Café	804 967 9052
Staunton, VA	CyberCafé	540 887 8402
Bellingham, WA	Tony's Internet Café	360 733 5662
Bremerton, WA	Higashi Kaze	360 377 4170
Seattle, WA	Internet Café	206 323 7202
Seattle, WA	Speakeasy Café	206 728 9770

Venezuela

Caracas	Cyber Café Collins	2 267 1721

Cyberia, London: world's first Cyber Cafe

Acknowledgments

In London, thanks to everyone at Internet magazine, particularly Roger Green, for laying on a speedy link to the Internet and daily news; Neil, Gail and David for letting me practically camp in the office; and the Duke lemmings, Paul, Darren and Craig. To Karen Williams (plus one) for shacking me up in a difficult time; John Trudgian for an endless stream of anomalies and bacon sandwiches; Garret Keogh for tuning me in to the pulse; the Lahore Kebab House for nutrition; broadcasting legend Matt Hall; Arthur Neame; Pipex Dial's Matt Townend; and Andrew Hatton. Special thanks to Tamsin Hughes, the world's sharpest Net critic, for bringing me back to speed on the Web after being offline; and roving super-editor Lisa Hughes for setting the original high standards. Plus CompuServe, for getting me online instantly no matter where; Easynet, for fast reliable mail; and Netcom, AOL, Pipex and Microsoft for access.

In the US, thanks to Jean Marie Kelly and Jeff Kaye at Rough Guides NY; Gerry Browne for a teched-out US base, fajitas and quick answers to impossible TCP/IP questions; and Jeff Davis for his skewed views. In Australia, thanks to Felicity Downey at Penguin; Rosanne Bersten of Internet.au, for inspiration and permission to reprint parts of the HTML chapter; Jane Fish; John Hooper for his verandah; Jo Chichester at the ABC; Sophie Parer; a droog called Alex; Christopher Carrigan and the HCC; Pete Withey; Shelley; Katie Sedgwick; and most of all my parents for always being there when I needed them. And in Hong Kong, thanks to Kylie and Ben, for way past perfect hospitality.

But the top-shelf thanks must go to the Rough Guides and Penguin in London. Especially Mark for stretching deadlines, decoding convoluted copy, and keeping me primed; Kate for an eagle-eyed proofing; Henry for working around the clock to get it perfect; Simon for sending us up bestsellers lists; Richard for getting us translated; Al for forwarding weird mail, and sharing his HTML expertise; and Susanne for getting it all on paper in the nick of time.

Angus Kennedy
angus@easynet.co.uk

HELP US UPDATE

Trying to keep up with the ever-changing Internet is a near impossible task. So don't be alarmed if you find a few addresses that don't work, or dubious recommendations. It was all correct at time of press. Honest. But it's sure to change. So, if something's not right, or you think we could've explained it better, please let us know via email at: internet@roughtravl.co.uk and we'll attend to it in the next edition.

In the meantime, for updates, keep an eye on: http://www.roughguides.com/net/

Index

R

S

T

U

V

W